One Minute Plays

D1558410

Can you really write a play that lasts a minute?

The one minute play offers a unique challenge to actors, directors and writers: how do you create a whole world, where actors have room to perform and where audiences have a true experience all in 60 seconds?

One Minute Plays: A Practical Guide to Tiny Theatre demystifies the super-short-form play, demonstrating that this rich, accessible format offers great energy and variety not only to audiences but to everyone involved in its creation and performance. This handbook includes:

- An anthology of 200 one-minute plays selected from the annual Gone in 60 Seconds festival.

- A toolbox of exercises, methodologies and techniques for educators, practitioners and workshop leaders at all levels.

- Tips and advice on the demands of storytelling, inclusivity and creative challenges.

- Detailed practical information about creating your own minute festival, including play selection, running order, staging and marketing.

Drawing on a wealth of experience, Steve Ansell and Rose Burnett Bonczek present an invaluable guide for anyone intrigued by the art of creating, producing and performing a one minute play.

Steve Ansell is a professional theatre director and the artistic director of stage@leeds at the University of Leeds, UK. He is also artistic director of Screaming Media Productions, and founder of Gi60 (Gone in 60 Seconds): The International One Minute Play Festival.

Rose Burnett Bonczek is director of the BFA Acting program and a professor at Brooklyn College, City University of New York, US. She is also the festival director and producer of Gi60 (Gone in 60 Seconds): The International One Minute Play Festival, US Edition. She is the co-author of *Ensemble Theatre Making: A Practical Guide* with David Storck.

One Minute Plays

A Practical Guide to Tiny Theatre

By Steve Ansell and
Rose Burnett Bonczek

Jan Ansell and Mike Flanagan,
Associate Editors

5/1/17
To Dahlen!
Thank you for all the beautiful
creative work during your years
with GiGO – you are in these pages
my friend – heart + soul!
Love, Rose

Routledge
Taylor & Francis Group

LONDON AND NEW YORK

First published 2017
by Routledge
2 Park Square, Milton Park, Abingdon, Oxon OX14 4RN

and by Routledge
711 Third Avenue, New York, NY 10017

Routledge is an imprint of the Taylor & Francis Group, an informa business

British Library Cataloguing in Publication Data
A catalogue record for this book is available from the British Library

Library of Congress Cataloging in Publication Data
A catalog record for this book has been requested

ISBN: 978-1-138-67505-6 (hbk)
ISBN: 978-1-138-67506-3 (pbk)
ISBN: 978-1-315-56087-8 (ebk)

Typeset in Joanna
by Deanta Global Publishing Services, Chennai, India

Printed and bound by CPI Group (UK) Ltd, Croydon, CR0 4YY

Contents

Acknowledgments

....

The authors would like to gratefully acknowledge the following people:

Jan Ansell and Mike Flanagan, without whom this book truly would not have happened ...

Anthony Ponzio, whose amazing spirit and creativity brings Gi60 to life each year

Those whose contributions made all the difference:

Anastasia Bell, Alex Bernstein, Bobby Brook, Hedley Brown, Joe Bryant, Ally Callaghan, Sabrina Cataudella, Ruben Carbajal, Nancy Brewka-Clark, Kevin Clyne, Catherine Clyne, Michael Colby Jones, Patrick Delaney, Helen Elliott, Tara Elliot, Kayla Feldman, Ramona Floyd, Samantha Fontana, Joshua Gold, Sarah Good, Madeleine Gray, Jonathan Hadley, Mark Harvey Levine, Paul Herbig, Vera Khodasevich, Arthur Kriklivy, Stacey Lane, Joan Lunoe, Meron Langsner, Jim MacNerland, Rosanne Manfredi, Jay Nickerson, Michael Raine, Walter Petryk, Mickey Ryan, Alexandra Slater, Adam Smith, Aurora Stewart de Peña, David Storck, Madeleine Thorn, John Weagly

Support:

Thanks to Christopher Thomasson, whose technical virtuosity and editing skills allow the world to see tiny theatre, Professor Kip Marsh and the Department of Theatre at Brooklyn College for their continued commitment to Gi60; Jackie Smerling: the president of the Gi60 Fan Club; Kat Ostrova, Frank Angel, Richard Grossberg and the staff at Brooklyn Center for the Performing Arts at Brooklyn College, Becca Guskin, Katherine Harte-DeCoux, Deb Hertzberg, Michael Hairston, Eugene Solfanelli, Jeffrey Steifel, John Tsang, John Vetter

Thanks to Vic Allen, Dee Grijak, and everybody at Dean Clough, Halifax for your amazing support and for giving Gi60 UK a home. To Bobby Brook, Robin Burch, Natalie McLoughlin, Emma Cook, Chloe Oldridge, Claire Lightfoot, Madeline Thorne, and Chris Nriapia. To the theatre and technical staff at stage@leeds, School of Performance and Cultural Industries, University of Leeds, Leeds Beckett University and to Chris Nriapia, BBC Big Screen for your support.

Our deep thanks to Ben Piggott and Kate Edwards for their unwavering support of this book, and their invaluable guidance and wisdom that made it a better book.

Introduction

Welcome to the world of tiny plays – it's actually a pretty big place with room for plenty of creativity and joy. If you're new to the realm of one minute plays, first of all, you're in for a great journey, and second, you aren't late to a party that started two hours ago. Though the increase of one minute play festivals in the last 10 years may make it feel as if this is a new phenomenon, they've been around for a long time. In fact, in our research we found *One Minute Plays Requiring No Rehearsal* by Fred L. Pauly – published in 1937! (We would argue with Fred about the wisdom of *not* rehearsing a one minute play ...) You may be a playwright, a teacher, a director, or a student curious about this particular form: "Can you really tell a story in one minute? Could I write a one minute play? Could I create a festival with my company/class/ friends?" The answers are yes, yes, and absolutely yes.

We've been happily making one minute theatre for nearly 15 years as Gi60: The International One Minute Theatre Festival. Gi60's global mission is to promote new writing and provide opportunities for writers; we annually accept between 700 and 900 submissions worldwide and perform 50 original plays in the UK, 50 in the US, and now 50 with Gi60 New Zealand. The festivals are performed live, live streamed, and filmed, and the footage is edited down to individual single play format and then uploaded to the Gi60 Channel on YouTube for viewing. We have worked with actors and directors on both sides of the Atlantic and the Pacific, and with writers from Australia to Israel, and from Los Angeles to London. We've produced and performed roughly 1,500 plays since 2004 (most available for viewing on the Gi60 Channel), and our experience of creating that much theatre on multiple platforms with an international community has taught us a thing or two. First, initial reaction to the form is nearly universal; people are curious, perhaps skeptical, or just plain confused by the idea of a one minute play. However, once they experience it, there is a transformation. Audience members, writers, and performers quickly realize the vitality, vibrancy, craft, and creative challenge of this unique theatrical form. Second, once that realization kicks in, people return for more. And more. We have dedicated audience members who do not miss a single Gi60, telling us, "You know? I don't go to much theatre. But I wouldn't miss this for the world. We look forward to it every year." That transformation is also witnessed in the increased success that one minute play festivals have enjoyed in the past 10 years or so. From Gi60 in Leeds and Brooklyn, to the Artswell Festival of All Things in Canada (celebrating 17 years of their one minute play festival), the form affords theatre companies and schools the opportunity to share a wide variety of voices and stories, and allows a dynamic experience for an audience.

This book is the first publication to focus on the one minute play as a creative form in its own right, and we feel that recognition of tiny theatre is long overdue (sorry, we've been busy!). Our shared experiences and the extensive examples in this book can be supportive at all levels, and this democracy of access is central to the potency and importance of the one minute format as a creative platform. We've created for you – educators, writers, directors, actors, readers – a clear and supportive guide to the skills essential to the creation, performance, and production of the one minute play, as well as ways of applying its benefits to the classroom. This practical guide will start you – or support you – on your own one minute theatre journey. When you see the richness and accessibility of the one minute play as both a written and a performed creative art form, you'll discover its potency as an artistic and educational tool. This book will empower you with a toolbox from which you can create your own one minute theatre, and will help prepare you for nearly any circumstance (just ask Steve about the time their theatre flooded and lost power on the day of the show and they had to find a new theatre in a matter of hours. And yes, they *did* successfully relocate and perform 50 plays that night). In the final section, you'll also find 200 brilliant plays that Gi60 has produced in the US and the UK. It was incredibly hard to choose – nobody wants to admit to having a favorite child. But. We've endeavored to offer a fair and broad representation of voices, a range of topics both serious and comedic, and a variety of characters, cast sizes, and visual challenges (zombies, security guards, and goldfish, oh my …). We've also noted plays that we feel are "family friendly" for younger actors and audiences.

Your one minute play tour guides

Steve Ansell

At the start of 2003 I was offered the position of Director of Education at a regional theatre in the north of England. The role involved overseeing all of the theatre's educational and outreach activities, including its new writing programme. The programme consisted principally of some weekly writing groups for adults and the theatre's youth theatre members and a small annual new writing festival dedicated largely to the work of the aforementioned groups. The theatre was a popular and busy venue with a huge regional impact, attracting audiences from far and wide, but the writing festival itself was clearly of interest only to those involved. This seemed like a lost opportunity to me.

I wanted to share new writing with a much broader audience and give more people the opportunity to write for the stage and see their work performed. The problem was that I didn't have the right vehicle. The answer came when I was leafing through an anthology of Christopher Durang plays looking for some interesting scenes for a senior youth group class. I came across a play simply called "One Minute Play," which Durang had written for the American Repertory Theatre in Massachusetts for a One Minute Play festival in the 1990s. The idea of a one minute play, which I had never previously heard of, immediately excited me, and the idea of a one minute play festival excited me even more. It seemed like the perfect vehicle to offer more opportunity to writers and provide audiences with something a little out of the ordinary and unexpected.

I soon started to become a little anxious about the one minute length. In his notes for *One Minute Play*, Durang had stated that the first time the American Repertory Theatre had asked him for a one minute play, it actually lasted seven minutes, so clearly a play in 60 seconds was a challenge. The combined result of my enthusiasm and angst was "120 Seconds," a two minute play festival!

120 Seconds proved to be a huge success with both audiences and writers, and proved to me that short format theatre worked, and also that it was a distinct and novel form of theatre and one that provided an accessible route into new writing for audiences and writers alike. It was clear that I was on to something. There was a real enthusiasm for this new (well, new to me at least) form of tiny theatre. I decided that the following year's festival would be a one minute theatre event. In 2004, the first Gi60 (Gone In Sixty Seconds) One Minute Theatre Festival took place in Harrogate, UK. Over 90 plays were performed, and once again the shows were sell-outs. Although the event was a huge success, it became apparent that 90 different narratives, voices, and stories were just too much in a single sitting. Even though the overall length of the performance was not much longer than the previous year's 120 Seconds performance, I felt that both cast and audiences were fatigued by the end of the event. This left me with a dilemma: how do you keep the same number of plays, or better yet increase them, while still keeping the event manageable for both artists and audiences?

Once again I stumbled on the answer almost by accident. We had decided to record the Gi60 performance and had strapped a camera to one of the handrails in the theatre. A writer had asked if it would be possible to get a copy, and as one of the company members worked in I.T, I asked if it would be possible to put the plays online so that writers would be able to share their work. I purchased some web space and a URL, and we managed to make the individual plays available for (painfully slow) download. Although we now accept online video sharing as part of our daily lives, with mainstream theatre now offering shows live online and in movie theatres, in 2004 this was an idea in its infancy and quite groundbreaking. In fact, our Gi60 video sharing experiment *preceded* the official launch of YouTube by about three months!

Having put the plays online, I decided to try and download one for myself. I had just purchased a shiny new cell phone, which could store up to "one minute" of video! Getting the footage on the phone took an interminable length of time, but at the end of it I had a one minute play that I had directed on my cell phone that I could show friends: "What have I been doing, you ask? Why, I have been directing one minute plays, that's right, a one minute play! Look, I can show you on my phone!" I was genuinely excited by this idea of theatre in my pocket, and it was the combination of these two pieces of technology – the cell phone and the internet – that led to the next phase of Gi60.

In late 2004 I emailed my colleague and old friend Rose Burnett Bonczek at Brooklyn College in New York. The email was mostly about my upcoming wedding, which Rose was attending, but at the end of the email I wrote: "Would you like to do an international one minute theatre festival?" It is a testament to Rose's spirit of adventure and her faith in me that she simply replied "yes" without ever questioning what she was letting herself in for. No questions about logistics, cost, practicality; these came later, but that "yes" changed our lives.

The idea was simple, in my mind at least. If 90 plays in one evening was too much, but we still wanted to do more than 90 plays at each festival, then we should have more than one show; and if we were going to have more than one show, why not have the second one on a different continent? The plan was to host the festival in both the UK and the US, with each venue performing 50 tiny plays, filming each event, and then making the plays available online. Once this had been decided, it became obvious that all play entries should be received online as well, which made it easier for writers from various countries to submit their work directly and easily. We moved from the website to a dedicated YouTube channel, and at the time of writing we have more than 1,000 plays available for viewing. Looking back, I think Rose's enthusiasm and excitement to enter the unknown and to take a chance is at the heart of what appeals to people about short form theatre. When an audience are told that they're going to be seeing 50 different plays that night, there's nothing but The Unknown. "Wow, that was amazing. I wonder what comes next?" "Oh, that was heartbreaking. I wonder what the next one's about?" "Ah! That was a laugh – oh, there are still 30 more to go! I wonder …?" There is no single linear play for the evening's entertainment – our brain can't predict what lies around the corner, because the previous play is, well, *over*. However, the whole evening of plays does tell a single story about a moment in time. What are writers from around the globe concerned about? What stories are they burning to tell at this moment in time? It provides a snapshot into a zeitgeist that we all can share, whether we're watching live in a theatre in Leeds or Brooklyn, or watching the stream from Alaska.

Rose Burnett Bonczek

When people ask me how I started my journey on Gi60 and one minute plays, I say with absolute honesty that Steve is the kind of person that if he asks you to join him in something – an artistic project, or an adventure – you just say yes. Because you know it's going to be an amazing time, no matter what. Steve's mind works at RPMs that haven't yet been discovered by scientists, and his creativity and imagination radiate out like some personal Big Bang event. That is, there must have been an initial explosion of artistic goo at some point early in his life, I'm sure, because through all the years I've known him, his creativity keeps expanding outward with increasing velocity and strength and includes theatre, music, literature, science, film, and an encyclopedic knowledge of all things Terry Pratchett and Bill Hicks. He's frighteningly talented at everything he does, and he has a whacking good time doing it all. So when he emailed me about the details of his wedding to the amazing and equally talented Jan Wilson, and mentioned in the final few lines, Oh, one minute play festival, New York and UK, next spring, interested? I said yes. Yes, and …, actually. The "and" being "and … what exactly are one minute plays?"

Our department of theatre at Brooklyn College was enthusiastic and supportive (and has continued to be). I gathered some students, some alums, and some dear friends and fellow artists who were always up for an adventure. We had absolutely no idea what we were doing, but we were willing to figure it out. We rehearsed 50 plays, and on opening night waited to see if anyone would walk through the door of the New Workshop Theatre. The audience that came that night broke all attendance records – because I'm a fire warden I'm not at liberty to say how many people were sitting in the aisles or swinging from the light poles or standing in the back of the house – but we broke a lot of rules that night. In more ways than one.

We'd never seen or experienced anything like it. The audience response was crazy; despite assumptions of one minute plays "being for the short attention span," the opposite was true. The audience were completely hooked in to every moment, hanging on as if it were a rollercoaster. They were audibly and visibly sending energy to the actors onstage, engaged completely with hearts and minds. Their presence and response fed the actors, and the plays themselves. Mickey Ryan, a member of the acting company since that first show in 2005, said:

> I have felt a palpable momentum build during an evening, between an audience and cast that is hard to describe. Ultimately that bond between performers and spectators is what pulls me back in year after year.

Our experience told us this was a form of storytelling and performance that was worth digging into further. It's now 2016, and we're still discovering things. The annual Gi60 Festival at Brooklyn College has raised thousands of dollars in scholarship monies, has introduced our students and audiences to hundreds of playwrights from around the world, and has created international collaborations among artists in the global community. A group of dedicated actors and directors return every year to create Gi60 with me, and some have dubbed it a "summer camp for actors," which delights me, thinking of how Steve and I met at Bucks Rock Camp for the Arts.

2005 seems like a long time ago, and since then we have produced over 1,500 tiny plays. Gi60 was the first one minute play festival in New York and in the UK, has been featured on National Public Radio and various other media outlets, and has now been produced and performed on three continents. It is the longest-running one minute theatre festival in the UK and in New York (and with due respect to festivals who claim "the first" or "the oldest" – we're pretty sure our old friend Fred holds those titles …). Our mission continues to be absolutely inclusive; Gi60 is open to anyone of any age from anywhere, it is wholly run by volunteers, and the plays can be about anything so long as they are wholly original. We are extremely proud of the creative community of writers, performers, and artists that has grown up around this annual event. From the simple idea of trying to provide more opportunities for writers, it has blossomed and expanded since 2003, not unlike its own Big Bang event.

So, you might ask, what are the differences between the needs of a traditional-length play and a one minute or very short-length play? The most obvious difference is that traditional-length plays have the luxury of time, breath, and space. They simply have more room to give exposition, provide detailed given circumstances, develop a range of character traits, and build complex character relationships. There's more available dialogue and language to help build plot, character, and theme. Traditional-length plays have a longer process of building dramatic tension, including the ability to add a range of complexity to the conflicts in the story. Now, a one minute play compresses all of that. It still possesses all of the elements of plot, character, conflict, theme; but it's simply a more compact package.

Another difference is that a traditional-length play is presented as a stand-alone in a single evening (or matinee!). It takes several hours (usually) to experience the single story it has to tell, to discover the one world that the playwright and her collaborators have created together. Sometimes it's a world premiere; often it's a production of a play that has already established itself in the theatre world, and we have knowledge of the story in advance. A one minute play festival introduces the audience to anywhere from 25 to 80 original stories in a single sitting every year. For example, Gi60 US and UK produce 50 new plays each for their festivals, and one of the few rules is that the play must be wholly original, and must not have been previously produced.

A full length play introduces you to a world. An evening of one minute plays introduces you to a universe of worlds.

(David Storck, Gi60 actor, director, playwright)

The breadth and range of the plays include themes of love, death, fear, and justice, and each year it's as if we take the global pulse to see what is guiding our universal heart and conscience. The collection of 50 stories connects the artists and the audience to the big questions (and potential solutions) on everyone's mind. There is a clear sense of a zeitgeist – that is, what is the mood, intellectual and cultural climate, collective consciousness, or spirit of this moment in this time – and the stories express that. And, because every year the plays are new, they express that zeitgeist in an immediate and present way.

And that is one of several advantages of the one minute play. It's nimble enough to express multiple, heartfelt moments of life that unfold into the unique experience of a collage of plays. The smaller time frame allows you to present a larger collection of those moments and stories, so you have a greater chance of capturing everyone in an audience. A single play in an evening stands a good chance of engaging most audience members, but there will always be someone who says, "It just doesn't grab me." An evening of one minute plays is practically guaranteed to engage the entire audience at some point in the evening. With 50 different plays, there's no way there isn't a story for everyone.

Putting on a night of one minute plays is like a fireworks display. One goes off, bang!, right after the other, and each one gets its point across, whereas a full-length play is like waiting for the sunrise. The brilliance is there but it will reveal itself in its own time.

(Nancy Brewka-Clark, Gi60 playwright)

And that's the strongest point we want to make – you may have an idea, a curiosity, or a notion about starting your own short play festival, launching your own workshop, or starting a creative project like this in your school. It *can* be done, you *can* do it, and you've come to the right place to find out more. Now, we are not offering a precise prescription of how to create and produce one minute plays; we're offering methods, stories, observations, and exercises from our years of combined experience that will give you the tools and support you need to create your own experience and support your own vision within the world of tiny theatre. And it may be easier than you think. Simply gather a few people you enjoy collaborating with, and begin to read …

PART ONE

CHAPTER ONE
Writing for short form theatre

Why a one minute play?

> A good one minute play is like a shooting star, it burns bright, and then it's gone. … but it remains in the memory forever.
>
> (Jan Wilson, Gi60 director)

The one minute play is the theatrical equivalent of a classic rock'n'roll 45. It makes its point quickly, it's irreverent, it comes in many flavors, it doesn't always follow the rules, and most importantly, it's got something for everybody. The history of popular music and the pop charts is filled with humor, pathos, love, politics, novelty, one-hit wonders, and of course, legendary talents. The melting pot of creativity, diversity, and freedom that typifies the pop charts' hey-days, where Elvis Presley's visceral *Hard Headed Woman* can sit happily alongside *The Purple People Eater*, can also be seen in a one minute theatre festival.

Popular music was initially dismissed as little more than a fad for the newly invented "teenagers" in the 1950s. Those (now quite mature) teenagers never stopped listening, and popular music has become the most enduring, accessible, and ubiquitous form of creative expression in Western society. This short form of (musical) expression, "the three minute single," can handle the most serious and the most nuanced of subjects as well as the most esoteric and silly. When Neil Young penned *Ohio* in June 1970 as a response to the student shootings at Kent State University, he didn't write a book or pen a letter to Congress; instead, he managed to shine a light on a dark moment in American history and articulate the anger and despair of a nation in just under three minutes. No symphony or concerto could have made a more powerful or singular emotional statement.

Steve

When I heard Billy Bragg sing St Swithin's Day *for the first time, it said more to me about love and heartbreak in two and a half minutes than any opera or theatrical musical could ever hope to do. Young and Bragg's vehicle for expression is "popular" music, so called because it's open to everyone and was therefore viewed, in certain quarters, as not serious. Pop music now forms an integral part of our lives.*

The one minute play may never be viewed with the same reverence that popular music rightfully enjoys, but the one minute play holds the same opportunities as the pop song. Its strength lies, like that of the pop song, in its irreverence: its ability to tackle any and all subjects, no matter how high minded, surreal, metaphysical, or just downright silly.

Detractors seem keen to dismiss the one minute play as not serious and little more than a sketch show for those with limited concentration spans. When the first Gi60 festival took place in 2004, one local newspaper proclaimed from billboards in the town that "Theatre experiments with tiny plays." The publicity was really appreciated, but using the word "experiment" somehow made it sound as if we were doing something sinister, perhaps lurking in a darkened rehearsal room armed with scissors and crazy glue ready to mutilate unsuspecting plays like the playwriting equivalent of The Island of Doctor Moreau. A few years later, a local journalist wrote an article that seemed to suggest that the one minute play was a clear indicator that theatre, and possibly society itself, was in ruins. Once again, we were reminded of popular music's early years and society's outrage at the "bad influence" of rock'n'roll. Seemingly, a very small play can cause very big emotions. The one minute play is brash, unapologetic, and to some the "enfant terrible" of the theatre world (we'll take that as a compliment). Rather than dismiss the form's detractors, we consider that their fears and concerns go a long way toward explaining the potency and power of the one minute play and, perhaps more importantly, what makes it such a vibrant and exciting form.

The most usual argument fired at short format theatre is that 60 seconds or a single page of text cannot possibly provide a platform for serious writing. This is evidenced by citing the fact that so many one minute scripts are humorous. There may be some merit in this: many one minute plays do take the narrative arc of a "joke" or a "sketch" with a single punch line. The comedy sketch is by definition a short form performance, and the classic format of a joke – "set up," "punch line," "tag" – can work beautifully in a one minute play format, such as Inverse Ninja Law by Russ Thorne, Slam Poetry by Dwayne Yancey, and many more. These are very funny pieces of theatre and also completely valid as "serious" writing. "Comedy is a serious business," to quote W. C. Fields. Short form theatre, like all forms of theatre, runs the gamut of human emotions. We see tiny plays of immense beauty, pathos, tragedy, and ingenuity. Helen Elliot's The Collective Memory of Humans, Being ..., Sean Burn's Mistah, Ruben Carbajal's Moment Before Impact, and the poignant Stating the Obvious by Meron Langsner are all deeply moving, fully realized pieces of theatre. Tiny plays can handle emotions big and little; they can be funny or sad, deep or shallow; they can make an important point or be irreverently pointless; but then, to be fair, so can other theatrical formats, so the next question worth asking is …

Why do people write one minute plays?

> My favorite thing about Gi60 is that it drives people to write, not just writers, but all kinds of people. People who might not normally attempt it, who are not necessarily from an academic background. I'm a mechanic by trade. My only college education is one writing course from Old Dominion University that I took while I was in the Navy in Virginia. But Gi60 appeals to people like me. It speaks to, and is open to everyone. All you really need is to have a story to tell, or something that you really want to say.
>
> (Kevin Clyne, Gi60 playwright)

We have been asked that question many times over the years, and it's an excellent starting point for understanding how to write a one minute play. Gi60 writer Kevin Clyne states his own reasons for writing a one minute play very clearly: "it drives people to write, not just writers ..." The one minute play format is a great way to encourage people to start writing. Every year, the submissions for Gi60 include people with little or no previous writing experience and writers from other backgrounds who have never considered writing for the stage before. Sometimes, the freshest plays and most potent stories come from those who are new to writing. This short form is a "way in," an achievable goal, and is a format that can be tackled by almost anybody, irrespective of age, creed, experience, or culture. It opens a door for people to more readily access and share the stories they have within: stories they may be dying to tell, but have been too daunted to write down because of the expectations of the traditional form. Our own Gi60 International One Minute Theatre Festival was created largely along these egalitarian lines. We wanted to encourage as many people, from as many backgrounds as possible, to write for the stage with the opportunity of having their work performed.

Kevin Clyne's quote is a great example of the ability of this format to encourage and nurture new writers. In fact, his first play Nothing was featured on National Public Radio's program The Takeaway when it featured a story on Gi60. Kevin describes how he nearly drove off the road when he heard his play on national radio; and, of course, it gave him even more encouragement to write. However, his perspective represents only a part of the picture. After more than a decade of directing one minute theatre festivals, it's quite clear that the one minute play format appeals to writers across the spectrum. It's easy to understand its appeal to new writers, but what does the tiny play offer the experienced writer? And why do writers, including many successful published writers, continue submitting scripts to us year after year?

Steve

I once asked a world-renowned British playwright (who shall remain nameless) if he would consider submitting a one minute play to our festival. He was kind enough to reply with a handwritten note in which he politely declined our offer, saying (and I'm paraphrasing here) that in his experience, the one minute play could be a bit of a trap, because the shorter the play, the greater the challenge to the playwright. This may very well have been simply an eloquent way of saying "thanks, but no thanks," but it highlight's the very real challenge a one minute play presents for an experienced writer.

For a new writer, the one minute play is the nursery slope of playwriting, easy to negotiate, not too long, and with a soft landing if you should fall. Conversely, for an experienced writer, the one minute play can be like skiing down Everest on a tea tray: a 60-second white knuckle ride with nowhere to hide, where character development, narrative structure, emotional engagement, subtext, and much more have to be explored and honed with clarity, economy, and flair in just one minute.

> A one minute play is meant to stand alone and leave a single impression. A full length that leaves a single impression has most likely failed.
>
> (Meron Langsner, Gi60 playwright)

The one minute play demands clarity: clarity of thought, clarity of idea, clarity of structure and story, and clarity of character. Starting with thought, idea, structure, and story, how can you begin to create and shape it into a play?

- Finish this single sentence: "This story is about ..."

- What's the essential conflict or problem you're writing about? Can you compress it to the "creative math," i.e. the "x vs. y = "? What two forces are in opposition? Innocence vs. Corruption? Ignorance vs. Enlightenment? Illusion vs. Reality?

- What is the journey of the story itself? If the story is a road map, do we begin in one place and arrive somewhere different by the end? Does the story cycle back around and bring us – purposefully – to the same place where we began? Does your story contain journeys where characters start and finish in separate places, only meeting briefly as their journeys cross?

- What specific location does this story need to be set in? And what are the "rules" of that world of the play? Even if it's a "magical realm" – every world of every play has its own set of rules. Define the rules of the world of your play, e.g. "In this world, the characters have the power to make time stand still." "In this world, Bigfoot and The Loch Ness Monster not only exist, but prove their existence." "In this world, the dead can freely move among the living."

- What time period is your play set in, and how does that time support the story? Is it happening at night? Morning? In Dwayne Yancey's play Sunset in North Dakota, two aging minor league baseball players debate the limited time they have left in their athletic careers. The writer's choice to set the play at sunset adds a specific poignancy to their fears and hopes.

- Why are you telling this story at this moment in time? Why is it meaningful to you?

- Why might this story only be able to be told in 60 seconds? How does the 60-second time compress the power or the stakes of your story?

- In a perfect world, your play has just been performed – lights down on the actors, lights up on the audience – what is the first action you would like an audience member to take after having received your story (and we don't mean applause, though that's always nice …)? For example, a story about a parent and child reuniting after a lengthy estrangement might inspire someone to make their own phone call to reconnect with a loved one after leaving the theatre. A play about a missed moment of love that changes someone's life might inspire a theatre-goer to take a chance on love in their own life. Though writers should not try to write for "results" (i.e. manipulation of emotions and such), you should know what and whom you want to affect with your story. How might another person be helped by knowing what you know? What change might you be able to make in the world, or in another person, by sharing this 60-second story?

Considering these questions will help you focus on the content and meaning of your play(s), and will support you in being as specific as possible with your choices. Now, what about the people we will meet who are telling your story?

- Who are your characters? What personality traits do they have? What marks and scars has life left on them? Why do we meet them now?

- What do they need? Why do they need it? What are the imagined consequences if they fail to get what they need?

- What are they prepared to do to get it? How do the actions that they're willing to take in order to get what they want communicate who they are at their core?

- How old are they? How does the age of your character affect their perspective on the situation at hand?

- What is their socio-economic background? Does that affect the story in any way?

- What are their relationships with one another? Not simply "brother and sister" or "parent and child." Those are titles, not relationship descriptions. How do they feel about one another? Are they strangers who are afraid of one another; are they siblings who care deeply about each other? Do they have a history together, and if so, how does that history impact this specific moment in their lives? What is their status with one another? Are they always vying for higher status when they're together? Does the relationship change in this play?

- Are your characters changed by the end of the play? If not, are they purposefully static, or are they struggling to make a personal change? Take a risk? Admit that they're wrong about something?

Yes, All this in 60 seconds. For the experienced writer, the tiny play offers the opportunity to try something that might not work or might be lost in a longer format (two donuts talking, the plight of lost luggage) or concentrate on a very specific moment, unfettered by the need for a larger narrative (the moment a child is born, the exact second that love begins, a doctor entering a mammography waiting room, calling out a woman's name). For the inexperienced writer, it offers a manageable structure that frees the imagination to consider the countless stories they've experienced that occur in a matter of seconds. It gives them the confidence that they can create a fully realized story that can be read and performed. For the experienced writer, the one minute play offers a different environment in which to create, one where the necessitated constraints of time (one minute) can nurture creative invention, providing the challenge and thrill of creating an entire world in 60 seconds.

For me it is about the discovery of that emotional moment; "a failing poltergeist has a moment of success," "a doctor carries with him all the deaths he's known and sighs." Comedy, drama, tragedy, farce all have a discovery moment in the one minute play.

(Jim MacNerland, Gi60 playwright)

A well-written one minute play makes a distinct point with total clarity, unencumbered by the need to justify or apologize. It can highlight the problem without needing to provide the solution. For some people this is problematic, cited as a flaw in tiny plays, but as Jim MacNerland says,

One minute plays are like a bullet, sometimes the aftermath creates more drama than the actual piece. I like that, too. I guess I'm a trouble maker.

One minute plays have the ability to stir things up and cause trouble because they focus on a moment: the battle, not the war. Or, perhaps more accurately, one single soldier loading the first bullet into their rifle. The one minute play challenges and focuses the writer to make a singular point that is clear and concise, but it also offers the freedom to explore territory and ideas that might not be suitable or sustainable in longer forms. A quick look at the diversity of characters, themes, and settings for the plays contained in this book clearly shows how much of a sandbox opportunity the one minute play format is, and I think this is why experienced writers return to the form again and again.

The most satisfying element of writing a one minute play is how even the smallest of ideas work in this format. So that phrase, event, or conceit you've never found a place for can fit perfectly without the baggage of having to be expanded way beyond its usefulness and outstay its welcome.

(Jim MacNerland, Gi60 playwright)

How to write a great one minute play?

There is no one way to write a great tiny play. Creativity doesn't have a road map or GPS, and although there are some key elements that you need to consider when writing a tiny play, ultimately it's your journey and your choice. So turn off the highway, drive across the grass, and if you knock over the fire hydrant or a garden gnome, don't let it get you down. We have now read over 7,000 one minute plays since Gi60 started, and we can honestly say that two things have become very clear. First, you have to kiss a lot of frogs before you find your prince or, indeed, your princess, and second, the ability of a 60-second play to surprise, delight, shock, or move you makes all that frog kissing totally worthwhile. In the spirit of creating a prince(ss) and not a frog, there are a number of key ingredients that recur in successful one minute plays.

I think my favorite play has got to be *School of Thought* by Mark Harvey Levine. It seemed to typify exactly what the one minute play does brilliantly. A high concept, with immense potential for staging and perfectly formed to last one minute.

(Hedley Brown, Gi60 actor, playwright, assistant director)

School of Thought by Mark Harvey Levine casts a school of fish in the role of the "prevailing political landscape." As the fish change direction, so their leadership and the political policy change with them. The play is an excellent example of the 60-second format, because it is concise and clear in all of its elements and contains the key ingredients we see again and again in good one minute plays:

- Clarity of idea: The flip-flop nature of the political landscape illuminated by the metaphor of a school of fish swimming and changing direction in the changing currents of the ocean.

- Clarity of character(s): A school of fish representing our political leaders and parties.

- Clarity of staging: A school of fish swimming. By using a school of fish as characters and metaphor for the piece, we are provided with clear staging opportunities. The specific physical actions demanded for the movement of a school of fish in the water afford directors and performers a great deal of scope to play with shape and form. In short, this is the kind of one minute play you want to direct and perform.

- Clarity of location: A body of water representative of any country or culture from any period in history.

- No need for long stage directions.

The joy of short form festivals is that you are likely to get many more applications than you would for one-act or full-length submission opportunities, and with short form theatre you can read the entire play rather than a synopsis. Because of this, the writer's previous work and background are less important in the process. The reality of play selection for Gi60 has always been both a pragmatic and an ideological endeavor. When selecting one minute plays for a festival, we are interested in only one thing: "Is the play any good?" Pragmatically speaking, with 100 new plays a year to select for performance from a submitted selection of 700–900 plays, we simply don't have time to look at anything other than the plays themselves. Ideologically, the play should come first. We get submissions from well-known writers, returning writers, new writers, writers young and old, and writers from across the globe. It would be easy to just cherry pick the plays from those playwrights we know or those playwrights who are well known, but it wouldn't be fair, and frankly, we wouldn't make the best selection if this were our process. You have read the entire play; you therefore know all you need to know.

As we've written, there is no one road map for a successful one minute play. Perhaps a better analogy would be that there is no single recipe. Many ingredients, when combined, taste great, and an equal number do not. In an attempt to help you avoid putting anchovies in your chocolate pudding, we have listed some handy "Do's and don'ts of tiny plays":

Things that you SHOULD DO when writing a tiny play

- Make sure you have a very clear idea of what you are trying to say. "I want to be a seagull because I would be free to fly and I enjoy eating fish." "I'm dying and I need to finally tell you that I'm proud of who you have become."

- Be theatrical, dream big; don't be constrained by theme or character. Let the Atheist Parrot talk to God, let the advancing horde stop for a latte and a heated discussion about the pitfalls of industrialized milk production. Be real, be surreal, be brave.

- Create clear, defined characters. I am the moon and I'm insecure about my relationship with the earth. I am John, my father left me when I was 14, and I live on the street.

- Be specific; try to avoid overly long or complex stage directions. Examples of strong, economic, and clear stage directions: five minutes before the world ends; a hospital corridor; in a car moments before a collision. Set the scene with the same economy and clarity as your play.

- Have a clear narrative arc with a beginning, a middle, and an end. It seems obvious, but so many tiny plays that we read have a beginning and a middle, but no resolution or conclusion. Make sure you know where your destination is before setting off.

- Ask yourself whether your play reads well off the page. Would a stranger who picked up your script immediately understand both the words you have written and those you have not? Use of local slang or patois may give your character extra color and depth, but if the terminology is alien to your reader, you may need to provide a footnote (e.g. Ginnel: noun, Northern English: a narrow passage between buildings; an alley) or use a less nuanced word. The simplest way to do this is to get a friend to read your script, or, even better, read the script out loud with them. Sometimes what works well on the page doesn't work as well when said aloud.

- Remember that what you *don't* write is as important as what you do. The spaces between the lines are where actors earn their money. A single look can do the job of a page of text in the hands of good actors. Ask yourself: "Do I need to write this or is it implied?" Trust; if your writing is strong enough and your narrative arc is clear, your actors will tell your story, and those words you chose not to write will give the actors the freedom to practice their craft.

- Is your metaphor clear? Do we understand that "the sheep" are representative of the Oscar nominees on the red carpet? Have you included enough specifics for us to draw the line between the herd mentality of the sheep and the herd mentality of the celebrities and paparazzi crowding in front of the Hollywood Bowl? If you find yourself explaining the metaphor in the stage directions, then the sheep are probably just sheep, and you may need to rewrite for clarity and impact.

- Cut, cut, cut. It is surprising how often the phrase "I like it, but it drags a bit" can be applied to a tiny play. Remember that one page does *not* equal one minute. Read your play out loud, in real time. Are you over-explaining things? Have confidence in your abilities. Trust that you can clearly communicate with fewer words than you *think* you need. If you're reading this book in a public area right now, take a moment to put the book down, and look up. Observe the body language of the people around you. That couple sitting close to one another on the subway seat directly across from you: are their bodies relaxed and intimate? Are they leaning into each other, or avoiding each other's eyes? If you're in a coffee shop, look at the young man sitting alone. Is he glancing about, anxiously waiting for someone? Is he openly staring with menace at the barista behind the counter? Is he absently scrolling through his phone, a worried tightness around his mouth, not seeing the message he needs? Look around you; right now, in *this* minute. How many stories can you tell about the relationships and physical language of the people around you? Now imagine what you can achieve in 60 seconds, with clear story, characters, and ideas, and a few words on the page.

Rose

Living in New York City, I love to observe the small stories that happen around me on a daily basis. I was once on a packed subway car near Wall Street just after 5:00 pm, and everyone was really tense, guarded, and grouchy. There was a businessman who was furiously poring through a fistful of papers that he was trying to hold onto, while he was constricted by the mass of people, trying not to lose his grip on the pole. A little girl about 6 or 7 years old pointed at him and started saying, "Mister? Mister?" He did the classic New York "In my world, you don't exist" move; bringing the papers closer to his face and gluing his eyes to the pages. But she was undeterred. Her voice got louder as she tried to get his attention, "Mister?? Mister??" Her voice rose higher and higher above the subway noise until he finally gave up in exasperation, looked at her, and impatiently said, "Yes??" She smiled and said, "You got a lotta homework. But don't worry. It'll be okay." The businessman – and everyone in the car – melted. That little girl's sheer insistence on reaching out to a struggling, unhappy human being – well, it moved us, and created a bond with every stranger in that car. Now, that whole story took maybe 30 seconds, not 60. Think of all the stories we might be missing ...

- Start at the end. As mentioned earlier, if you don't know where you're going, you will almost certainly not arrive. If the play is about two people saying goodbye forever at an airport, don't spend 58 seconds on the car journey to the terminal. If the play is about saying goodbye, start at the terminal gate, concentrate on that moment. Will she get on the plane? Is this actually goodbye forever? That's up to you, but whatever the outcome, your audience will get to experience that destination.

- Go back and rewrite, check your grammar, and ensure every word you use is the strongest word or combination of words. With such a short form, every word has to earn its place. Just because the play lasts only 60 seconds, it doesn't mean you should take less time to polish it.

- Heed the words of Jim MacNerland: "A minute is always longer than you think and shorter than you want."

Things to try to AVOID when writing a tiny play

- Including excessive stage directions. If your dialogue doesn't tell the reader all they need to know about your characters, their location, and their situation, perhaps you need to go back and see if the script can be revised so that these things are clear. Long stage directions are never a substitute for a well-written script.

- Rehashing clichés or well-known scenarios. Some jokes are as old as the hills, and some are worth repeating, but try to avoid staging an old joke or comedic scenario that everyone has heard or seen before. If you do want to retell a story or a joke, then make sure you bring something new to the party. Interpretation is much more appealing than repetition. What draws you to that familiar territory? What specifically resonates for you in those situations, and what fresh point of view do you have on it? Sure, everyone has seen the sketch in which a man slips on a banana peel; but have they seen that story from the banana peel's perspective? Make your script as distinct and interesting as you are.

- Unless you have a specific reason for doing so, try to avoid calling characters names like "him," "her," "A," "B," "One," or "Two." While, in certain circumstances, this can be an effective way to name characters and help illuminate a script, often ambiguous character names are the result of an ambiguous script rather than the result of specific choices. Character names are very important; even the spelling of names should be closely considered. In such a short format, every word you write is considered. Names can tell us – and the actors – a great deal about a person. Nationality, family background, culture, even social status can be conveyed by a name. In Tom Carrozza's play *Old Italians in Lawn Chairs*, the characters are named Josephine, Nella, Philomena, and Pippo. There is a sense of an "old world" to these names; they communicate an age and a weighty feeling. The names make you think of old Brooklyn or Little Italy in New York, or *Godfather* II when they're back in the 1920s. And, at least in the US, you wouldn't name a child Philomena or Pippo, unless you want them to grow up feeling old with a name like that. Imagine them being named Denise, Marie, Tony, and Joey instead; completely different images come to mind. Which set of names more aptly evokes "old" Italians in lawn chairs? Having said that, the ambiguity afforded by "A" and "B" naming can be useful, particularly where there is a wish to represent an "Everyman" character. However, this could also lead to actors failing to connect with characters and/or make strong choices, which could render Everyman as "no one in particular".

- Having the characters speak extensively about other characters whom we'll never meet in this story, and who don't really drive the action forward. If your protagonist confronts another person and starts with "This is just like the time you and Drew and Mildred borrowed that crappy old car from Miklos instead of renting something decent, and it broke down in front of Amy's house, and you had to call Ally to come pick you all up and bring you to my wedding to Connor." The audience is trying to keep up with who these people are, whether they're pertinent to the story we're actually seeing, and wondering if we're ever going to meet these people. The brain is a funny thing; we hear something, and we're not so quick to let it go, especially with a one minute play. We think we're going to need that piece of information in the next few seconds. Meanwhile, we're missing the story that's actually happening because we've been bogged down with unnecessary people and facts that are essentially a "data dump" weighing down the story. The whole run-on sentence above is about someone being confronted about their poor judgment. If the character begins with "Susan, you promised you would be on time for my wedding. I'll never trust you again," Susan now needs to plead for forgiveness. You're immediately placed in a classic "Please/No" conflict. (See Appendix A for this exercise in establishing clear conflict and objectives.)

- Writing a monologue instead of a play. A monologue is different and distinct from a play where only one character speaks. Monologues have their place, and we have staged many fantastic ones over the years, but a monologue doesn't allow interaction with other characters, and that is what makes a play a play.

- Using expletives unless you need them. All too often, expletives are used in the place of true emotion. If your character is swearing, ask yourself whether she is doing so because no other words will fully convey what's being said, or whether the expletive is being used as a short cut to or a substitution for the emotion you're trying to convey. The unnecessary misuse of expletives is one of the most common problems with scripts, of all lengths, that we read. More often than not, the use of an expletive covers the fact that the character's emotional journey has not been fully realized. Remove the expletive and reread your work: is the character still in the same emotional place without the expletive? If they are, then let them curse. If they are not, then they never had a good enough reason to curse in the first place. Sometimes people swear because it's part of the rhythm of their speech. If your character needs to swear, by all means let them swear, but ensure that the swearing is grounded in the truth of the character.

- Ranting. If you are going to tackle a subject that makes your blood boil (and good for you if you do), you will need to climb down from the soap box long enough to ask yourself "Am I writing a pithy one minute play that articulates my point, or am I just angry?" If it's the latter, you might want to consider a rethink. Turn your anger into actions, and allow the characters to inhabit those actions to tell a fully realized story that communicates your point to an audience.

- Writing a play that exists only so you can use a clever "switch" at the end. We also call those the "ba da bump" plays. For example, two people are having a debate about killing a human being; we think we're in a rough neighborhood in a big city; then, in the very last sentence, they reveal they're really lions in the jungle about to pounce on a safari guide. The play exists only for the twist "they're really lions" in the final moment. Another example is two people meeting on a blind date; they don't hit it off and immediately get into an argument about something. In the final sentences, someone invariably says "I'm sorry I agreed to meet you, Joanna." "I'm not Joanna, my name is Annabelle." Sheepish exits. Or, one scenario we've read on multiple occasions finds a heated discussion among some people who've died. They're moaning about how disappointed they are with heaven, only for it to be revealed in the final moment that they're in "The Other Place." Having a clever idea for an ending is no substitution for a strong story that leads to a solid conclusion.

Supportive exercises

There really isn't a single way to write a one minute play, and that's exactly how it should be; however, there are times when you need a little kick start to get the creative juices flowing and to defeat the blank white page (or, more accurately, blank white screen). The exercises below can be done alone, or can be used in a classroom setting for groups. These exercises work equally well for young or old, for novice or experienced writer. The examples listed here can be expanded or changed and are offered as a supportive reference to help get you started. In addition to providing some individual writing stimulus, these exercises can be used to encourage writers to work collaboratively, particularly in a classroom setting.

Exercise 1: Pen head (generating content)

You will need:

Paper, pen, and stopwatch or other device with an alarm/stopwatch function.

1. Set the alarm for one minute.

2. As soon as you start the stopwatch, you must start writing anything and everything that pops into your head, and you must write continually, without stopping, thinking, or considering, for one minute. Don't take your pen off of the page and don't question what you are writing, just write.

3. At the end of the minute, stop writing and review your work. If you are doing this as a group, read some of the pieces out loud and discuss what has been written.

What is the purpose of this exercise?

By writing freely under pressure for one minute, the act of writing itself becomes the focus rather than the content of what's being written. This refocusing away from conscious narrative can free the writer from the constraints of storytelling, leading to unexpected discoveries. Most of what you write may be of little or no use, but often writers find the germ of an idea or a narrative possibility hidden in the gibberish.

The second reason for this exercise is that it illustrates to someone how much time a minute really is, and how many words and ideas can be crammed into that small amount of time. Writers are often surprised at how long a minute seems when they take part in this exercise. They are also often surprised at what was bubbling in their subconscious. If you are in the mood for writing but out of ideas, this can be a fantastic exercise.

Exercise 2: The ballad of X & Y? (generating content)

You will need:

Paper and pen for each participant and some large sheets for the group.

The aim of this exercise is to open the door to writing by creating collaboratively without pressure or expectation. This exercise is a twist on the traditional writing game "Consequences." Give each writer in the group (unlike all the others, this exercise requires two or more participants) a strip of paper. Photocopier paper folded down its length, then cut, works very well.

- Ask the group to tell you some of their favorite words. Words that have a flavor or are fun to say, and also personal words that might be local or slang words or perhaps only used by their family. Write these down on the large sheet of paper and display so that all the group can see them.

Steve

I love this exercise as it really generates some interesting words and conversations. I always give the example of strudel because it's just so much fun to say (you're trying it now, aren't you?) and loquacious because it sounds so beautiful and I prefer being called loquacious rather than a big mouth! Slang, local, and family words are also great for generating character and bringing the group together (set some rules about slang words). You may want to give an example to get the ball rolling. For instance, in our house we call the TV remote the pointy-press, and in my part of the world a passageway or an alleyway is known as a ginnel or a snicket.

- Ask each person to write a name at the top of the page (i.e. Michael or Carlos or Juanita) Then fold the paper so that the name cannot be seen. Each participant then passes their paper to the person on their left.

- Repeat step one and pass the papers to the left. You should now have two names on each paper.

- Ask the group to write a line of dialogue, which must contain one of the words you wrote down at the start of the exercise (e.g. "Where does that snicket lead to?" or "Have you seen the pointy-press? I'm sure I left it on the table." Once everybody has written their line of dialogue, fold the paper so that the line cannot be seen and pass to the left.

- Continue this process using words from the create list until you reach the end of the sheets of paper and pass to the left one final time.

- Ask your participants to read out these newly created works of theatre. Get two group members to take the parts of the character, so that in *The Ballad of Michael and Juanita* one group member would take the role of Michael and the other Juanita.

Some of the ballads may make little or no sense or raise a smile, and in rare cases some quite moving dialogue can be created. When you have finished reading the ballads, encourage the groups to scrunch the papers into a ball and throw them into the middle of the room. This symbolic act can be very freeing (especially for more seasoned writers). Make sure you keep your list of personal, slang, and local words, as these can be used in the following exercises.

Exercise 3: What's in a name? (generating character)

You will need:

Paper (large sheets for group work), pens, dice, stopwatch or other device with an alarm/stopwatch function.

The aim of this exercise is to help you quickly generate new characters with which you can work. If you are working alone, you use the name lists below to start generating characters immediately; if you are working as part of a group, it's often more fun to generate names together using the methods described below.

Category 1

Happy	Mike	Badger
Susie	Rocky	Stig
Lucinda	Pumpkin	Doreen
Ernst	Bruce	Rusty
Beishung	Nan	Fridey
Kolya	Samson	Luca
Beba	Catia	Dillon
Coco	Mena	Bernie
Mandy	George	Larry
Jan	Daisy	Zebedee

Category 2

Simon	Gitter	Burton
Penn	Clegg	Bulova
Nightingale	Baverstock	Matzke
Cleary	Butterworth	Winchcombe
Harris	Wilson	Banks
Smith	Upchurch	Hart
Seidan	Budd	Wallace Hoare
Olivia	Lamby	Smith
Blumberg	Hobbs	Segal
Yockers	Krantz	Green

- Pick a name from Category 1, or ask group members to pick a number between 1 and 30 if working in a group (if you are working in a group, do not show the names to group members until all the names have been used).

- Do the same for Category 2.

- Join the two words together and repeat as many times as you need (if you are writing on your own, generate at least half a dozen names).

You will now have generated a diverse, rich, and at times just plain strange list of names. Pick one name that interests or inspires you and set the stopwatch for five minutes. Now, write in as much detail as possible about a character bearing that name. Before starting this exercise, take a quick look at our notes about character, or if you are leading a group, get the group to read these notes out loud. Five minutes should be enough time to write a short but detailed synopsis about your new character, including their age, gender, occupation, relationship status, the clothes they are wearing, where they are living, their health, finances, favorite foods, allergies, and any other specifics that add detail and color.

If you are working alone, repeat this process with another character. If you are working in a group, share the details of each character created, and then write down their name with a simple description on large sheets of paper that everybody can see.

ALTERNATE METHODS OF GENERATING NAMES

The names listed above were generated via social media. We asked people on social media to tell us their first pet's name and the surname of their first love. If you are working in a group, you can do the same. Names of pets, the name of your first boss or first boyfriend/girlfriend, or your mother's maiden name can all be used (be creative). Any of these will provide you with some interesting and colorful nomenclature. You could also split your participants up into two groups. Take a forename from Group One and add it to a surname in Group Two.

Group 1:

Christopher Thomasson

Joel Dean

Group 2:

Anthony Ponzio

Madeleine Frost

You might end up with "Christopher Frost" or "Madeleine Dean" or "Joel Ponzio" (1940s failed boxer now living on the upper east side of Manhattan …).

The names you generate, no matter which methods you use, will have their own Identity. Some characters may feel very familiar, and some may seem quite distant, but each new character provides you with a possible story yet to be told.

Exercise 4: What's in the box? (generating content and character)

You will need:

Paper (large sheets for group work), pens, stopwatch or other device with an alarm/stopwatch function.

This exercise is designed to help create content and theatrical tension. If you are working with a group, ask them to think of an item from childhood that was important to them, maybe a gift from a loved one that was unique. Maybe a piece of jewelry or a music box (ask them to avoid obvious items like stuffed toys, technology, etc.). If you are working alone, you can use one of the items from the list below.

A piece of crystal	A banjo	A children's picture book
A catcher's mitt	A compact (mirror)	A bottle cap
A silver cross	A bookmark	A tobacco tin
A doll's head	A pack of cards	A scarf
A Miles Davis LP	A conductor's baton	An egg timer
A cat's skull	A tiny metal dragon	A fountain pen
A pair of gloves	A baseball card	A music box
A kaleidoscope	A perfume bottle	A key
A necklace	A stone	A cassette mix tape
A shark's tooth	A strand of hair	A flag

Set the stopwatch for five minutes and write about the item in as much detail as possible. Describe the item's size, weight, feel, age, temperature, and appearance. Describe how you came to own it (fictionally if you are using our list, factually if you are writing about a personal possession), what it means to you emotionally, and anything else you can without actually mentioning what the item is. At the end of five minutes, if you are working in a group, ask participants to read out their description and allow the other participants to discuss what the item is. Write down each item with a short description on the large sheets of paper. If you are working alone, find somebody to read your description to, and see if they can work out your item from what you have written.

Exercise 5: Have we met? (generating narrative)

You will need:

Paper and pens.

This exercise brings together the work done in Exercises 2 and 3 in narrative form.

Whether you are working alone or in a group, you will now have created at least two new characters and have a detailed description of an item.

- Write a short 100–150-word description of how the item (group participants may pick any item other than their own) relates to one of the characters.

- Write approximately one minute of dialogue that involves a meeting between the character with the item you just wrote about and one of the other characters.

If you are working as part of a group, why not perform these newly created plays? And if you are working alone, you deserve a break, so print out two copies of your new play and head to a friend's house. If the final result is good, you could always submit it to a one minute play festival.

Steve

I love these exercises because you don't need to be precious about what you are writing. If you are doing the exercises in a group, one writer may generate a character but another write a play about them. At the end of the session, anything you don't want you just discard. When I use these exercises with writing groups, I encourage writers (of all ages) to throw what they've written into the center of the room once we've used it (unless they wish to keep it). The act of discarding can initially be stressful, but once people embrace the idea it's very liberating.

The exercises above are not designed to show you how to write a one minute play (that's your job). They are designed to put words on a blank page and to offer up character and narrative ideas that were lurking in your subconscious that you might otherwise have missed. Mostly they are designed to make writing fun and accessible. The exercises can be done alone (except in one case) or in a group setting. They work equally well for young or old, for novice or experienced writers. The examples listed here are only a starting point, and you can expand, change, and tailor the exercises quite easily so that they work for you and your particular set of circumstances. All of these can be used in conjunction with the syllabus/scheme of work example we have included in Appendix B.

CHAPTER TWO
Acting and directing in short form theatre

Being able to jump from play to play means being able to jump from actor to actor and dynamic to dynamic without blinking. Rehearsing for Gi60 is like mingling at a dinner party with 20 different people, except the mingling isn't just small talk – it's admitting your deepest secrets, sharing your most vulnerable truths, and laughing your absolute hardest and least polite laughs … one must be focused, flexible, playful, attentive, and intuitive with your partners. This allows the play to keep evolving and the characters and their relationships to keep growing.

(Anastasia Bell, Gi60 actor)

Dynamic and intense conflicts, lightning-fast changes, suspended moments of heartbreak, earth-shattering decisions, whiplash reversals, breathtaking revelations, all in 60 seconds or less. Directing and acting for one minute plays is not quite like anything else. Though director Mike Flanagan once said, "It's pretty much the same as any other play. But shorter. A lot shorter…," a one minute play demands that we use our acting and directing skills differently. Look at it this way; we might approach a musical or a straight play similarly as far as creative philosophy goes, but a musical asks us to work different muscles than the straight play, and vice versa. Similarly, one minute plays have all the elements of a traditional-length play (plot, character, conflict, theme), but they're more compact. We like to compare it to when Superman picks up a lump of coal and squeezes it with his superpowers. The elemental properties don't change, but when Superman opens his hand, he reveals a spectacular diamond. Multi-faceted, shiny, beautiful, and small. That's a one minute play. Its compressed nature determines the muscles we need to focus on in rehearsal and production, because it is the directors' and actors' laser eyes that reveal the clarity and make the cuts to make the diamond shine.

The plays come to us in a form which needs a clear hand and actions to make it come into its own. They don't all show up as diamonds, but when we mount them they are. Whether it is just a polish or maybe a light cut, the directors and actors shine the light through the diamond's prism to show the most clarity and brilliance – the true story of the play.

(Michael Colby Jones, Gi60 director)

So, it's not that the skills actors and directors need for traditional-length and one minute plays are different; but performing in and directing 60-second plays demands a higher concentration of those skills so that the play and its story can shine bright. Think of Superman and the diamond. The strength and precision Superman needs to make that diamond has the same source as the strength and precision that Clark Kent uses when writing at his typewriter (for us, Clark Kent will always be at a typewriter and not a laptop). Strength and precision are always strength and precision, but how they're employed makes all the difference in the world. One minute plays compel us to commit our artistic choices to every single moment within each play. When a story must be told in 60 seconds (or less!), there is simply no time or energy to waste.

Everything is going so fast … you need to be all there. You can't miss anything … or you're wasting precious time. You're going to want that time.

(Walter Petryk, Gi60 actor, playwright)

Whether you're a seasoned theatre practitioner about to perform in or direct a one minute play festival, or an early career drama teacher designing a one minute play project for your students, we're here to help guide you through the process. For the experienced theatre practitioner, these ideas and concepts will be familiar. For those of you who may be at the beginning of your journey in theatre, we include a series of exercises in the Appendices to help you explore these skills with your students or company of players. So, what are those essential skills and attributes that actors and directors require to create the phone booth needed for their inner Clark Kent to more readily become Superman?

Skills and attributes for actors in one minute plays (but directors, please take note!)

- being 100% present in a moment; listening, listening, listening
- focus, awareness, and observation
- commitment
- specificity
- powerful imagination
- risk taking
- adaptability
- versatility
- physical storytelling
- strong and supple vocal instrument
- stamina
- a generous and collaborative spirit
- being grounded and calm, no matter what is going on around you
- trust, trust, and more trust

Being present in the moment, and listening

> One must be totally-completely-mind-spirit-and-body present. Because if you fall out of it, or you blink, it's over.
>
> (Anastasia Bell, Gi60 actor)

Being present and listening go in hand. And yes, actors should *always* be present and truthfully responding to their partner's choices in the moment. But let's face it; with full-length plays, whether in rehearsal or in performance, there are times when an actor can check out: they might have a few pages between lines, something steals their focus, or they have a false sense that their thoughts can wander without consequences. "Hmm, Henry seems a little off today. I wonder if he's OK?" or "Wow, that's the best that Frankie and Artie's scene has gone yet; man, I never thought they'd break through … Hey, why is it so quiet …? Oops …"

A well-written 60-second story is filled to the brim with given circumstances, character traits, and actions, so actors must listen and be alert for every nuance. If focus wanders even for a moment, they'll miss an essential piece of character and story that they might not be able to recover in the remaining moments of the play. An entire relationship can shift with one word, or an essential plot twist will reveal itself in a sentence instead of a lengthy monologue. The economy of the story gets us "there" more quickly, and the actors must take us there. Being present and listening ensures that every moment is alive, connected, and truthful, and that those moments will be clear and will help tell the story to the audience.

Now, performing a one minute play can have a weird effect on actors; they sometimes experience the time going by so quickly that they get the feeling they've missed something or dropped a line. And then, boom; they stop themselves for no reason. Sometimes that's simply because they need to become more familiar with the rhythms and tempos of the short play, but it also comes back to whether they are listening, connecting, and being present. And even when actors do stay connected, the brevity of each story can feel counter-intuitive, and peculiar doubts can pop up. To counter this, we recommend that each time the play is rehearsed, be sure to run the whole thing several times. Even if you just want to touch up a few moments or fix a piece of blocking, make sure you run the play in its entirety, and at the end of each rehearsal, run all the plays that you've worked in that particular session. This helps the actors discover the natural rhythm of the piece early in the process, and it helps directors see where they need to focus their attention at the play's next rehearsal.

> The most challenging part about performing a one minute play is that there is no "right" way to do it. Even after running a certain play 20 or 30 times, it still might not feel quite "right." It can be difficult to "crack" some of these tiny stories, or to capture the heart of them in so little time. Sometimes it feels like you'll never have enough time … and the show just has to go on!
>
> (Anastasia Bell, Gi60 actor)

Focus, awareness, observation

> Living so many diverse characters in a single evening, so quickly, puts all your senses on red alert. Listening, focus, timing. There is no landing strip. You must drop in, fully present. It's thrilling.
>
> (Ramona Floyd, Gi60 actor, playwright)

Now, to be present and listening in a one minute play, actors need a heightened focus, a hyper-awareness, and to be keenly observant at all times. Every choice that actors commit to is an opportunity to strengthen a relationship, clarify a point of view, or draw attention to a key plot element. Also, in a full program of one minute plays, directors might cast a single actor in anywhere from 5 to 15 plays. Awareness of the rhythm of the entire program/running order itself will help an actor be prepared for each play that they appear in, both for practical purposes and for psychological preparation. Have you ever watched kids on a playground playing double-dutch jump rope? Look at the girl waiting to "jump in" – she's keenly alert, watching everything; you see her physically listening to the rhythm of the people swinging the ropes, and you see her intense awareness of the rhythm of the person who is about to "jump out." Her focus is laser tight, her body starts to sway with the rhythm, and at exactly the right moment, she jumps in – flawlessly avoiding the ropes that could trip her at the ankles, and immediately beginning her own double-dutch dance.

That's what we're talking about with one minute plays. Actors need to reach a level of awareness so that they can work with the ropes swirling around them, while executing the actions necessary for the plays they're in.

Now, losing focus in a one minute play can be deadly. If you trip on those ropes, it could mean dropping a key relationship dynamic, or losing the turning point in a relationship, and the whole purpose of the play could be lost. Losing focus or being unobservant has the potential for a short play festival to turn into a disaster. Ten minute play festivals often produce five to seven plays in a night. One minute play festivals produce anywhere from 25 to 80 plays in a single night. Though it has only happened three times in 13 years of Gi60, an unfocused actor has indeed run onstage into the wrong play. Fortunately, each time there was a group of focused actors waiting to whoosh them right off again, usually with a clever improv moment relating to the play they're all supposed to be in.

The other potential nightmare is if an actor misses an entrance for a play they're *supposed* to be in. Not only does a loss of focus mean you risk missing an entrance, but you risk missing an entire *play*. We've seen (and been told about afterwards!) many a close call averted because the cast of 14–16 actors are so vigilant on everyone's behalf, they become keenly aware of *everyone's* entrances and exits, not simply their own. This creates a collective sense of ownership of the evening of theatre that is truly thrilling. And trust us; it helps the directors sleep easier at night …

Steve

As a director I rely on the actors to let me know "where they are" in any given moment. It's not unusual to hear comments like "I can't come on from stage left as I am just leaving stage right." Or "I can't pass them the sword as I'm supposed to be lying dead on the stage at the time." Your actors, as always, are your greatest asset; empower them in the process. Many of the actors I work with are seasoned one minute performers and we have a working relationship that has been built up over many years. Our working process is fast and efficient. This could be very daunting to new company members, but I have always found that those more experienced company members will offer their support and advice, allowing those new to the process to settle in quickly and find their feet.

Commitment

There's something about a one minute play that means in the very instant an actor has not committed to a choice, everybody sees it and feels it; there's nowhere to hide. Commitment: commitment to specificity, to objectives and actions (what does this character want, why, and what are they willing to do to get it?), to physical and vocal choices, and commitment from the first second that the play begins. There's no time to "slide" into the world of the play; actors need to firmly land with both feet on the ground and make it as clear as possible to the audience where the play is set, who these people are, and what their story is. Anything vague creates confusion and risks audience members "dropping out." If the audience lose attention at the beginning of a one minute play, there's a good chance they'll check out for the *entire* play, simply telling themselves "Ah, I'll catch up with the next one." Commitment. Don't leave home without it.

Specificity

> Only the most significant words can be used – there is nothing wasted or thrown away. Everything that is said has a very specific purpose.
>
> (Catherine Clyne, Gi60 playwright)

> I love to see how much I can take away without the structure collapsing.
>
> (Ruben Carbajal, Gi60 playwright)

Specificity of words and language impacts actors and audience; every single word carries a potent weight. We've seen actors "skim" over words in full-length plays; not so in a one minute play. There's no fat on the bone; every choice has to be filled with specificity of purpose. The devil may be in the details, but the angels are there too. Committing to distinct choices in each moment clarifies the journey of the character, their relationships, and the arc of the story itself. We've also found that with younger actors, when they discover the significance of the choices they make in this form, it strengthens their overall confidence and reduces doubt and "the enoughs" ("is my choice strong enough? Clever enough?").

They can see and sense the impact of their choices clearly and more quickly, and that nurtures self-confidence in all of their work.

> I do my best to physically differentiate my characters. Finding how they carry themselves, where their strength is, and where their voice originates from can really help with that. Some of my favorite characters have no lines. There is a physical freedom that comes from the limitation of creating a character without the use of language.
>
> (Adam Thomas Smith, Gi60 actor)

Now, one of the most fun and exciting challenges of Gi60 is that our playwrights love to write about fantastical creatures and realms. We've produced plays about mice at a funeral, birds fighting over a hedge, and talking suitcases trapped on an airport carousel, and on Halloween in 2010 we devoted an entire festival to ghosts and the supernatural. We've had Death go to the movies and accidentally take out an entire row of patrons through his bumbling, an offended gorilla chastise (and educate!) a group of school kids who called her a "monkey," and most poignantly, we've seen a couple in a frozen moment reflect on life just before they perish in a car crash. We love producing these plays; they're a wonderful challenge to the idea of specificity and imagination. How can a clear physical tableau communicate that we're at a wedding and that Cristina is the bride? How can a particular intonation of a line help place Sofiya at a city bus station and not a school bus stop? How can a quick and specific scratch behind the ear show us that Kate is a velociraptor and not a cat? It's exciting to find solutions in the fantasy plays, though we'd be lying if we said that a small investment in a bag of mouse noses doesn't help …

> When you're performing in a one minute play, your choices have to be even stronger and sharper … You must drive your action home every moment you're on stage – not because time is running out, but because if you don't stay as present as possible, you're wasting this One Minute Play's precious time. Performing in a one minute play is a reminder of how strong your choices should ALWAYS be.
>
> (Samantha Fontana, Gi60 actor)

Without specificity, you have 60 seconds of mud; it's that simple. A single evening of multiple plays will have stories about loving relationships, interstellar visitations, family crises, ocean voyages, and actors playing everything from people to chickens to zombies. Short form writers are adventurous and imaginative, and they need the actors and directors to make sense of their adventurous and compact stories. There's no time for elaborate costumes or scenic elements to help clarify that we're at a funeral parlor, on a starship, or underwater. There isn't a second or third act to further clarify whether these two people love or hate each other. Each one minute play needs to have its specific story realized, and each play must be distinct from the others. You can't afford to say, "Ah, here's another timid-nerd character. I'll just do what I did before." Any "sameness" can trigger an audience member into thinking, "Oh, this is a recurring character – how interesting! Wait, why is he in a field of tomatoes?" Remember, 60 seconds doesn't mean you have less to do; you actually have more to do. Which leads us to …

Powerful imagination

Gi60 actors are inspired by the few dynamic words on the page, and the feelings and images they get from those words. They create a history, relationships, actions, and a home life; in short, they create essential given circumstances from their imaginations, because the play doesn't have the time to provide very much about them. As long as the text that is there supports their decisions, the imaginative choices help ground the actors in a more fully realized world of the play. This leads to a personalization and deeper ownership of the material, which helps audiences connect to the actors and the stories. However, actors then need to allow their imaginations to expand and soar from that point of personalization in order to bring the many varied characters and worlds to full life.

> The plays always work better if the actor is connecting to the material on a personal level, but with the short form the opportunity for broad stylistic differences requires broad imagination. So plays

that are in some way personalized for the actor to ease the empathic availability for the audience but are then expanded dynamically thru imagination allow for the breadth of character, style, and creativity that a short play festival requires. Connected, but expanded. Otherwise the play can fall flat and miss the mark in the short time afforded.

(Michael Colby Jones, Gi60 director)

We can sometimes focus so intently on actions, staging, and language that our oldest and dearest childhood friend – Imagination – gets pushed down the list of consideration. Or, Imagination's presence is "assumed" and we don't bring it up. Though we use our imagination constantly, we often take it for granted and rarely give ourselves time to nurture it and allow it to play freely. Because one minute plays need actors and directors to ask "what could it be?" with such frequency, imaginations get some real time on the playground. Stretching those legs with so many plays also creates an environment of freedom, free play, and risk taking. Imagination can be such a private experience for people, so we recommend you encourage actors to explore theirs in a safe and supportive environment that you create. It will benefit the specific plays and the overall rehearsal process, and will strengthen the imagination muscles for the future.

And, of course, strong imagination helps when you're playing a bored chicken crossing the road in one play, and a guilty cow in the next.

Risk taking

I love chaos. I can make sense of it, and it's generally more exciting.

(Walter Petryk, Gi60 actor, playwright)

It takes a particular kind of constitution to create 10–14 characters in a program of 50 plays. Gi60 actors have described it as a "concert for actors," a "roller coaster," a "haunted house fun ride," and "a terrifying parachute drop where you hope you never hit the ground." Emotionally and physically investing in that many characters and stories takes a lot of courage, fortitude, stamina, and a willingness to take Big Risks. Trusting the broad spectrum and specificity of your choices also asks you to be quite vulnerable. Committing to plays in which the characters can be absurd (talking doormats, ghosts, and Giant Vending Machine Snacks who are stuck in their chute) requires a level of confidence and willingness to face one's fear of looking silly. All of this equals risk taking.

[A]cting in a one minute play requires a lot of the same skills you use in improv. It calls on the part of you that makes big, bold choices. It really works best when you swing for the fences and you miss the mark; you can just take what you've learned from that and apply it to your next big choice.

(Adam Thomas Smith, Gi60 actor)

Actors have often said that one of the things they love the most about Gi60 is the extremes to which the plays go. They enjoy how liberating it is to play a dog desperate to prove his love and loyalty to his owner, and then play a Nightmare who is having an existential crisis about whether to frighten a child or not. For some, it's been a long time since they had the freedom to swing from flat out comedy, to fantasy, to heartbreaking drama in a single night.

And that's probably the biggest risk of all; actors need to emotionally and personally invest in so many different characters and worlds. Some plays are tragedies that focus on the despair of a single moment; a break up, the loss of a parent, or a deadly diagnosis from a doctor. Others are about the discovery of love, a comedy of errors on a first date, or the hilarious frustration of a student being denied entry by a campus security guard after zombies have just been given a free pass. Actors don't get a lot of recovery time when going from one play to the next; they risk their hearts in being completely open to what each play needs. A one minute play doesn't have time to build you up to the emotional moment.

It has to hit you hard and fast. Whether it is sadness, excitement, anger, or laughter … you will feel it.

(Walter Petryk, Gi60 actor, playwright)

And when the play ends, actors can't afford to linger with those emotions; they need to move on to the next story. That, too, requires a vulnerability that is at the core of risk taking.

Steve

I worked with an actor on Gi60 whom I had worked with previously on a full-length production. He's a fine actor and a great company member, but about halfway through the rehearsal process I could tell everything was not alright, and so at the end of a rehearsal I took him aside and asked what was wrong. He told me that he was concerned about the "serious" plays and wouldn't it be better if we just did the comedic and outrageous pieces. He was scared of making a fool of himself on stage, worried that what we were doing "wouldn't work." It's something I have come across more than once. This format asks for a great deal from those involved. Comedy gives instant reward in the rehearsal room. You know if you are being funny. Dramatic, thoughtful pieces do not provide such tangible feedback, and this can be unsettling for an actor. Your actors are taking risks; you need to support that risk taking. The actor in question has now taken part in many Gi60 festivals and is one of the most supportive company members we have.

Adaptability

Actors for one minute plays need to be as versatile as a Swiss army knife, and as elastic as a rubber band. The average Gi60 festival features 10–16 actors, 3–6 directors, several designers, camera operators, and usually one stage manager with nerves of steel. It's a miracle how right each festival goes, considering … Actors play lead roles in roughly 7–9 plays, and appear as secondary characters in another 5–6 for a rough total of 15 plays each. Each story and collection of characters must be distinct from one another, and that requires an actor to quickly adapt to each new set of given circumstances, and make each new palette of choices different from the previous ones.

> Centers of energy and physicality can go a long way in discerning different characters from each other. The part of my body that I lead from both physically and verbally changes with each character, and informs every decision I make … This helps when trying to create many distinct characters. If you let your body make the decisions for you, the rest will follow and will be completely apparent to the audience.
>
> (Anastasia Bell, Gi60 actor)

Versatility

Now, it's one thing to make clear choices in rehearsal; but running multiple plays together can sometimes cause an actor to "neutralize" their choices. Versatility helps an actor to work with ease when creating multiple contrasting choices in quick succession. Adaptability is needed for actors to execute those choices with consistency in every play. Flexibility allows an actor to let go of previous choices and commit fully when transforming from one character and world to the next.

> I remember being so impressed (and a little intimidated) by the actors who had been doing Gi60 for years because there was so much ease in their performance. They swung from character to character like it was nothing and they breathed through each moment with a fullness and a commitment that made each story land on me. It was unlike anything I had ever seen.
>
> (Anastasia Bell, Gi60 actor)

Along with creating and executing choices for each play, actors need to be able to let go of each character and story the moment that it's done in order to make room for the next play. Once they hit their final beat, they need to quickly switch gears and begin their process for the next. Having an emotional "hangover" from one story to the next isn't an option; neither is that time-honored tradition of beating yourself up when you make a mistake in live theatre.

> The thing that Gi60 has engendered in me is the ability to move on if something doesn't work. Letting go of mistakes and not letting them interfere with the progress of another play.
>
> (Mickey Ryan, Gi60 actor, playwright)

Developing and learning to trust, how to fully commit, listen, let go, and move on in one minute plays will strengthen an actor's ability to be grounded in the moment, always.

Physical storytelling

Specificity, flexibility, commitment, and imagination are cornerstones for the foundation of physical storytelling. When playing multiple characters, actors must go the extra mile to create specific centers of energy, movement, gestures, and body language that can only belong to that specific character. If your character who has been pulled over by a cop is a wild gesticulator, it's best if your other character who passionately argues with his child's teacher has a different physical vocabulary. Even if that same "wild gesticulator" could work for both characters, you can't. Audiences crave and seek connections, and you risk plays being associated with each other as if they were a "series" within the evening.

> When a character seems similar to another ... you can find little things to differentiate them. Maybe one is British, one is American. One tucks their shirt in, one doesn't. One has a nervous tic, one keeps perfect composure at all times.
>
> (Walter Petryk, Gi60 actor, playwright)

> I give myself a specific trigger for each character. It can be a posture, a gesture, a vocal choice ... Something that immediately triggers the character to life. After all, it's likely that I was recently inhabiting a different character and I don't want that character to appear in the next play.
>
> (David Storck, Gi60 director, actor, playwright)

Also, Gi60 uses minimal, ubiquitous set pieces (more on that later) – usually a series of cubes/blocks – to create each world of the play. Specificity of physical storytelling helps audiences quickly land in the story. The actor's bodies and physical choices are the prime visual element that allows Gi60 to change worlds 50 times in a night. Any physical choice that is too casual works against the clarity of character and story in the world of the play.

Strong and supple vocal instrument

The flexibility and adaptability we wrote of earlier extends to vocal work as well. If physical storytelling is a primary visual element to support the distinct worlds of each play, then an actor's vocal choices provide the auditory experience for the audience to distinguish characters and settings. Good old-fashioned clear and crisp articulation and annunciation will support the storytelling even more than usual. Remember that audiences are trying to connect with a new set of characters and voices every 60 seconds, so actors must deliver whatever they're saying (and in whatever vocal color they're choosing) with clarity of articulation from first word to last. It can make a world of difference in the comprehension of each story for the audience and their ears.

Dialects can also provide a shorthand to help audiences understand where a play is set as well as what the status of each character might be. Having plays from so many parts of the world lends its own inspiration. A play written by a British author gives US actors the opportunity to apply a dialect (or not); and the specificity of a character's "posh" London dialect juxtaposed against a character with a "Cockney" or south London accent can communicate status, class, and a potential conflict between characters. Sometimes when you're trying to "crack the code" of a play, an actor will break it open by simply saying, "Why don't we try it with accents?"

The demands of these vocal gymnastics mean that actors must commit to healthy vocal practice (doing comprehensive warm ups, avoiding foods/drink that impact the vocal chords, etc.) to have their full instrument available to them, and to avoid injury to that instrument while executing a wide variety of vocal choices. Breathing and breath support are key; allowing breath through to the ends of lines, strong and consistent breath support (short bursts of lines are not uncommon), and literally breathing through each play to build stamina for the evening. The number of plays, and the pace of a program of short plays itself, can contribute to stress or anxiety, and usually the first thing that happens is that an actor stops breathing. Literally. They tend to hold their breath while they "check in": "Did I enter into the correct play … yes! I did! Whew!" "Did Jay put the hockey puck where I need it for the next? Yes!! (exhale)," "Do I have the scarf I need to hand off to Sabrina at the end of this play? Yes! Back pocket! (exhale)." Literally, if an actor is "holding their breath," they're going to lose energy, strength, and focus for the play marathon.

Stamina

Stamina is one of those things that we all think we have, but until we're put to the test, we can't really know our strength. Few things test the physical and emotional staying power of an actor more than performing multiple plays/characters, one after the other. Actors should always practice good health and fitness in order to build strength and stamina, but as languishing gym memberships will attest, that's not always the case. Stamina is one of the most important skills that is challenged in one minute play festivals, and actors know pretty quickly if they've prepared adequately or not. You might run a mile or two if you get the urge to prove you're in shape; but you wouldn't run a marathon without months and months of intensive training.

Rose

Believe me, I've watched my sister Maureen run the New York City Marathon several times; she finishes (and finishes well) because she commits to building her body and mind and spirit over a period of many months.

Those who design marathon routes make sure they plan variety for the physical challenge for the runners. There are steep hills, flat plains, a series of gently rolling hills, etc. The runners need to prepare themselves for all of these challenges to run sequentially; no marathon is going to be all hills, or all flat (unless you're in Kansas …). Likewise, actors need to prepare for the variety of plays and for the pace at which they'll be performed. Yes, the director can conduct exercises throughout the course of rehearsal that will help, but actors should find their own version of the treadmill in working up to performances. (See Appendices C, E and F.)

Steve

The Gi60 UK rehearsal process is quite intensive; whether we rehearse in a single block or over a longer period, the time in the rehearsal room is usually 40 hours. New actors are always shocked about how quickly we work. They find it hard to accept that 50 one minute plays can be fully realized in a little over a week's rehearsal. They are also often surprised at the mental and physical challenge of the process. It's not just on stage that the actors have to be present, focused, and "on it." If a Gi60 performance is the marathon, then the entire process is an Iron Man Challenge; three disciplines all linked: "Rehearse the parts, understand the blocking and scenes, now perform."

Strength might get you through one challenging short play. Stamina will successfully get you through a whole evening of them.

A generous and collaborative spirit

Theatre is a collaborative art form, end of discussion. But it is the beginning of a story; a story about people willing to sacrifice their shining moment for the artistic goal's shining moment. When working with the sheer number of people who are needed for a short play festival, the potential for conflicts simply increases with the numbers involved. Tiny play festivals benefit from working with an ensemble of artists who value working as a team, who are open and receptive to others, who are willing and eager to listen, who are dedicated to the process of collaboration, who are willing to sacrifice their shining moment for the play's shining moment, and who truly enjoy this kind of work. That is, they enjoy working with a new play and a new cast every few minutes, and thrive on the unique challenges.

> [T]he theatre is buzzing; the actors, directors, and audience are fully present because you must be in order to witness and participate in these 60-second pieces of theatre, and that presence that we all bring is a tangible, palpable energy that fills the space in a way a full-length play does not.
>
> (Anastasia Bell, Gi60 actor)

The rehearsal processes for a one minute play festival can vary from town to town, and from country to country. Gi60 US rehearses anywhere from 12 to 18 plays each evening in 20–40-minute rehearsal blocks over a three-week period. Gi60 UK usually rehearses with all actors and directors in the room together, often over the course of a single week, working eight-hour days. (See Chapter 4 for further examples.) No matter which process you use, that's a pretty concentrated period of time, with many interlocking gears that can't afford to jam. Festivals of tiny plays put actors in a series of roles with different casts once every few minutes. Generous and collaborative actors are essential to a play that demands 16 people create the bodies of two dinosaurs in less than five seconds, and it ensures that the ensemble is prepared to roll with whatever may happen in the evening (including success or chaos). "The plate you need for the 'restaurant' didn't make it onstage? No worries, I'll be a waiter and bring it to you." "Someone forgot their block move assignment? I'm in the next play, I'll get it."

Rose

Though we've all seen our share of conflicts in rehearsal and performance processes, I don't think I've ever seen "The Blame Game" played in Gi60 (who forgot to do what assignment, who dropped a line, etc.) – if something comes up, someone fixes it and everyone gets on with it. And I don't think that it's because "there's no time for blame." I believe it's because Gi60 is an attractive project to actors for whom generosity and collaborative ensemble work truly matters.

> Collaboration is key. You will never be the star. The PLAY is the star.
>
> (Samantha Fontana, Gi60 actor)

Being grounded and calm

Short play festivals thrive when the participating artists are grounded, supportive, giving, and centered. It helps everyone do their best work. Things can go "wrong," or, perhaps more accurately, things can evolve and change pretty quickly. The ability to be calm and grounded allows actors to accept each "surprise" as it may occur; it's the ultimate exercise of "yes, and …." If everyone commits to that philosophy, then everyone continues to make discoveries, embrace each moment as an opportunity, take risks, play, and bring the entire evening to life.

I love working with cast members who say "yes and." When the cast in a one minute play is saying "yes and," the possibilities of what can happen on stage are endless. So when the entire cast in a one minute play festival is a supportive yes-and ensemble, you will without a doubt have a kick-ass show.

(Samantha Fontana, Gi60 Actor)

Trust, trust, and more trust

Commitment, sacrifice and support are the qualities upon which trust is built. Honor those qualities and you build trust; violate them, and you lose that trust. In ensemble, trust is the coin of the realm; with it, members can truly risk, fail, play, discover, and create. Trust is the recognizable form that the bond takes; it's how we know the ensemble is bonded.

(*Ensemble Theatre Making: A Practical Guide* by Rose Burnett Bonczek and David Storck)

Enough said.

That's a pretty healthy list for actors, but don't worry, directors – we didn't forget about you.

Skills and Attributes for Directors (and actors, please take note too!)

Directing a one minute play festival is a lot like running the New York City marathon. It's a daunting task that involves a lot of mental and physical preparation, quite a bit of running around, a greatly rewarding conclusion, and when you tell people you're going to do it, they either say, "Wow, that's amazing. I can't wait to be there and support you." Or they simply ask, "Why, dude?"

(Mike Flanagan, Gi60 director, playwright, associate producer)

Rose

I've loved the challenges of directing one minute plays; as a professor of mine once said, "Economy equals impact." He was actually trying to get me to "get to the point already" in my research paper on Medea, but I took his idea into my directing and teaching. How can getting to the bones of a story and character make the play clearer, and amplify its meaning? After exploring "economy equals impact" for several years in traditional one acts and full lengths, I found that the shorter plays made me employ my inner Superman instead of my Clark Kent. The shorter the plays got, the more concentrated my directing skills became, and I discovered that choices seemed to carry more "weight;" every single moment and word counted.

When Steve invited me to join the international Gi60 team, I knew it would be an opportunity to test my ability to make those diamonds. For one evening of plays, a director might be responsible for directing anywhere from 5 to 25 plays each. That's a lot of sparklers ....

Steve

Directing one minute plays is, for me at least, an exhilarating, challenging, and liberating experience. The challenge of creating 50 distinct worlds, inhabited by equally distinct characters each telling a unique story, can be quite sobering as you look at the pile of untested scripts on the first day of rehearsal; but what an opportunity! Fifty new worlds to explore, hundreds of characters (animal, vegetable, and mineral) to develop, and all with just the actors in front of you and a few wooden boxes (or chairs or whatever you choose to use). Every year when I'm selecting plays I will have a day when I think, "Why am I doing this?" but from the moment the 50 plays are selected I'm excited, excited to share the plays with the company, excited to start creating worlds, and excited to bring those worlds to an audience. Gi60 and the tiny play format have taught and continue to teach me valuable lessons about the craft of the director.

Most people choose to direct because of their pure love for stories and storytelling. In traditional practice, a director works on one story at a time. It's possible you could be in rehearsal for one project and developing a contract for the next, or directing one show and squeezing in a staged reading or workshop, but by and large, you're working on one story at a time; and you may have been doing preparation for that single story for several months. If you're directing in a one minute play festival, you could be working on anywhere from 5 to 35 stories (or more!). Play selection tends to happen fairly close to the start of the rehearsal process; you probably have a pre-prescribed set (rehearsal blocks, chairs, etc.) and you will probably be working with a different combination of actors for each play you're directing. Any research and prep you're doing for the story itself is multiplied by the number of plays you've been assigned. This way of working is a departure from what most directors are probably familiar with.

This next section offers some thoughts and advice based on our own experience working with short form plays and festivals. Similarly to what we've outlined above for actors, plays of any length will, of course, ask directors to engage in their key skills (communicating and collaborating with actors, making specific choices, awareness, being efficient time managers, etc.). Directing one minute plays asks for a higher concentration and particular application of those skills (remember the typewriter and the diamond!):

- clear communication
- specificity and clarity
- collaborative spirit and support
- ability to analyze what is in the text and use imagination for what is not
- flexibility, adaptability, versatility
- focus, awareness, and observation
- time management
- visual storytelling
- being grounded, calm, and patient
- inspiration and motivation
- trust, trust, and more trust

Clear communication

One of the greatest benefits from working on Gi60 for so many years has been discovering how much clearer and more efficient it makes communication skills. Directors often enjoy the discussion process – sometimes a bit too much – chatting and circling round the subject until we finally arrive at the point we're trying to get to.

> # Rose
>
> *I clearly remember one day in my first Gi60 festival, my synapses snapped to attention and my brain said, "You can't take the scenic route; go straight down the highway." Getting to the point with the actors quickly and concisely doesn't take away from the discovery process, at all. In fact, getting to each point on the highway of the play's story got us farther down the road, and when we reached the destination it allowed the actors to sink into the details of that destination. Clear and specific communication allows us to get to the destination wisely; and that leaves us time to thoroughly flesh out and build details in that destination.*

You may well find that the process of directing short form plays will help you become more aware of how you've been employing your own communication skills. "Did I really need all of those words to make that point? Did I have to share three analogies, where one would have done the trick?" That "compression" that we spoke of earlier will help you be more effective "moment to moment," and this leads to more efficient time management, with more time to explore choices within the clear framework of the world of the play.

Specificity and clarity

Do please read what we've written previously for actors. There's no fat on the bone; every word counts, and is an opportunity for you to make clear and specific choices that clarify story and theme. Don't be tempted to "leave something open"; that is, "let's keep playing with that moment and see what happens in performance." Short form plays heighten the need for specificity, especially for actors. It can be an odd experience, for them and for you, to work on a play whose length prohibits the writer from providing substantial given circumstances. Directors and actors can choose to create those together, or it could be left to the actors to create their own given circumstances. We recommend you do it together for continuity and consistency and for pure collaboration's sake. Actors can be shy about what they feel might be "imposing" on a script. Help them to be clear that they're not imposing, but simply supplying answers and context for questions the playwright raises but hasn't provided concrete answers to. There's a difference; you're not asking your actors to draw a new picture, merely to make some decisions about the color and shading on the picture you already have. Actors, particularly those new to the form, may well need your help or "permission" to discover and offer those choices. Deciding that John Proctor from The Crucible is actually guilty of being a witch would be imposing a narrative that clearly isn't in the original text, and by doing so, you would be knowingly altering the playwright's meaning. In Mark Harvey Levine's one minute play Plato's Cave (see page 149), Gary might or might not be in a coma; the director and actors have to make a specific choice, clarifying the point of view.

Many short form plays leave open questions. The playwrights have found strong ways of giving enough specifics, with room for the actors and director to glean what else could be true. Also, it's good practice for directors to commit to specific choices quickly. Every play has a buffet line of choices, but some buffet lines need to move more quickly than others.

Collaborative spirit and support

One minute play festivals need directors who are skilled at, and enjoy, building ensembles; not only creating ensembles from play to play and cast to cast, but for the entire company of actors, directors, stage managers, etc. Remember, an ensemble doesn't begin with the people; it begins with a clear goal that is shared by everyone involved. What are the goals of the plays you're directing, yes; but what is the goal of the whole event? And how can you best support that, in your rehearsals and beyond? (For some specific exercises, see Appendix B, C and E.)

Directors have the unique vantage point of seeing the bigger picture long before the actors get into the room together. Plan accordingly, and when you do meet, take the time to create the bonds necessary for the entire festival, not only for the plays you direct. Be mindful not to get too crazy with the dark side of "ownership" when directing several plays in an evening. That is, you might be responsible for directing multiple plays, but the festival is a *single event* that "your" plays are a part of. Collaborating also means making choices in the plays you direct that will support the whole evening. This could be as simple as creating a physical setup in one play that supports the needs of the next play, or alternatively, making sure that you don't add excessive visual elements (props, costume pieces) that will take too much time to strike at play's end. Be generous; do good work, but remember that these plays will combine to tell one larger story that night.

Steve

Gi60 UK usually has up to three directors and operates as a "democratic monarchy," by which I mean we all (directors, actors, stage manager) have equal status in terms of developing the 50 plays, but ultimately I will make the final decision. At a certain point somebody has to take responsibility for the overall festival and the way it feels and the way it flows. This might mean a small change in how a play is staged or where characters enter or exit, or in certain rare cases a need to rethink a one minute play so that it works as part of the whole. This big picture or mise en scène is the vessel that holds all the tiny plays together; it's important that somebody has the job of making sure that vessel looks good and is seaworthy.

Collaboration and generosity are essential, and this extends to your fellow directors in the festival. Directing can be a lonely profession; it's rare to have more than one director on-site for a process. Treat this as a great opportunity to work collaboratively and offer support to one another. "Hey Michael, would you mind taking a look at *Shoebox* with me? I'm struggling with the physical shape and could use your fresh eyes." "Jan, I have nothing left in the tank … I know this play is really good though. Can you take a shot at it?" "Eugene, you're an expert at stage combat – can you choreograph this moth fight?" (true story …) Let's face it: many directors have been trained to be wary of "adding cooks to the broth." The concept makes good sense – a team responds best to a single voice rather than a many-headed hydra; unfortunately, it can also lead to a director feeling embarrassed or prideful at the very thought of asking for help. One minute play festivals foster collaboration, and they're an excellent place for young or emerging directors to hone the craft *and* healthy skills of collaborating. It's also a great opportunity for experienced directors to see other directors in action and perhaps add something to their own directing arsenal.

Ability to analyze what is in the text and use imagination for what is not

What's the conflict? Who are these characters? What's really at stake? Where are they? How do environment and relationship impact what they're fighting for? Short plays challenge a director's analytical skills in delicious ways. Each story gives strong, spare details with clear conflicts. However, the brevity of each tale also means there are "enigmatic" moments. That is, we see the characters and the scenario, but how and why have they gotten to where they are? And how can that influence the outcome? As we've previously written, sometimes the director and actors needs to glean what they can from the given text, and then look beyond to the subtext and perhaps even further to consider what things could be. This creates rich, imaginative layers that help the world of the play become fully realized. For those who have trained as directors, this will probably be very familiar. For those who haven't, these questions below will help you create a foundation and framework for each play.

- What is this story about? What is the X vs Y conflict (e.g. Illusion vs. Reality, Innocence vs. Corruption, Ignorance vs. Enlightenment)?

- Who is each character? What are their personality traits? Not emotional states: traits. Being "depressed" or "angry" is a passing condition – what character traits are fixed throughout? What's their background? How might their history impact the actions we see them taking in this play?

- What are the characters' relationships to one another? Brother, father, best friend are only titles; dig into details about the nature of each relationship. Sometimes characters are strangers – but every encounter with strangers is different. Some are exhilarating, some are frightening. What's at the source of that?

- What do they want? Objectives? Keep this direct and strong. "I want …" If the actors are saying, "I want them to understand …" "I want them to know …" "I just want to …," imagine a loud game show buzzer sounding off and a voice saying, "Too passive!" Short plays demand specific and direct wants: "I want an apology." "I want her to say yes to my proposal." "I want my daughter's forgiveness." "I want my dad to accept that I'm an adult."

- What are they willing to do to get what they want? How do they go about getting it? What actions or tactics do they employ? ("To intimidate, to cajole, to seduce …")

- Where is the play set? How does that environment influence the story and characters? If the setting isn't defined, how can you choose a location that best supports the story?

- Time of day? Is the play set late at night, or at sunrise? How does time affect behavior and actions (and not just for vampire stories)?

- For one minute plays particularly: is the playwright making a point about time itself? Is he or she acknowledging the truth of a 60-second structure within the story itself, and expressing something about the limitations of 60 seconds, the wonder of what can happen in 60 seconds, the tragedy of how life can be turned upside down in 60 seconds?

- What's the theme of the play? What message do you feel the playwright is trying to convey?

- Why are you directing this play at this moment in time? What do you feel you uniquely can bring to the telling of this story to make it come to life?

You can always go further, but these few suggestions are a good start. Having concise notes about each play with you in rehearsal – including x vs. y conflict, one sentence about theme, one sentence about story, one sentence about each character and each relationship – may also help you clarify each play you're directing. If your rehearsal structure asks you to rehearse multiple plays in one evening, these notes can help ground you at the start of each play's rehearsal.

Based on your analysis of what the playwright gives, decide what this play is about and then create the given circumstances that best support that analysis. As long as the text supports it, give yourself the freedom to add to a world, and help it create its own fullness, beauty, and rules.

Steve

I love to use company members to provide background or what I have come to think of as "depth of field" for plays. If the play calls for two trees to have a conversation, why not use the entire company and make a forest? If you have a play featuring two birds, perhaps they are flying through that same forest, or perhaps they are part of a flock or...? I have used the ensemble to create the physicality and atmosphere of a spacecraft, a full subway train, dragons, and more. If two characters meet on a city street corner, don't be afraid to make it a busy street ... with a hot dog stand ... and a mime ....

Flexibility, adaptability, versatility

Even the rehearsal process adds to the insanity, and calls upon your abilities to be flexible and work fast ... since you are usually scheduled back to back with the plays you're directing .... The skills that Improv teaches you, such as making clear, bold choices, making them quickly and sticking with them, being flexible with time, space, and language, communicating with very few or no words, and of course the principle of "Yes And," are absolutely invaluable to creating and performing in a one minute play.

(Jonathan Hadley, Gi60 director, actor)

One minute play festivals give directors the unique opportunity to work on plays with a broad range of subjects. Is directing comedy one of your strengths, but you have always wanted to try working on tragic material? Are you known as a "movement-based" director, but you've wanted to stretch your muscles with a play that uses stillness and heightened language? The fantastic thing about this form is that you can direct multiple genres of plays at the same time. Talk about stretching your artistic muscles ....

Rose

In 2015 I directed a play about a widowed dad accepting that his adult daughter was no longer a little girl, one in which six artistic muses bemoaned the fact that painters got all the credit for the art, and a one minute fact-based Historical Scottish play with more violent stage combat crammed into 60 seconds than I've seen in a full length. If one minute play festivals are concerts for actors, they're also a director's gymnasium. You will never, ever get to tell that wide a range of different stories for a single event anywhere else.

Now, rehearsing that diverse pool of plays can also give you whiplash. Flexibility, adaptability, and an excellent set of notes can help you successfully shift from play to play when in rehearsal.

[N]ot all ensembles are the same; different ensembles will require you to adapt your leadership skills and style to suit their needs ... You must meet them where they are. Engage your listening and observation skills to discover the group's identity and who the individual members are (or think they are), and what they need ... Then you can begin to figure out how you might bring them what they need.

(*Ensemble Theatre Making: A Practical Guide* by Rose Burnett Bonczek and David Storck)

Though it can be unnerving at times, ultimately it's a thrill to rehearse with a new cast and story every few minutes. Each new group of actors will look to the director to set the tone – so you can't afford to be scattered. Give yourself what you need to ground yourself in each rehearsal, in the same way as the actors must ground themselves in each first moment of the play. Practicing commitment and specificity from play to play will strengthen your adaptability and versatility. The ability to quickly shift gears is a skill that pays off in many ways (especially when you return to directing plays of traditional length). Along with the flexibility and adaptability you'll need for multiple changes of cast and play, you also need …

Focus, awareness, and observation

Directors need to keep their eyes on multiple balls being juggled in the air at all times. Given the compression of the one minute play process, you better eat your carrots. Directing multiple plays with multiple casts requires you to maintain heightened focus and awareness, and your powers of observation will be challenged.

Awareness: awareness of whether the play is progressing or stagnating, awareness of the rhythm of each play and the plays in your running order, and awareness of all dynamics – character dynamics, and actor dynamics. Who might be struggling with the challenges of this rehearsal process? Is somebody behaving in an uncharacteristic way? Are they less enthusiastic than at the last rehearsal, is a cast member suddenly less willing to take direction or make changes? It may be that an actor thinks they are struggling, but in fact they are at the same place everybody else is. Make sure you are there to provide the support needed. This is a new experience for many actors, and so they may need more assurance (after all, they are the ones going out on stage dressed as a chicken). Can you identify an actor in your ensemble who could be a supportive guide for them? Sometimes actors struggle with the tiny play structure, but can't admit it. They may be reluctant to say they don't "get" a one minute play; something about the play's length makes them feel embarrassed for not understanding something so short. In fact, the brevity of the plays actually can make it more challenging to understand, especially if it's one of the more enigmatic plays.

> I love fighting with the word or phrases to make it fit inside the minute. How can I say that line, convey that meaning in fewer words? I've even gone to the thesaurus to find words that mean the same thing with fewer syllables.
>
> (Rosanne Manfredi, Gi60 playwright)

Awareness is not only essential for observing what's right in front of you, but also means you need to listen and be sensitive to rhythm and tempo. Are the actors rushing moments because they want to get the play under 60 seconds? Does the rhythm of the language ring true, or are actors stumbling over words because the play was written by an international author for whom English may not be their first language, and there are "extra beats" in a sentence? Now consider the rhythm and tempo for the whole running order of the program: have you put all fast-paced pieces together, and is it creating an unhelpful momentum? Have you put the tragic pieces back to back, and there's an emotional "sad zone" that brings things to a halt in the middle of the program? Finding gentle rises and falls, while maintaining a concrete build, climax, and conclusion to a program, is also one of the strongest supports you can give to the collection of plays being performed together. We talk more about creating effective running orders in Chapter 4; but you add to a play's potential for the power of its story by being aware of where to perform it in a running order.

Focus: remember how challenging it is for all of you to shift gears from play to play in a rehearsal session. Help the actors ground and focus themselves with each play's rehearsal – what would you do if it were a rehearsal for a traditional-length play? Would you take a moment to check in to see how the actor's day was? Would you review the plan for that specific rehearsal? Would you do a brief exercise that connects the partners? Would you run something to help the actors warm up and get focused? You can – and should – still adhere to whatever process works best for you and the actors – it will simply be shorter. And finding consistency, or even a ritual that focuses everyone, will help provide a structure within the structure that can help focus and concentration.

Be mindful of your own focus as well; know your limits and your own stamina. If you've worked on several plays in a row, there's wisdom in taking a break instead of muscling through. It's not dissimilar to working on the same scene for a traditional-length play for too long a session. You can run that thing for another hour and still not make any headway. But – if you stop for the night, or take a break to rest your brain and shift gears, you'll gain more ground when you return to it.

Rose

Observation: This is a particular challenge; when running short plays or segments of short plays, it goes so fast that I find I sometimes feel an observation before I see it or intellectually register it. Almost like catching something out of the corner of my eye; something happened, it needs attention, but I don't quite know what it is yet. When directing in this form, I find that observations made through intuition and instinct are way ahead of observations made visually or intellectually.

Time management

Whether you are part of a school or a theatre company, you're going to have your own rehearsal process determined in part by your organization's resources, and by your available time. Whichever process works best for you, your students, or your company, you'll most certainly be producing multiple plays, and you'll need to be efficient with planning and time. Every logistical reality creates a creative one for the director.

When directing a full-length play, you quickly develop a sense of "where we are" in the process. Most directors will have experienced that moment when they realize the big scene at the end of the second act still hasn't been tackled because they may have spent too much time on Act One. Rehearsal schedules get adjusted, and the scene gets its time in the rehearsal room. With a one minute play festival, that big scene in Act Two might be 15–20 plays. From the very first rehearsal, one minute festival directors need to be aware of exactly where they are. For instance, if you have a five-day rehearsal process (Monday to Friday) with your dress rehearsal on the Friday evening and your performance on the Saturday and you have 50 plays to work on, you might adopt the following strategy:

Monday:	9.00 am – 5.00 pm	Rehearse and block 20 plays
Tuesday:	9.00 am – 5.00 pm	Rehearse and block 20 plays
Wednesday:	9.00 am – 5.00 pm (morning)	Rehearse and block the final ten plays
		(afternoon) Run the first 25 plays and make fixes
Thursday:	9.00 am – 5.00 pm	(morning) Run the remaining 25 plays and make fixes
		(afternoon) Run whole show
Friday:	9.00 am – 10.00 pm	(morning) Make any last minute fixes and changes
		(afternoon) Run full show
		(evening) Dress rehearsal
Saturday:		Performance

As you can see from this rehearsal plot (which was actually used), you may need to block 20 plays a day, or about one every 20 minutes if you prefer, from day one of rehearsal. Add warm-ups, lunch, and late comers, and it's clear that you have a challenging schedule. If you are not keenly aware of the time, you simply won't get a chance to run the festival before the audience are taking their seats. This example is particularly tight and is by no means ideal, but as an example it does highlight the very real challenge you face and the need for directors (and actors) to focus and be aware of the process. You also need to ensure that your actors understand that when you say "be 'off book' on scenes for the next rehearsal" you really mean it!

Create clear goals for each rehearsal, and trust us, write them down because it goes by fast. Know which elements you're going to work on for each session, and move the rehearsal action forward with consideration but with efficiency. Be willing to start and end on time. Be open to scheduling additional time for some plays if they need it (that big ensemble opera piece might just take a little longer) – make sure that the time length doesn't make you feel that a one minute play shouldn't need much time to put together. Sometimes the conflict is clear and works like clockwork. Other times there are layers to relationships and moments that take time to tease apart. Give yourself that time; and if you manage it well, you won't feel rushed.

> I look to avoid the trap of having every play be fast paced. A slow moving one minute play is remarkable. When one minute feels like an eternity, I find it very compelling.
> (David Storck, Gi60 director, actor, playwright)

We recommend that you do make the time at the start of each rehearsal to do the normal checking in: "hi how are you, how was your day?" But shorter. Collaborators still need that moment to gather and connect with each other. Again, the needs and skills don't change; simply how they're applied.

Visual storytelling

Visual storytelling is one of the clearest ways to help the audience immediately understand the world of each play. Directors often function as their own "set designer," using simple elements to help define a location and circumstances. Two stacked cubes become a McDonald's counter. Two women wearing simple patient's gowns while holding magazines? A doctor's waiting room. And two people wearing enormous puffy winter coats places us outside on a freezing day (in 2015, Boston playwrights wrote many plays about their record-breaking snowstorms – residents were literally jumping out of second story windows into snow banks). Specific tangible details help audiences make connections to their known world, and this helps take them on the journey of the play.

Clear physical blocking and gestures also help establish a specific world and atmosphere. A man pacing frenetically at the top of a play set in a maternity ward; a woman anxiously tapping her foot and looking sideways to the distance is at a bus stop (and that bus is late!). We wrote earlier about physical storytelling helping to establish character; it also creates environment, relationship to environment, and even time of day (see Appendix E for suggestions about ways to create simple and specific environments/locations).

Rose

Stillness in a single locale can be powerful. When I directed Moment Before Impact *by Ruben Carbajal, the two actors sat simply side by side as if in a car. We meet the couple in the moment before their car crashes and they are killed together. Because the actors established that locale, the audience recognized what "car" meant (confined environment), then everything the actors did with their voices, upper bodies, and faces counted for so much more. Audiences "settled in" because an expectation was created for them in the first moment. The rest of the play became about the couple's relationship, told through physical touch, language of course, and facial and physical expression.*

Though there certainly isn't time to set up realistic set pieces in between all the plays you do, you can be inventive with very simple objects. For Gi60, both US and UK use cubes of various sizes that become park benches, restaurant seating, a counter in a shop, an office setting. But, we use them very differently. Gi60 US pre-sets the cubes in different locales on the stage: and though we do make small adjustments – stacking, pushing two together – by and large we leave the arrangements pre-set for expediency's sake and allow those arrangements to determine the play's environment and location on the stage. See Chapter 4 for more examples of this. Though the stage never goes to black, the lights dim to blues at the end of each play while actors enter into the next play's location. Gi60 UK employs an entirely different application of the cubes:

Steve

In the UK edition of Gi60 there is generally no blackout at the end of each play, so the theatre blocks and their movement from one scene to the next have become an integral part of the show and its shape. Actors transform the blocks from mountains to spaceships to offices and subway trains in a matter of seconds. UK company members will often talk in hushed tones to "virgin" Gi60 cast members; warning them about the challenges of "the block rehearsal" and the shared responsibility of the "ballet of the blocks."

Small costume pieces can also be worth their weight in gold for visual storytelling, especially for students or young actors in training who may not yet have strong physical storytelling skills. They serve as a visual clue for audience members to understand a character's age, status, and profession. Hats, scarves, eyeglasses, and suit jackets are quick and easy communicators. An actor throwing on a shawl and eye glasses is suddenly elderly. A smart suit jacket creates a professional or business person. In Aurora Stewart de Peña's play *Ghosts*, we brainstormed about how to communicate that all the people hanging out in the living room of a terrified homeowner are actually ghosts. The characters are written to indicate that they are doing mundane human things like reading the newspaper, working out, and playing Connect the Dots; so running around and shouting "Boo!" wasn't the answer. We decided they would all wear matching scarves – we won't spoil the end of the play, but there's another reason the visual element helped. (See page 353.)

Being grounded and calm

> My wonderful old boss, Rosabel Wang, once said, "The fish rots from the head." I blanched a little at her visceral description, but I never forgot her meaning.
>
> (Rose)

Successfully guiding actors and stage managers through a rehearsal process for multiple plays is one thing; giving them the confidence and trust to perform all the plays in a single event can be quite another. When you start to run the entire program together for the first time, there may be questions, a lot of questions. "How is this going to work? Is it OK if we post the running order backstage?" Actors can lose a little trust in themselves and in all of their good work when they look at the totality of their responsibilities for a full festival. Give them the confidence and reassurance they need, in abundance. Honestly, don't joke about how "impossible" it may seem, and don't even think of teasing them about what could go wrong. They're already trying to come to terms with how they can possibly get a program of 25–50 plays right.

We can't stress enough how far support, enthusiasm, a calm exterior, and having complete confidence in a positive outcome really go for a cast and crew. And isn't that a direct reflection of having confidence in your own work? Give yourself what you need in order to be the confident and grounded leader that your collaborators need you to be. Fill each moment with absolute faith in everyone's ability to do their work. The hard part? Even if you *see* the potential for disaster, you need to squelch your own nerves and fears, and trust that with time, practice, and repetition, all the work done throughout the rehearsal process will shine through. If you find that you're beating yourself up for something you feel you neglected or missed, you can't. Fear is contagious.

Steve

The one piece of direction I have given more than any other in my career, and the older (more experienced?) I get the more I find myself saying it, is "Perform the play we rehearsed." There is a tendency when actors become agitated, nervous, or excited to be "better." Better than in rehearsal, better than it's been done before, better than... All too often "better" simply means trying too hard, "better" almost never means "better." Let your actors know that the performance you have created together is the performance that you are proud of and the one you wish to share, nothing more and nothing less.

Be patient with the actors, and with yourself. In a first run through, if you see the choices flatline or disappear, don't react. Really. Truly. Underline these sentences. Do not react. Remain calm. Remind yourself that you really have been spending that much time rehearsing that many plays, you didn't dream it. The cast is simply focused only on how the running order works, how they're going to get from Point A to B, and if they're saying the right lines for the right play. Once they've had the opportunity to run the entire event, they'll breathe a big sigh of relief, relax, and get back to the richness of their choices. Take only technical notes in those early stumble/run throughs, even if it kills you. Trust them, trust the work you've done together; and take notes on actor choices and blocking at the next run through.

Rose

I'm really lucky in that Gi60 US has had several actors who perform in the festival every year. Their maturity and experience, their incredible generosity and humor, and (seemingly!) calm exteriors do as much, if not more, to inspire newer cast members than I ever could. Sabrina Cataudella, Joan Lunoe, Mickey Ryan, Jay Nickerson, Cristina Pitter, Mack Exilus, and others do an amazing job to keep the confidence levels high for everyone. They're always present, listening, and completely working in the moment. One thing they do brilliantly is embrace mistakes as they happen. Dropped a line? Improvise. Moustache fell off? Carefully pick it up, tuck it in a pocket, and say, "I shall need that later." They don't ignore it when things go awry, they embrace it and use it to make the moment even stronger. Because our cast is comprised of current acting students as well as experienced actors, our students learn, and learn from the best. It's one thing to perform well when things are going as planned; it's a different lesson on how to do grounded work when things are falling apart.

Inspiration and motivation

Inspire each group of actors you work with, and tailor that to who they are, and to the work you're doing together. In rehearsal, bring in ideas or exercises that are fun; surprise them, create an environment of ease within the structure, and you'll encourage creativity and risk taking. Listen to the actors, and even though the time is brief, don't rush the process itself. Being efficient doesn't mean you have to cut out parts of the creative collaborative process. Again, you're compressing skills, not eliminating them for time's sake.

Help the actors connect with one another. Do exercises, table work, whatever you observe that your specific cast needs. This pays off in your rehearsal, and for the entire program. Most of all, motivate actors by helping them see the value in each other, in each play – create a No Judgment Zone – and lead them in a coordinated effort of mutual support. No matter how tight schedules may seem, there is always time for support, communication, collaboration, and play. And fun. Have we mentioned how fun it is?

Steve

My final cast note is usually "Enjoy it, this is the fun part!" Often actors will have focused so much on the challenges they face and will have been so committed to making sure that they are ready for the performance that they will actually forget why they chose to act in the first place. Making theatre is fun (that's why so many people want to do it) and an actor who is happy in their skin and happy on stage is an actor who can communicate much more effectively with their fellow cast members and the audience. Give your actors permission to have fun.

Trust, trust, and more trust

See what we wrote above for actors. Ditto. Trust your choices of plays, and then let go of any judgment of those choices. Trust your casting choices, trust that the actors will do their work with joy and professionalism and that they will not fall apart when things get moving, trust the playwrights, and trust yourself. Remember that trust is earned, and you're responsible for building that trust.

> For me, it has happened that I read a play, knew it was a right one for selection and that I was the right director for it, but didn't have a clue as to how I should do it. Total passion selection without clarity on HOW to do it. And within this form we have the gift of being able to take a piece that is for many reasons scary but still chase it. Not because there is no consequence if we fail, but rather because the festival format is one in which we have the resources and framework wherein we can explore and ask for help. It's a creative dream. And therefore, the play is realized and your risk is validated. What a great way to go thru life and craft!
>
> (Michael Colby Jones, Gi60 director)

Conclusion

> I think it's important to treat a one minute play with the same respect one would give to Hamlet. It's easy to underestimate a one minute play. You cannot rely on good writing or brevity to do more than their share of making a play effective. If a story is not well told, audiences won't respond as fully as they might.
>
> (David Storck, Gi60 director, actor, playwright)

What we've shared here can be applied to all directing and acting, regardless of the type of play you're working on. Working with one minute plays can help improve existing skills, and it can illuminate our strengths, whether we're teachers, students, or theatre practitioners. It helps us become more aware of the strength and precision of how we're applying our artistic abilities in the service of a play, and when an adjustment of those strengths is needed. Sometimes you need coal. Sometimes you need diamonds.

CHAPTER THREE
Using one minute plays in the classroom

Every year, we are contacted about Gi60 and the one minute play format by an increasing number of teachers, educators, and youth theatre leaders from both sides of the Atlantic. The enquiries come from all sectors of the education community, from kindergarten to college, from youth theatres to graduate writing programs. We hear from writing instructors, acting teachers, directing programs, community groups, and professional theatres. Gi60 obviously resonates with educators, who can see the potential and flexibility of the one minute play format and its potential to inspire students in a variety of subjects. We are asked about getting permissions to use Gi60 plays in the classroom, creating one minute theatre festivals, and exercises for classes and groups. After many years of replying to enquiries, emailing educators and playwrights, and supporting their partnerships, we realized: "You know, this would be a lot easier if we put it all in a book for everyone...."

There are many reasons why one minute plays are so appealing to educators. Whether you are teaching literacy, creative writing, acting, directing, or English as a foreign language, the compact, economic nature of the one minute play format (writing that needs to be performed) and the fact that the form can be tailored to any age, group, or subject makes short form theatre a fantastic tool for educators. No two classrooms are alike, but many share the same challenges: the high school classroom with 30 students rather than 20, the college acting class with 20 students instead of 14, or the youth theatre group with 20 or more students ranging in age from 11 to 18 years. It's a familiar story; you're supposed to teach your students multiple skills (the principles of playwriting, acting, directing, story structure, grammar, spelling, sentence construction, collaboration, team building, status, the list is endless) in a prescribed amount of time; but achieving that goal and doing so in an exciting and compelling way for those you teach can be extremely difficult (and this is why educators are the real superheroes). When was the last time you heard a teacher say, "I have *way* too *much* time for that lesson, I guess I could pull out another exercise or two to kill time ...?" You may only meet your students for a couple of hours a week. How can you provide every one of them with the opportunity to actively explore and achieve their potential in such a short time span? Enter the One Minute Play ... whose clarity, specificity, and flexibility provide students (of all ages and experience) with the same opportunity to explore complex ideas as a traditional-length play, but the economy of each story allows more students to be able to work on these concepts in the limited classroom time.

> The one minute format is excellent for modern teaching, where you can be often asked to deliver 45-minute classes. Students can struggle to get into lengthy work and get frustrated about not creating an "end product" in the time frame; the one minute play can be both written and performed in the same class, giving the student instant gratification and feedback.
>
> As a teacher of age 16+ in a General Further Education College, I have used Gi60 as a format for teaching writing and direction for the past decade. Simply because it is such a diverse tool that can be applied to any ability group. Students for a variety of reasons are often fearful of writing text, and I have found that by applying a "playful" approach (as detailed in some of the exercises in this book) it quickly breaks down the barriers to the written word and opens the imagination, providing some outstanding results.
>
> (Jan Ansell, York College, UK)

Additionally, classrooms increasingly have a multicultural population and demographic. Teachers are working with students from a wide range of nationalities and cultures and face a constant challenge. These teachers seek ways to introduce their students to one another's cultures and languages while still teaching their subject. The one minute play can be an effective tool for schools with a diverse student population or for educators looking to explore different cultures. What makes a play specifically Greek, Polish, Canadian, or Chinese? What makes a play specifically rural or urban? What does the writer mention that might be unfamiliar to an audience outside their home environment? Whether using existing one minute plays or ones generated by the classroom participants themselves, short form theatre is an excellent way to articulate and discuss these questions and our cultural similarities and differences. Additionally, it has the potential to empower students from various backgrounds to teach others about the vitality of their heritage.

For example, the play *Deep into October* by Dwayne Yancey (Anthology p. 117) is a quintessentially American play. It focuses on a middle-aged man fantasizing about being on the pitcher's mound in a baseball game. In this fantasy, this is not just any baseball game, but the last pitch at the bottom of the ninth inning in the final game of the World Series, with legendary New York Yankees pitcher Don Larsen whispering in his ear. The play captures a specific aspect of growing up, and growing old, in America. A majority of young boys (and now girls) play baseball at all levels, evolving from Little League to high school baseball, and many young men dream of one day playing in the minor leagues and then the majors. For many Americans, baseball is a rite of passage and an experience and memory that connect many men to their own youth and dreams. *Deep into October* is about a father passing those American dreams on to his son, upon realizing that his own time for those dreams has come and gone.

A contrasting but thematically connected example is *Run!* by James Harvey (Anthology p. 306). A young man stands on the stage preparing for battle with his foe; he describes his feelings and the tension he feels as he prepares to fight. As he advances across the stage, describing in detail the explosive moment when he will strike, we begin to realize that this is not a soldier preparing for conflict but the bowler in a cricket match preparing to unleash the ball on his opponent. The quintessentially British image of the gentle village cricket match is replaced with the tension and ferocity of Roman gladiatorial combat. The play shows how the perception of cricket as a gentle Sunday afternoon sport is at odds with the reality of a game that is played and supported passionately across the UK, India, and Australia. James Harvey articulates this passion in such a way that an audience watching the play in Brooklyn or Rio de Janeiro can appreciate the subject matter as easily as audiences from Yorkshire, Delhi, or Melbourne.

These examples reflect our own particular heritages, but hopefully illustrate the point. A one minute play can capture the essence of place and time.

> Using the Gi60 writing exercises in our workshop with the group of over 65s allowed us to explore their memories in a way they had never encountered before. This workshop formed the basis of five further hours of reminiscence work and was a great foundation for us; I would definitely use it again!
>
> (Lauren Scrivens, University of Leeds)

Using the anthology and the huge number of plays available on the Gi60 YouTube channel, there is also the option of exploring a range of plays from within a given submission year. What were the defining socio-political events of that time? In what ways does this series of plays reflect those events? As mentioned earlier, simply because there was a global financial crisis in 2008, it doesn't follow that every play is going to be about economic ruin or the evils of the global banking system. In 2009, the plays we received actually focused on love and family – possibly a reaction to, rather than a comment on, the socio-political climate.

That is perhaps one of the more important things that a collection of one minute plays can do that a traditional-length play cannot. A collection of tiny plays read together in a class or workshop can illustrate a global or communal response to world or local events, illuminating connections and demonstrating a wider range of impressions than a single play can.

Rose

In a recent class presentation, I introduced three plays that had been written after the Boston Marathon bombing in the US to our graduate directors. One play focuses on a man taking refuge in a baseball stadium on a freezing January day arguing with a security guard who is trying to make him leave; the second focuses on a young woman scared to step off a bus in The Big City for the first time, because the bus is in an ugly place and she fears if her first step is on that spot it could hurt her dreams; the third play introduces an optimistic man at a creek encountering a brooding man who states that "the devil is in the water" and he is watching the sins from a baptism upstream wash away. These three plays were written by people from different parts of the US at a specific time in its history. Though none of these plays specifically focuses on a terrorist event, they all actually fit the classic "seven types of stories" (see Appendix G) category of "Overcoming the Monster." In the first play, the traumatized man pleads to the guard that baseball is the only thing that makes sense in the world; so instead of kicking him out, the security guard joins the freezing man on the bench, and they bond by talking about their team's World Series victory. In the second, a young man offers to carry the young woman on his back until she finds the perfect place to take her first step in The Big City, avowing that he won't let the city crush her dreams. In the third play, the brooding man tricks the optimistic man to bring his face close to the water to see the devil in the creek, and the brooding man grabs his head and holds him underwater until he drowns, saying, "I told you the devil was in that water." Each play focuses on a "monster" – a threatening outside force that the characters can choose to fight, succumb to, or seek an ally to help fight it. This lesson sought to illustrate connections to world events that may not be overtly in the text. If you look at a collection of stories from a specific time, it can open the door to see how artists express their responses to world events without specifically mentioning them. Again, the lesson is learned by reading or viewing the collection of plays from different cities and countries, not simply looking at a single play.

Writing skills in the classroom

Writers of all ages can be daunted by the prospect of writing a full-length story; however, ask a student to try writing a play that is only one minute in length, and they may not only find the confidence to try; they may also start to find their own writer's voice. It's simply easier to tackle a story with this time limit. You need the cauldron to make the alchemy, and this structure actually frees up the creative impulses for first-time writers. The idea that the one minute play is like a song rather than a whole album helps to focus young and/or emerging writers on a moment: a simple and powerful event that happens in a single moment in time. If you are working with experienced writing students, the exercises starting on page 18 in Chapter 1 provide a dynamic and fun way to challenge students to look more deeply at narrative, economy of expression, content, and collaboration. If you are working with younger students or youth groups, or are looking simply to bring drama into the classroom, the following section offers our thoughts, ideas, and suggestions to guide and support you. It's a smorgasbord of information, so eat what suits your palette best (let's face it, not everybody likes broccoli, even if it is good for you).

Specifics for younger students

People write what they know, and children are people. We've produced many plays written by authors as young as seven years old. An example of one of the strongest was *Should I Stay or Should I Go?* written by

13-year-old Natasha Geffen (see Anthology p. 344). The story focuses on a young girl nervously preparing to attend her first-ever party, trying to get the attention of her parents, who are both glued to the television set. She is neglected, lonely, and desperately trying to get her parents to stop looking at the screen and help her decide if she should go to the party. When she fails to get their attention, she is defeated, and she squeezes onto the couch, takes the TV remote control, and joins them. She immediately loses herself to the flickering screen. The final image is all three staring at a screen, and not at one another. This was a prescient play written in 2009. After experiencing an increase in play submissions from young writers for Gi60, company member and theatre teacher Vera Khodasevich proposed the development of a one minute play festival solely for her younger students at Acting Out! (a private conservatory in Brooklyn, NY). Gi60 #NextGen is now produced annually with students 9–14 years of age, performing plays written by peers (and some adults as well). Ms Khodasevich experienced the benefit of young people performing stories written by those their own age, and also found that it supported the development of other skills:

> Most of the actors that we have in the #NextGen ensemble are acting students, and therefore are still learning and growing their craft, and we've seen over the years how participating in Gi60 #NextGen has benefited their growth. The pace of Gi60 is such that it really challenges our young students to step up their game. With stories, characters, and conflicts changing literally from minute to minute the actors have to be able to quickly shed the skin of their previous play and start anew the next time they step on stage.
>
> (Vera Khodasevich, Gi60 actor, and Gi60 #NextGen director, teacher)

You can use one minute playwriting exercises with students of any age, from kindergarten to college (see Chapter 1). However, it can be particularly useful in classrooms where students are being introduced to, or are working on, writing and literacy. A student might be reluctant to write a personal essay or a journal about a life experience. But, give them the opportunity to create fictional characters that they can bring to life and can serve as surrogates for their voice, their worries and dreams – and they have a "mask" that protects them while freeing the story that they want to tell. An eight-year-old may not be ready to write their first Harry Potter novel or become the next Tolkien, but they *can* write a one minute play about a magical student who saves their classmates from an evil teacher. Even a classroom the size of 25 children can be asked to write one minute plays, and then read and share each other's work (see Appendix B). To experienced educators, the benefits are readily apparent; for those of you perhaps newer to the profession, or if you are considering bringing theatre into your classroom for the first time, the benefits include:

- Students learn how to create characters and dialogue. How do they speak? How do their specific choices of words help tell us who their character is, and how do those words help move the story forward in the narrow time frame? How are they becoming more aware of the power of language itself? And how can a deeper exploration of multiple dialogues support reading comprehension and analysis skills when students return to reading novels, histories, and biographies?

- Students learn the essentials of good storytelling; good old plot, theme, structure. What is their story about? What about Daniela's play? Or Jonathan's play? Or …? It gives them 25 different stories to read, discuss, and act out. Again, the length of the plays allows that to happen in regular class time.

- Students learn about their own voice and identity. Writing their first play empowers them to tell their unique story. What ideas are important to them? What kinds of stories do they feel are important to tell? How is their story different from or similar to those of others in class? You can learn a great deal about students by their choices in this exercise. Their plays can be a window into their lives, their joys and personal challenges. Having that level of personal information can guide you in teaching and reaching them. But don't forget the role of imagination – sometimes young Connor may write about a dragon devouring his parents just because he thought it would make for a cool movie version.

- The variety and number of stories can spark the curiosity of students to read (and write!) even more. It introduces and reinforces the idea that the world is filled with stories and storytellers, and that stories are a huge part of what makes us human (for further information see *The Storytelling Animal: How Stories Make Us Human* by Jonathan Gottschall, Mariner Books).

- Writing and sharing stories promotes literacy. As a child is writing, of course they're thinking carefully about language, how to use it, and their choice of words on that page.

- The fact that these stories are "plays" that will be read and/or performed aloud is really important. By bringing their words to life, young writers can see the tangible effect of what they have written. Making your peers laugh or think or maybe even cry with the words you have written and the characters you have created can be a very empowering experience.

- Reading plays out loud helps to develop confidence and fluency, and in reading plays with multiple characters, the shared reading helps students support each other and learn from one another. Plays may well introduce students to a wider vocabulary, and the variety of topics that the students choose to write about helps to spark curiosity about those new subjects. You can also incorporate simple literacy exercises within the one minute play exploration:

  o After reading each play, ask students "what do you think happens next?" It asks them to use the body of knowledge they already have, and make a judgment in trying to predict where the character's behavior or given circumstances will lead. Practice with making such predictions or judgments develops critical thinking and nurtures curiosity.

  o Ask your group to visualize where they think the play is taking place. What surrounds the characters? When you put the play on its feet, are there simple objects in the classroom that can represent any of the things the students described? Visualization strengthens comprehension and retention of details.

  o If the play is about a strong conflict, there are likely powerful emotions in the story. Ask your students to discuss what they think the characters are feeling, and why. Good conflict and clear emotions draw people into a story and make them want to know more.

  o Are there any words in the play that they don't know? What part of the play do they have questions about? These discussions help listeners (and readers) to synthesize the information, which again strengthens comprehension and critical thinking.

- Introducing concepts of team building, listening, and being respectful of one another's choices. The most fun and direct way to achieve this is to have the students perform each other's plays. Rehearsal and performance teaches our students:

  o Creativity (creating an imaginary world, characters and relationships) and collaboration.

  o Problem solving. How can I truthfully communicate that character's personality trait of being shy? How do I pick up that book to make the audience understand that it's precious to my character?

  o Close listening, awareness, and collaboration. In rehearsal and performance, students need to listen to their partners, be aware of everyone's contribution, and be respectful of everyone's choices in serving the common goal of telling the story.

  o Dedication and work ethic. Rehearsing/performing a play requires students to honor a time schedule, and to commit fully each time they work on that play. It demonstrates that with repetition, ideas and choices become clearer. Also, by "trying it again" they learn the benefits of not giving up on themselves, or on another person. They learn the difference between "my choice is stupid" and a choice they're simply not committing to yet. A choice can *feel* stupid if they're only committing half way; dedication and practice help them take the risk of committing fully to their idea.

  o Physical awareness and stamina. Plays are active; characters have physical lives, and ideas are communicated through actions. Exploring physical action and gesture (through multiple rehearsals) helps young people understand the power of physical storytelling, body language, and how much they're capable of communicating with their body as well as their voice.

○ Self-confidence, self-confidence, and more self-confidence. Rehearsals are all about trying things that don't work half the time, accepting that they're not working, and then having the courage to try something else. Performance allows students to experience being in front of groups and accepting their reactions (whether applause or constructive critique). Performance is also all about (supported) risk taking – and the more risks we take, the more we redefine what risk means to us as individuals. That is, once we experience it, what seemed risky a short while ago now feels comfortable, and things that may have once seemed scary, no longer are. The rehearsal and performance process teaches this to young students in a fun, safe, and supportive way, and it helps them develop their personal confidence.

> Gi60 has given my students the chance to dip their toe in the water. Shy, and "I'll never go on stage" students, those who would rather have a triple root canal than to read aloud, find that they have a wonderful time playing parts in one minute plays. Plays that their classmates have written, classmates that they hang out with every day. "How can a friend make me feel foolish, look silly, oh what the hell let me give this a try …"

> They love when they can go from the good guy to the bad guy in less than two minutes. They get lost in the group one minute plays … this gives them the confidence to do regular plays and longer scenes, and to push out the limits of their talents.
>
> (Ed Clarkson-Farrell, theatre/drama teacher, at AB Davis Middle School, Mt Vernon, NY)

Acting skills in the classroom

The one minute play can be the saving grace for the acting teacher who consistently runs out of time for students to get on their feet to work. Many beginning college or high school acting classes have anywhere from 14 to 22 participants, and meet for an average of two or three hours each week. A traditional scene is two or three pages, and five to eight minutes in length. If a teacher is an excellent time manager (and most are), they might get half of the students working scenes on a given day. A one minute play is a *complete* story, and allows the student to investigate the basic concepts of acting while economizing on time in the classroom. Exploring a one minute play instead of a five- to eight-minute scene allows the instructor more time to work with the students moment to moment on character, objectives and actions, and relationships. There is more available time to work on the practical components of acting. For students, the one minute play is an appealing form because, unlike individual scene study, the one minute play provides beginning, middle, and end, offering students the chance to fully realize their performance.

And in the same way that a student may have more confidence in attempting to write a one minute play vs. a traditional-length play, a student new to acting may have more courage in attempting to perform a one minute play instead of a longer scene. The "smaller bite" can make it less daunting. Students who are new to memorization and character and play analysis have a stronger chance of succeeding with a shorter piece of material. In countless Intro classes, we've seen beginning students spend half of their time struggling to remember lines, and the other half of their time beating themselves up because they're afraid they're going to forget the lines they do know. How much time and energy does a new student have to investigate complex concepts of acting if they've devoted most of the time to simply trying to remember what to say? (Side note: Rose is currently also working with colleagues on a book that focuses on the impact of excessive use of smartphones and internet on actor training skills; research shows what the top skills acting teachers feel are diminishing in student actors are stamina, awareness, and ability to memorize lines.)

> One of the most beneficial things about using one minute plays … was the fact that the scripts are not daunting. These students were nonmajors, most of whom were terrified about the project. One of their biggest worries, of course, was that they could not learn lines, and anything more than what they could see on one page in front of them may have caused a rebellion. What they learned

(and what I learned thankfully) was that, yes, they can learn lines. Not only that, but they can design a whole show. ... [and] ... when students couldn't remember the lines, they could still remember what was supposed to be happening. My lesson there was that as actors, they're already grasping the most important part, which is telling the story.

(Paul Herbig, actor, teacher University of South Florida Sarasota-Manatee, USA)

One minute plays can be excellent resources to explore concepts of status, relationships, and interpretation.[1] For example,

Rose

When I teach status in improvisation class, I bring in a stack of one minute two-character plays for the students to use. For example, I use the play Nothing *by Kevin Clyne found on page 143. Two students are asked to perform the play, and are instructed to simply follow their impulses. Then, two new students are asked to read the play, but are given assigned contrasting statuses – one high, one low. Two more students begin the same play, and are given high/high or low/low, and so on. The class quickly sees how the play works every time, but the story is different each time because of the changes brought about by the character's status. One isn't better or worse than the other; the points of view have simply changed. It's an exciting, quick, and direct way to teach students about the power of status, and to reinforce the concepts of interpretation and embracing one's individual choices without judgment. It helps to fight the "my character would never do that" syndrome, and opens them up to possibilities: "what conditions would need to exist for my character to take that action?" For more exercises, please see Appendix I.*

Directing skills in the classroom

Similarly to acting classes, the compact nature of one minute plays allows students to delve more deeply into a wider variety of stories in a directing class. Again, it affords the instructor the time to work with more students on specific directorial skills during limited class time. Many college level undergraduate directing classes meet weekly for perhaps two and a half to three hours. As with acting classes, much of the time can be spent on: "Did the actors know their lines? Did the basic blocking support the story? What do you feel this story is about?" As we wrote in Chapter 2, the format allows directing students to cultivate specificity of directorial choices, focus clarity of point of view, explore imagination, and deepen communication skills, and allows more time to experiment with ways of telling a story. The compression of story allows the students to focus more intently on each moment of action and spend more time advancing their visual and physical storytelling skills. Students can go so much farther than "memorize your lines and let's get this baby on its feet ..." – they can dig into advanced directorial concepts while allowing essential time for critical feedback. Especially in undergraduate directing classes, the spare nature of the one minute play cultivates the imagination and helps students discover ways to add flesh to the bones of the story. And yes, 10 directing students will have time to present 10 scenes in a single class.

Another useful thing about using short scripts instead of scenes is that everything that the students needed to understand about the play was right there. The rest was up to them to make choices about.

(Paul Herbig, actor, teacher University of South Florida Sarasota-Manatee, USA)

Rose

At the time of this writing, I'm developing a new course on story and storytelling with our wonderful MFA graduate directing students. We've been investigating elements of story, types and archetypes of stories, relationship of story to mythology, what makes a "good" story, etc. After several weeks of investigating connections between story and myth, traditional categories of stories (Hero's Journey, Overcoming the Monster, Voyage and Return, etc.), we returned to theater and plays. I brought in a stack of roughly 20–30 one minute plays to serve as samples for exploration. In one three-hour class, they read them out loud, analyzed what category of story they felt they belonged to, discussed specific story elements to justify their choices, compared the multiple stories with one another for greater clarification, determined whether each play was a story they would want to direct, and why. Whew! The quality of the plays and the brevity allowed the directors to explore multiple examples of story types and express their personal insights, with the remainder of the class devoted to in-depth discussions of their understanding of categories of stories and myths. Because of the diversity of culture and backgrounds of the playwrights, it also opened the discussion up as to whether certain parts of the world seem to yield a particular type of story, or not.

One week after this class, the directors had their thesis presentations; i.e. they pitch three plays each to the Faculty Committee so that one can be approved as the capstone project to their Master's Degree. All three reported that the depth and variety of stories we examined in our class together made it "incredibly easy" when they returned to the three full-length plays each was presenting. They felt clearer and more confident about what kind of story the play was telling and how that story "fit" into the stories being told in society today. The class work focused their understanding of what the story meant to them and why they felt the need to tell that story at this moment in time. Because I was on that Committee, I could see their confidence, ease, and the joy they had in describing each of their proposals. I've served on that Committee for over 15 years; it was the most stress-free bunch of directors I'd ever seen.

One of the most important directorial concepts that one minute plays can illuminate is that of interpretation and discovering one's unique creative voice. We encourage you to have your students read a selection of one minute plays (perhaps 10–15) and ask them to choose a single play that every student would like to direct. They should all be working on the same play, so it may take a little trial and error to get consensus. Ask for volunteer actors to come in (acting students always champ at the bit for more time with directing students!), and depending on your class time, allow for one-third rehearsal time with directors/actors, one-third presentations with critical feedback from viewers, including the volunteer actors (see Appendix H, the Liz Lehrman *Critical Response Process*. We recommend this structure as it focuses the feedback on the work itself instead of on the artist's feelings), and one-third of class for discussion with only the directing students being present (don't send the actors the scripts in advance; have everyone start at the same place). What are the benefits?

- It allows the teacher to "float" from rehearsal to rehearsal in the room (hopefully you have a big classroom!). You have the opportunity to observe director/actor communication and relationship, to listen to the language being used (Clear? Constructive? Vague?), to see what kind of rehearsal environment the director creates, to note what circumstances seem to block them, or free up their creative impulses, and to observe one of the biggest directing bugaboos of all: time management. Are the directing students getting sidetracked with over-explaining things, or with personal anecdotes, and they're running out of time?

- When each play is performed, directors and actors see the same play as a different story every time. The concepts of interpretation and point of view are potently and clearly illuminated in the creative choices each director made with the exact same text. There's no right or wrong; there is only their artistic vision and how it's realized. The differences in the points of view and in the actions open up the door to countless possibilities for the students. This frees up their confidence in their creative and intuitive choices, and really helps to lessen the power of "the Judgment Monster." Sure, they might see something in a classmate's version and say, "I wish I'd done it that way." But ultimately, that's appreciation of their fellow director's imagination and unique perspective. You'll help them tease apart the difference. Also, a student may see a moment and say, "I would never have made the choice to do it that way. But you know what? It works."

Doing it differently doesn't mean "it's wrong;" it means you went with a choice that made sense to you; as Keith Johnstone says, "Dare to make the obvious choice" – that is, what is obvious to you. And that choice will not be obvious to anyone else. This is a vital lesson to all young artists as they get to know who they uniquely are as storytellers, and as human beings.

Rose

I did this exercise recently with the same MFA Directing class mentioned earlier. They chose the play Fishing for Men *by Dwayne Yancey (see Anthology page 275). Josh Gold's version told the story that Brooder (male) had "had his eye" on Sunny (female) for quite some time and had been waiting for this opportunity to murder her. Tara Elliot's version had Brooder (female) surprised by Sunny's (female) appearance, and the drowning was not premeditated. Michael Raine's version had Brooder (female) well prepared for the planned act against whomever showed up at that moment, and he incorporated specific props like a garrote to hold Sunny's (male) head under water. Each interpretation was exciting, wildly different from the others, with clear and specific choices made in each moment. The most thrilling comments were made when the actors left and the directors had the room to themselves. They looked at each other, exploded with laughter, and almost simultaneously pointed at one another, saying "Oh my god, that was so you!" The discussion that followed was one of the most exciting I'd ever witnessed in a directing class. They had such clear observations about one another's interpretations, and what each point of view said about them as storytellers. It was a beautiful example of owning and having confidence in one's unique artistic voice. And it was wonderful to see how incredibly supportive these directors were of each other in celebrating what makes them the unique storytellers that they are.*

Final thoughts (and not just ours!)

Whether you teach kindergarten or run a graduate program, one minute plays have the capacity to teach your students about stories, creativity, cultures, literacy, humanity, and most importantly, about themselves. You might choose to work from some of the 200 plays we include here, or you might ask your students to write their own plays for the classroom. Whatever you do, have your students present the plays to an audience of some kind. This could be to peers, parents, other teachers, the general public, or even the janitor. By performing their scripts live, students experience the unique empowerment, pride, fear, and thrill of theatre, as well as the feedback and affirmation that can only be experienced when work is placed in front of an audience. Performing live can be scary, especially for those not used to doing so; however, performance helps students confront their own fears of being "rejected" or "not worthy" or "not capable." In short, it gives them the chance to prove themselves wrong. When you were expecting ridicule, rejection, and recrimination, it's amazing the effect that a little laughter and applause can have on a student, whether it's from a class of your peers, a parent, or even the janitor.

Here are a few examples:

- Ed Clarkson-Farrell at AB Davis Middle School had his 11–13-year-old students write one minute plays, perform them in class, and then rehearse and present them for parents and the general public in a renovated auditorium. Parents and administrators get excited by projects that are low budget (you don't have to work with big complicated sets for multiple one minute plays!), allow involvement of larger numbers of students, and have incredibly flexible casting.

- Theatre instructor Paul Herbig, while working at University of South Florida Sarasota-Manatee, was teaching an Introduction to Theatre course to undergraduates. He wanted to challenge them to direct, perform, and design one short play each and then write about the experience. He had 18 students, and he wanted to show them how challenging it is to put on a play, even a one minute play. He selected 18 scripts from past Gi60 festivals, his students directed and acted in each other's plays in class, and then they took the big step of inviting other students and faculty to a studio performance of their work. None of these students were theatre majors; some reported to Paul that the process was "nerve wracking," but all felt that they learned invaluable lessons about the challenges it took to put on a play of any length.

- Jan Ansell, Head of Division (Media, Music and Performing Arts), York College, UK, used Gi60 in the classroom at two institutions, first with undergraduate students at Leeds Met University, who were confident in their skills in creating theatre and relished the challenge of producing ideas to put on stage. The aim of these classes was to develop concise plotlines and detailed characters. At York College, Jan uses one minute plays with 16–18 year olds, most of whom have not tried writing before. The focus of these sessions is centered on developing narrative and story ideas, understanding dramatic structure, and improving self-confidence. Jan says that the beauty of the Gi60 format means it can apply to any level of student, and meaningful lessons can be developed by the teacher.

- Roberta Loew and John Isgro, directors of the private school Acting Out!, attended the annual Gi60 festival several times. They loved it, and joined Gi60 company member and colleague Vera Khodasevich in believing it would be an ideal structure and platform for their younger students to learn from and apply their skills to. The curriculum at Acting Out! includes acting classes that focus on understanding character and story, movement, imagination, working as a team, and developing self-confidence; all things that the exploration of one minute plays can support and nurture. Vera had performed with Gi60 US for many years, and not only felt that the one minute plays could be beneficial in their classroom, but, as we mentioned earlier, believed that creating a festival specifically for this youth group would strengthen their skills even further. So, John, Roberta, and Vera (with the encouragement of Steve and Rose) launched Gi60 #NextGen, featuring 25 one minute plays performed by Acting Out! students aged 9–14. Each year, these young students take what they've learned at Acting Out! and apply it to the challenges that the 25 one minute plays provide. They follow the Gi60 structure in that they issue a call for play submissions with specific criteria for their students' age group, and writers from across the country and around the world submit plays for consideration. (See pages 317, 318 and 357 in the Anthology for some examples.)

Educators and youth group leaders of all age groups are often challenged to find projects that provide performance opportunities for students. Teachers and directors can be hard pressed to find a project that presents "equal" opportunity for all students, and there are many factors to consider in selecting the appropriate project. "Are there plenty of roles for girls/women? Is the cast size of this play big enough to accommodate the 20 students I have in the Drama Club? Does it have expensive design requirements?" Performing and presenting a collection of one minute plays has easy answers for all of those questions. Yes, yes, and no, it's cheap to produce. We have already mentioned the many benefits of live performance for writing, acting, and directing students, and hopefully you will experience, or may already have experienced, these benefits yourself. So, what if you want to take this further; how do you move from the classroom or the workshop to creating your own festival?

Keep reading!

Note

1 Status: The power differences between two people; social dominance or submission. Keith Johnstone writes that there are unwritten rules based on survival instincts focusing on dominance and strength. "These unwritten rules result in a 'pecking order' within a pack or tribe, wherein animals (and humans) can know their place and their value-to-the-pack without necessarily fighting physically. They will send each other 'signals' of communication (eye-contact, posture, stillness, etc.) during interaction in order to establish dominance or submission."

CHAPTER FOUR
Creating your own one minute play festival

By now, you're thinking of ways to create your own one minute theatre festival or project – and if you aren't, you *should*. We hope we've expressed to you the abundance of creativity, learning, discovery, community, and fellowship that is generated through working on one minute plays. However, we hear that little voice in some of your heads saying, "But organizing and curating something like this must be a logistical nightmare! How can you possibly get that many working parts to – well, *work*?" It is challenging, but the rewards are worth every breathless moment you're likely to spend putting it together. We're here to 1) tell you that it *can* be done and 2) offer you specific guidance and support on *how* to do it.

First and most importantly, decide what your goal is. Why are you planning to put on a one minute play festival or event? Are you a teacher or a summer camp counsellor who wants to create an event for which your students create and perform their own material for parents? Are you a college theatre professor who is looking for a project that will present "equal performance opportunities" for your students? Are you a theatre company, brainstorming about a fundraiser that will also feature the talent of your members? But because it's a fundraiser, the entertainment can't be *too* long? You might be seeking opportunities for your writing group or your community theatre, or you may want to commemorate a particular event, person, or place. You may want to start your own one minute play festival in your city and invite local or international artists to participate, or you might simply like tiny plays. Getting a clear goal is akin to writing a mission statement: try to be as specific, and personal, as possible.

- What is your purpose, and how can its needs be fulfilled by a one minute play festival?

- What are the advantages of your event being a one minute play festival (as opposed to a 10- or 15-minute play festival)? How can that specifically support your goal?

- What is the primary focus of this festival? To introduce new writers to audiences? To showcase actors and their skills? To give students an opportunity to publicly perform original works from their classes? To create national or international collaborations through working with large numbers of writers from far afield? To illuminate or celebrate a specific town's or city's persona by presenting plays that focus solely on that community and its identity?

- Who is the festival for? Who is the audience, and why is it important that this audience sees your event? This is a really important question, and one that if answered clearly will have a huge, positive impact on the shape and feel of your event. How many plays you perform, what kind of plays you choose, how you source your plays, where and when your event will take place, and even who will perform at the event will be affected by simply knowing who the festival is for and who your audience is. It's also a lot easier getting people to come to your event if you actually know who they are (there's no point sending invitations to a "round the world" race to the Flat Earth Society …).

- Do you think of this festival as a one-time only event, or would you like to establish an artistic endeavor that you hope will become a recurring event?

- What is special about your event? Marketing folk will often talk about USP (Unique Selling Point), and funders will often speak of a project's viability in terms of "need." In both cases, the same basic question is being asked. What makes your project different; what gap in the market is your project filling? Most of the time your "need" or "USP" is clear. "My class are doing a one minute theatre event; we have never done this before"; "We are celebrating the 500 Years of the Potato with a festival of one minute plays dedicated to potato-based snacks"; or "Class two have run a successful one minute play festival for the last few years; we would like to try this with class one as well." In these examples, each festival clearly identifies its USP. In the case of the two school-based examples, the USP and need relate to the participants (and presumably their families and peers). In the case of the One Minute Potato Snack Festival, the specificity of the event is obviously its USP. If you are starting a festival that you hope will become a recurring event, your USP and the identification of "need" become more important. Why is your festival different? Are there other events locally that are doing what you are doing, and if so, what makes your event different and special?

- A word of warning about USPs; try to avoid gimmicks. The best way to do this is to always look for the need alongside the USP. For example, you discover another one minute play festival in your town and think "hmm, we need to make sure that our event is not confused with theirs. I know! Let's do a 90-second play festival!" Your 90-second festival may have a (highly debatable) USP, but if you look at the "need" for your proposed event, the fact is that the town's original one minute festival already services the community's "need" for short plays. Look for the gap in the market; perhaps the town's other festival takes place in the summer, and therefore your festival could be staged in the winter? Perhaps the town's other festival is open only to commissioned writers and yours will be open to all? If you are planning to start a festival, investigate the cultural landscape that surrounds you; it may provide not only context but also inspiration.

- As you're shaping your goal, take a moment to consider who will be working with you. Do you have enough support to make this event happen as you currently envision it? Do you have directors, designers, publicity, and box office staff?

- Do you have the technical resources to support your vision and goal? If not, can you modify some aspects to simplify? Remember, as Shakespeare famously said, "The play's the thing." You may want to include impressive lighting, sound, projection, costumes, etc. These are all great, and all can be used to enhance the audience experience, but a well-written short play, beautifully acted and realized, is still theatre at its purest and best. Don't feel you need to "add" to make things better. Gi60 has always been based on the following formula: (Writers + actors + directors) × creativity = play festival.

Some specific examples

- You're a teacher and you've been asked to "create an event we can invite parents to." Aha! A one minute play festival could be perfect; your 25 students can learn and apply skills they're currently working on, and it would provide the opportunity for them to share and demonstrate these for parents and families. Working on the plays will give your students team-building skills and confidence (see Chapter 3); you have control over how many or few plays to produce, so the event can be whatever length you feel is appropriate; and you can tailor play selections for your specific students. You have an auditorium, some chairs, and a fellow teacher who has offered to help put up some lights and play some music. Options:

  ○ You can have your students write and perform the plays. Students will benefit from the exercise of writing their own stories, and they know who will be performing their stories: their classmates. Knowing who will be playing the characters of your play can also teach ways of finding the "natural voice" of a character, and can inspire ideas for personality traits and behaviors. Now, it takes time for this process (see Exercises in Chapter 1, etc.), and not every play that your students write will be ready for performance. Are you ready for that selection process, or do you make a decision in advance that every play that every student writes will be used, no matter the quality, content, or number of characters? This is likely several weeks of work prior to starting your rehearsals.

- ○ If time is limited, or your students are more interested in learning about performance than writing, you can choose plays from this book. There are many that involve large casts and age-appropriate scenarios. You may find an author in our anthology section whose writing you love – but, because we're trying to be fair, we may only include a limited number of plays from that author. Visit the Gi60 Channel on YouTube and type in that author's name – look at some of their other works. And then go ahead and contact that author directly (see page 384): trust us, they have many more terrific one minute plays, and 99% of the time they will be delighted to support your school project and grant you permission to use their work.

- ○ If the school event is meant for parents and community, do you want to create a playwriting competition for community members in order to involve them in your school's activities? Advertise a call for submissions along with the specific criteria, choose one minute plays from that pool, and have your students produce and perform the selected plays. Audiences will include writers and parents, your event will promote the talents and educational goals of your school, and you will celebrate your school's role in your community. You might even meet a few people who are teaching artists who could work with your students on other projects as a bonus.

- You're a new theatre company, and you want to showcase the talents of your members to your audiences. Or, you're an established theatre company that has just moved to a new location/theatre and you want to "introduce" yourselves to this new neighborhood, inviting them to get to know you. Or, you're a theatre company creating a fundraising event that will require minimal tech, and will be flexible in length so that part of your evening can be devoted to "Please get our your check book" speeches. A program of one minute plays can be designed to feature the specific strengths of your company, and will support your case as to why potential donors should support you (everyone likes to see a demonstration of something before they invest, especially in the arts). We suggest you produce a series of two- or three-person plays that allow a bit more depth, and round out your program with one or more large group plays that can showcase the strength of ensemble that your company enjoys. And if you're a company that's struggling with ensemble bonds, producing a one minute play festival will bring out the strongest collaborative skills in everyone. Options:

  - ○ If your company is known for its playwrights, write plays from within your group to demonstrate those strengths.

  - ○ If your company is known (or wants to be known) for its strong acting, then identify scripts that showcase those strengths.

  - ○ If your company is new and you have a wary community that needs to be "won over," this would not be the time to present a series of risqué or experimental pieces. Don't underestimate your audiences, but try to challenge them a little at a time. A one minute play festival in and of itself is *already* challenging as a format. Try a mix of plays about relationships, whimsical fantasies, and a healthy number of comedies about serious issues. Then, next time, you can include the play with the talking penis ….

- You run a youth theatre group with weekly classes and would like to showcase the work and talents of your students at the end of the term. A one minute play festival is a fantastic way to do this. Using your students' own writing or works from this volume (as discussed earlier) or a collection of both, you can host a festival in the same room where you hold your weekly sessions. You don't need a theatre studio or any extra technology, just a few chairs for your audience and your actors. A one minute play festival can last five minutes or two hours; it can be technically demanding or technology free. It's this absolute flexibility that makes it so useful as a form. If you run multiple classes with multiple age groups, it's not a problem, as plays can be sourced or created to suit all age groups. Your youngest group members might work together on a small number of family-friendly ensemble pieces while your senior group members, who may well have written their pieces themselves, can tackle more serious and demanding subjects. Alternatively, you may decide to bring all your groups together, with senior members perhaps directing some of the younger members; the options open to you are pretty much limitless and can be tailored to the particular skills of your students.

Steve

I included a musical score played on a bowed saw in a Gi60 piece once simply because I knew Gi60 actor and director Hedley Brown played the instrument. I have also used multiple ukuleles, juggling, banjos, singing, and mime because of the talents of those I'm working with. This is one of the great joys of the form: your actors can bring their full range of skills and have their chance to use them and hey, if it doesn't work on one play perhaps it will on another (for the record, the saw sounded great).

One of the great things about one minute theatre in a non-curricular setting such as a youth theatre group or a community group is the fact that even when group members fail to show up to rehearsals, the form is flexible enough to cope with this. There is nothing worse than preparing to rehearse a big scene in a traditional play only to find one of your main characters is ill and won't make rehearsal (or worse, the performance). In these cases, the group leader is faced with trying to work out how best to use the time, now that the planned session can't continue. If you have ever been in this position, you know how frustrating it is and how damaging it can be to the rehearsal process. With one minute theatre you don't have these problems in quite the same way. You can recast pieces quickly if members are not available, or you can simply rehearse the pieces the missing person is not in and add extra pieces if you need to. You always have the option of reshaping your performance.

Whatever your reasons for producing a festival, one thing is certain: those reasons and the specific goals you have identified will influence the way your plays are generated and/or how you choose your scripts. Once you're clear on the goal of your event, let those goals inform the plays you use and the process you employ to create or select those scripts.

Selecting plays

There are obviously many things to consider when choosing scripts, but the first and most important is how you interact with and treat your community of writers. Without scripts, your festival simply cannot exist, and the better the writing, the better the potential festival. Some one minute play events generate their scripts through an open competitive process, and some are generated within existing writing groups or community groups or in a classroom setting. Others are generated by commission (invitation only). Whatever your particular method of generating scripts, make sure your writers are clear about what you expect from them, what you are offering in return, and, equally importantly, what you are not offering. Here are some things you might want to consider when sourcing material for your festival:

If you're holding an open submission process:

- Is there a prize (other than that of being selected and having the play produced)? Is there financial payment?

- Have you clarified what criteria you are using for play selection?

  ○ Will you cut or alter scripts that exceed the length of one minute?

  ○ Do you ask for age-appropriate material?

  ○ Do you require a specific format and writing style for submissions?

  ○ Does your organization or school have any guidelines about sexual content or profanity?

- Will copyright remain with the author (we would always advise "yes")?

- How many performances will there be, what are the dates, and does the writer get free tickets to see their play if chosen?

If you're commissioning plays (invitation only), in addition to the above:

- Are you and your collaborators clear on the criteria for how you're selecting these specific writers? Why Jim MacNerland and Nancy Brewka-Clark and not Barry Hobbs? Are you focusing on "name" writers only, or are you mixing those choices with inviting early career playwrights?

- Are you setting specific criteria re. topics, cast size, etc.?

- Are you letting each invitee know who the other participants are in advance? That is, if a playwright of high profile says yes, is the next writer more apt to agree to write a play for you based on their participation?

When a writer submits a script, they hand over their creative work, like a parent leaving their small child at a friend's for sleepover for the first time. You, as guardian, need to make sure that the writer is happy for you to take care of their tiny play. For example, the Gi60 festival is open to everybody; we are clear about our criteria, rules, and regulations, and we make these easily accessible online for all to see. We reserve the right to cut material that is too long, and we interpret plays without the writer in the room, so we may not always produce the play the writer believes they have written. To be able to successfully produce the festival each year, we rely on our writers' continued goodwill and trust, even when our vision and the writers' might differ; information and clarity are key. When errors occur, and they do, we try to rectify the problem quickly and efficiently. Our writers have always been universally supportive even when problems have arisen, because they trust the festival and our aims and because we try to keep them informed. One main reason is the clarity of our stated goals, and our efforts to include the writers and promote their work to the best of our ability.

Your writers are the most important element of the event. Actors, lighting, sound, set, and props are all irrelevant without the creativity and support of your writing community. Nurture your writers and they will produce beautiful pieces of tiny theatre.

Having sourced and/or generated a large pile of tiny plays, you will be faced with the exciting, or possibly daunting, challenge of choosing which plays to select for performance. How and why you choose one play over another will depend on a number of factors, including who your writers are (a writing group, a class or community group, total strangers) and whether they have fulfilled the criteria of the brief (we still get many plays that are nearer ten minutes in length than one). Having taken into consideration these and any other factors particular to your event, you will still, no doubt, be faced with a pile of plays from which you have to select. We have read literally thousands of one minute plays over the years, so here are a few things we have learned about selecting one minute plays:

- Many plays you read will not be ready for performance. Anybody who has spent time as a play reader will tell you that good plays are in the minority and great plays are rare. Don't be disheartened if you read 10 plays before anything grabs you.

- Just because it might look odd on the page doesn't mean it won't work in the hands of actors. If a play appeals to you but you are not totally convinced it's going to work, read it aloud or take it to a rehearsal. You may be surprised.

- Two heads are better than one. Get lots of people to read the plays. Even if you are tackling the direction of the plays on your own, encourage other people to read the submissions. You will be guided by your own taste, and that's essential, but somebody else may see something in a play that you have missed (especially if you are reading a lot of tiny plays).

- Trust yourself; if you think it can work, it probably can. The nature of one minute plays means that there is rarely a great deal of background detail or description. Plays can therefore seem enigmatic, or just plain odd in some cases. This shouldn't be seen as a negative but, rather, as an opportunity. If you read something and it moves you or makes you laugh but you're concerned that others might not feel the same way, don't falter; go with your gut. These choices can often turn out to be some of the best you will make.

Steve

Gi60 submissions are made online, and the selection process is made the same way. Rose and I have been selecting plays together for over a decade using this method. We don't talk about our selections prior to making them, and the interesting thing is that in all that time, we have only had to fight over a handful of plays. This is partly because we understand each other and each other's festival environments, but I think it has more to do with the kind of work that appeals to us. I have watched plays performed by the Gi60 US cast that were funny, moving, and inspiring that didn't connect with me at all when I read them. Both Rose and myself now share our directing duties with associate directors, and I think this brings a richer, more diverse selection of plays to the stage.

Structure

When Steve made the decision to run a short form festival, he generated the scripts through writing groups. He did so with little thought about how he might structure the eventual live theatre event. When he invited Rose to join two years later in 2005, she said yes without really thinking it through either (we're both impulsive that way…!). She was lucky that as a director and acting teacher, she knew a lot of actors, and she had access to a theatre that was dark in the summer months. We've learned many things over the years, primarily that "you need the cauldron to make the alchemy." That is, structure will set you free for the rest of your process. Some key things to consider for your own supportive structure:

- How many plays will be performed?
- Who will be performing the plays (age, gender, cast number, etc.)?
- What is your rehearsal process for producing a festival of individual tiny plays (full-time intensive rehearsal, weekly sessions, full cast at all rehearsals, individual calls)?
- In what order should the plays be placed? How can that running order be shaped to tell a larger story beyond the individual stories?
- What (if any) lighting, sound, set, and props will be needed?

Your decisions about structure and the production of your festival will be guided by a combination of these pragmatic, aesthetic, creative, and personal considerations.

How many plays will be performed?

The number of plays you decide to produce is entirely up to you and will undoubtedly be guided by the reasons and goals you have clarified for yourself and your group. If you are working with a class or a community group, you have a defined number of participants, and this will dictate the number of plays you produce. If you are commemorating the centenary of an event, you might choose to produce 100 tiny plays, as this number is clearly appropriate. Whatever the number you settle on, it's worth considering the following:

- If you have 50 plays or fewer, you might consider running the event as if it were one continuous play, with all the scripts produced in a single sitting and no interval.

- If you have generated 60 plays or more, perhaps an event of two halves might provide a better structure. Having an intermission will also give audiences a chance to stretch their legs, share their thoughts and discuss what they've just seen, grab a quick drink if available, and also visit the rest room (audiences have needs too). An intermission often whets the appetite for the second half (rather than hurting any momentum gathered).

- If you have over 100 plays, then perhaps two separate performances on consecutive days (or different continents) would be the best model. It's not that the length of time would be prohibitive. A two-hour show with an intermission is fairly standard, but 100 different stories are a lot to absorb. Running that many one minute plays together in one event runs the risk of some of the stories being lost through sheer number and possible mental overload.

As a general rule, treat the total running time of all your plays in the same way you would a full-length play. Fifty one minute plays performed back to back with scenic changeovers will tend to run for about an hour. That's the length of a one-act play or the first half of a full-length play. Modern theatre audiences can start to become itchy in their seats after about an hour, and it's no surprise that many modern full-length scripts run for 1 hour and 45 minutes: the first half running for the full hour and the second half for 45 minutes. So, a festival containing 80 tiny plays might run best with 45 in the first half and 35 in the second. However, you may still wish to run the show with 40 in each half so that the programme looks balanced, or possibly because 40 were written by one group and 40 by another. Your choices will be affected by numerous factors specific and particular to your own circumstances. Just try to ensure that your structure values the "whole" as much as it does the "singular." Each individual play should have its own unique voice and color. All these voices are held within the vessel that is your event. The individual voices are important, very important, but they will not get to their destination if the vessel they sail in sinks. If you are the captain (director, teacher, etc.), remember that as captain you are responsible for both the passengers and the ship.

Who will be performing the plays (age, gender, cast size, etc.)?

The age range, gender, and size (that's quantity, not height!) of your cast will influence and guide the scripts you choose to produce. A mixed-gender cast with a wide age range is a very different proposition from a cast solely comprised of nine-year-old boys. The size of your acting company is also an important element to consider. It's easy to assume that the larger the company, the less each actor has to learn, and therefore, the easier the process. However, larger companies often mean more administration and a more complex rehearsal process, so you have to find the balance that works for you. Over the years, we have worked with cast sizes ranging from 9 to over 30. There are no absolutes, but if given the option, we would choose to work with a group of 12–14 actors of mixed age and gender.

When preparing for your casting:

- Will you have an open call for actors? If so, we encourage you to have group call-backs, and do some ensemble exercises so that you can see how these people who are new to you respond to one another. Are they skilled at listening, yes and, and collaboration? Do they have strong focus and awareness? Are they flexible and open? See Appendix C, D, E and F for some simple exercises you can include in your call-back process.

- Do you have an established acting company that you know well? Do they have established chemistry with one another that can be used to your advantage in a series of one minute plays? Chemistry can help actors easily establish the history of a relationship, and offer details not given in a script. Actors' familiarity and ease with one another can lead to greater risk taking earlier in the process, which gets the play farther, faster. This increases your chances of a fully realized story.

Rose

I'm so lucky that several of our actors have returned every year for 12 years. Over time, actors develop a beautiful chemistry, and a short-hand with one another. Two of the most talented actors I know are Mickey Ryan and Jay Nickerson – from the first time they hit the stage together, everyone in the room felt the "kapow!" of their connection. They both take huge creative risks, and have wicked senses of humor. They're supernaturally great listeners, and they are the penultimate "yes and" actors. And to be honest, they're good friends with a mischievous competition going on between them. One year, we produced Joel Dean's play Mr. James and Mr. Walker, a comedy about two aging ham actors who show up at a youth theatre audition and start showing off their skills, trying to win the lead parts (while small children around them are crying their eyes out). When Mickey and Jay hit the stage, the audience began laughing before a word was uttered. Their connection, physical storytelling and status work created an instant history between the characters; the sense of egotistical competition was established immediately and the rest was Jay and Mickey building upon the hysterically funny story. They are masters at economic storytelling, and believe me, they fill every single second of a one minute play.

- Do you have a diverse mix of actors? A balance of male and female? Resist the temptation to do a play you know you can't possibly do justice to.

When you have your cast assembled, devote some time for everyone to get to know one another. Doing that many plays has the potential for fragmentation to occur, so every effort to help the company bond with one another is important. A strong ensemble is essential, and it leads to everybody feeling equally connected to the project.

What is the rehearsal process for producing a festival of individual tiny plays?

Having chosen your plays and your cast, you now have the exciting prospect of rehearsing all of your plays for performance. There are many ways you might decide to approach this, and here again, your specific circumstances and goals will affect your decision. Are you yourself producing? Directing? Directing *and* producing? After the first few years of running one minute theatre festivals, we decided to work with associate directors. Now, it is possible to direct every play yourself, but the addition of extra directorial assistance provides the festival with more creative options. It also allows multiple plays to be rehearsed simultaneously, and if required, a larger company of actors can be accommodated. Once you have your actors and any additional directorial help, you will need to decide how you are going to cast the plays that you've selected from the pool of actors you've assembled.

Steve

My preferred method is to dedicate the first rehearsal to a read through of all the plays with the full company of actors and directors and then cast the roles at this read through. I have worked with many of the actors in the Gi60 company for quite a few years (actor Arthur Sutcliffe has appeared in every Gi60 UK performance) and because of this I already have a rough idea of some of the casting in my head, but I still like to hear the cast read, and there is always the chance that a new company member might make me rethink a play even at this early stage. Once we have read the first 20 to 25 plays and have roughly cast them, we check the balance of parts to ensure that one person isn't appearing in all 20 while another has failed to be cast. This process works for me for a number of reasons. I know many of the actors I'm working with and have already had thoughts about casting prior to first meeting; I like to hear the actors read for the first time and watch their choices regarding pieces (who has committed to what, who seems to have already made a character connection). I also like the opportunity to see new cast members and watch their reaction to this pressurized environment that asks them to simultaneously audition while at a read through. It allows me to start to understand who I am working with and shows the actors how intense and concentrated the process is. The most important reason that the process works so well is because we work together as a company. Actors (new and old) happily give up parts, swap roles, and express when they feel they are in too few or too many plays. I think the one minute play format offers such an opportunity and challenge for actors that the usual fears and issues of role size or "star" billing become irrelevant. In a one minute play festival, everybody is a star. The Gi60 UK company has always worked this way, and we all look forward to read-through day. It's a great chance to meet new cast members, catch up with old friends, and prepare for the process ahead before getting into full rehearsal mode. I love placing the huge pile of scripts on the table, and I love seeing and hearing the actors' reactions to the year's crop of tiny theatre. This method has always worked for us; it allows everyone to meet, hear the entire show, discuss parts, share out directing duties, and dip their feet in the waters of tiny theatre on day one. At the end of this first day we are all (hopefully) excited, on the same page, ready for the challenge, and clear about our shared responsibility to each other, our community of writers, and our audience. This is our process, and it really works for us, but it might not be the one you choose.

Rose

In the early years of Gi60 US we held open auditions, and it quickly became clear that this form demanded a very specific skill set from actors (See Chapter 2). Someone could audition and be a wonderful actor, but doing 50 plays in one night was something they just might not be built to do. Some actors are well suited to a single role in a single traditional-length play, and a rare group is eager and ready for the challenges of performing 50 plays in one go. I found that auditions could tell me how creative and talented someone was – but they didn't tell me if they were built for the demands of Gi60. So, I changed our system to simply inviting back returning actors, and once we knew who was able to return, we looked at "gaps" that needed to be filled, e.g. actors to cover the young roles up to mid-twenties, roles in the middle ground of thirties and forties, and those 50+. Then we invited additional actors who were current and/or former acting students (as well as some I knew from the professional world who were happy to go on this adventure). We emphasize improv and impulse work at Brooklyn College, and actors with strong improvisation skills excel with the one minute play format. We haven't had auditions in almost 10 years. We don't want to appear as if we're a closed club, but by the same token, those acting company members work their tails off to earn the experience and expertise it takes to do this work well, and I'd be crazy not to want to keep that around as long as possible. We add new actors every year. All of our proceeds go to a scholarship fund for theatre students, so it's also nice when I'm able to invite a current or former scholarship recipient to perform, and they enjoy "paying it forward" by volunteering their talents to help the next group of students ....

I love and agonize over casting our 50 plays; and I take days and days to do it. I see Gi60 as a rare opportunity to help create a "concert for actors" within the symphony of plays. So, I try to make sure that a) the actors are cast in a somewhat evenly divided number of plays; b) there are different pairings of actors, so that the audience doesn't start to make "associations" with one particular couple; c) younger actors are cast in plays with more experienced actors so that they have a nice mentoring experience; and d) actors are cast in a wide range of roles so that they stretch their acting muscles. If an actor plays variations of the same character type across their dozen plays, it gets boring for the actor and, again, can be confusing for the audience ("Is that the same geeky character from that other play, or a different nerd? Why does he have a sword in this one?"). The actors thrive on the variety, and I thrive on being that organized in advance (I so appreciate Steve's method, but as a director, I would have a coronary arrest if I went into a first rehearsal with 50 plays and 16 actors not knowing who would be playing what in advance). And, our audiences enjoy the fact that they can't pinpoint who will play what. Many audience members return every year, and love to talk with the actors afterwards and compare the roles they're playing this year with previous festivals. They love seeing Joan Lunoe play a heartbroken mother in one moment, and then perform a hilarious turn as a film noir, shoe-obsessed gang moll in the next (and Joan likes that too!).

We also get special requests from playwrights about casting; some will submit plays and write, "If you choose this play for Gi60 US, I think it would be great for Sabrina Cataudella!" or Cristina Pitter, etc. ... I love that the writers – some who have only ever seen our festival via live stream or YouTube – have gotten to know our actors and their specific abilities, and they start to write characters and plays with them in mind. It's fun ... and it helps me see the writer's vision more clearly if I know they heard that particular actor's voice while they were writing the story.

Steve

I find it really interesting that even though Rose and I seem to approach casting from almost opposite ends of the room, our results are almost identical. We both spread out our actors so that they have a combination of major and minor roles, and we try to ensure they work on a wide range of characters, genres, and storylines. We both have the same destination; we just choose to start in different places.

CREATING YOUR OWN ONE MINUTE PLAY FESTIVAL

Having cast your plays using whatever method works best for you, you will now have to work out the best way to schedule rehearsals. Your choices will, of course, be determined by the number of plays that you're producing, personnel, resources, available space, and available time. Here are two options:

Steve

I have always preferred to have the entire company present at all times. For many years I rehearsed the entire show in an intensive week of rehearsals. More recently I have worked across a much longer period of time rehearsing once and twice a week, but in both cases I called all actors to all rehearsals. This is once again a personal preference and one that has evolved over a number of years. Often my associate directors are also members of the acting company, so having everybody at all rehearsals allows smaller groups to break out to rehearse scenes while still being available if needed. I will often add actors into a scene to create depth (i.e. if a scene is set in a park where a couple are talking on a park bench, I might add somebody walking their dog or playing Frisbee or roller skating, etc., just to bring the scene to life). Having the company all together allows me this freedom. For the Gi60 2015 rehearsals, I made the decision that I would just call people for the scenes they were in so that I wasn't wasting their time. We rehearsed in the evenings once a week for three hours at a time over a period of six weeks. Even though they have jobs and other commitments, the entire cast just turned up to rehearsals anyway. It's that kind of commitment and enthusiasm that I look for in would-be cast members. As already stated, the one minute theatre format requires a certain kind of actor, one who is self-sufficient, totally focused, fearless, and caring. Every year that I work with the Gi60 Company, especially seasoned company members, I remember just how special they are.

I have always found the collaborative process in the Gi60 projects to be something that does not need to be worked at. Everyone comes to the rehearsals with a totally open mind and a work ethic I have rarely seen elsewhere. This makes collaborating a joy. So, while in other productions there might be a need to "manage" the differing temperaments and conflicting egos, a Gi60 cast is so easy to work with. Everyone feels comfortable in pitching ideas and none of the directors (I hope myself included) are too dictatorial as to accept other people's ideas and perspectives.

(Hedley Brown, Gi60 actor, director, writer)

Rose

The reality of working with actors in New York is that they are working on multiple projects at any given time. They're auditioning, doing readings, filming a commercial, performing in late night cabarets while also committed to your rehearsal schedule together. Oh yeah, and they're also working one or more survival jobs so they can pay the exorbitant thing we New Yorkers like to call "rent." Long way of saying, there's no way that Steve's method would work for us.

We do a variation of a more traditional rehearsal schedule. We rehearse the plays in 25-minute blocks in the evenings (usually for about two or three weeks prior to performance). We have anywhere from three to six directors each year, so we can run three or four rehearsals simultaneously in various studios. By rehearsing the plays individually, after a few days it becomes clear which ones will need more work than others, and then we can adjust additional call times for those plays. It sounds like madness – and it is – but we all really enjoy the wackiness of it. It compels us to be economic, there's no time for BS, the atmosphere is light because the situation is so unusual, and the time chunks are always enough to get a reasonable amount of work done. The actors also love that there's no time for a "hangover" from a previous play – they have to let go of whatever emotional life they were just working on, and make way for the new character and story in the next rehearsal studio.

The really mad part is the scheduling itself – this is the down side of this method. If you're scheduling three or four simultaneous rehearsals, and up to 15–20 plays in a single night, one small mistake and it can fall like a house of cards. BUT – once you find a system and a rhythm as to which plays can successfully be scheduled against each other, then it's like watching the innards of a Swiss watch.

These are just two approaches; your needs and resources will guide you to a process and system that work best for you and your collaborators. If it's a class project, all your rehearsal and prep time may happen during school hours. If you only have your theatre on weekends, then calling full company for those two days may be best. Again, note the number of plays you're doing, your personnel and resources, and your available time, and then decide what you are comfortable with and what process would best support your goals for the event.

In what order should the plays be placed, and do you need an interval/intermission?

There is absolutely an art to ordering these plays. I won't pretend to understand how best to do it, but in my experience there is an excitement created when a couple of plays of similar tone are followed by something completely different. It's a great way to highlight a point of a thought or even a question posed by a play.

(Adam Thomas Smith, Gi60 actor)

One of the most surprising elements of creating a one minute play festival is the challenge of putting so many different pieces of theatre in some kind of running order. There are a number of things that need to be considered, including:

- Does your play order allow your actors to enter and exit the stage in such a way that they are available for their next scene?

- Does your order spread out your actors' roles across the event rather than placing them all together?

- How will your chosen order affect any set and props you are using?

- Are there any plays that you really don't want next to each other? Because of content, or extreme differences in tone?

- Are there any plays you think would work well performed in close proximity?

The order of plays provides you as a director with an extra narrative tool. You may choose to cluster plays with a similar theme together. Four pieces set in an airport may become four pieces set in the same airport. You may choose to counterpoint work; a piece about death and grieving could be followed by a piece of high comedy involving two clowns. These choices shape the overall event and give the one minute theatre festival its sense of gestalt. This overarching "extra" narrative really does make the event more than the sum of its parts. You have the opportunity to create a single story from the collection of plays, and a play's specific placement in your running order can make all the difference. Give yourself the freedom to experiment and if things don't work, allow yourself enough time to change them. Maybe you need to give an actor more time to get to the right place on stage, or maybe you want to leave an actor on stage to improve the flow of the show. You will only see these issues when you run the full show, so give yourself some wriggle room by allowing space in your schedule to make changes in good time. Your actors are under pressure, so don't finish your dress rehearsal and then decide to make changes (you have been warned!).

People are often surprised that a very poignant and moving piece of theatre can co-exist with something genuinely silly and irreverent. Far from adversely affecting either piece, this kind of juxtaposition can actually benefit both.

Examples of a running order

The order in which plays are performed can have a significant effect on the audience's perception of the "larger" story you're telling. We crave connections, and in situations where no overall narrative exists, our imagination just makes one of our own. When watching a collection of 50 or 60 plays in a single sitting, audiences will seek meaning and method in how and why you have chosen to order your plays in a particular way.

The following is a series of potential running orders using 10 plays from the anthology section.

Sample 1:

This first sample is a collection of plays about love and relationships:

Running Order 1:	Running Order 2:	Running Order 3:
Sudden Death	Last Chance Saloon	Online Senior Date
A Doable Resolution	Mr & Mrs?	Love Finds a Way
Mr & Mrs?	Nothing	February 15
Last Chance Saloon	Love Finds a Way	Conversation
Nothing	February 15	Mr & Mrs?
February 15	Oh Baby!	A Doable Resolution
Love Finds a Way	Conversation	Oh Baby!
Oh Baby!	A Doable Resolution	Sudden Death
Conversation	Sudden Death	Nothing
Online Senior Date	Online Senior Date	Last Chance Saloon

Running Order 1:

This has been crafted to give a rise and fall to the nature of relationships. It begins with an argument that ends in a proposal, proceeds with a happy play about a pregnancy, then enters into a series of plays about relationship challenges, separations, and loss, culminating in a renewal of faith in love with *Online Senior Date*. The comedic pieces are spread throughout the more serious plays.

Running Order 2:

The focus here is on the need for relationships to rebuild and renew throughout, with plays about missed opportunities spread among the optimistic plays.

Running Order 3:

This is meant to be a cautionary tale. It begins with optimism, and slowly descends into stories about what can happen if someone doesn't attend to their love, or take action in the moment.

Sample 2

The second sample focuses on stories about life and death:

Running Order 1:	Running Order 2:	Running Order 3:
Going to Kevin's	Universal Conflict	GRTC
GRTC	Tree	In an Hour
Not Expecting That	Not Expecting That	Shoebox
In an Hour	Ghosts	Not Expecting That
Fishing for Men	Fishing for Men	Going to Kevin's
Shoebox	In an Hour	Ghosts
Ghosts	Sunset in North Dakota	Fishing for Men
Sunset in North Dakota	GRTC	Universal Conflict
Tree	Shoebox	Tree
Universal Conflict	Going to Kevin's	Sunset in North Dakota

Running Order 1:

This has some ebb and flow of comedic and serious plays, tracking life from the innocence of childhood, to serious discoveries about death, to lightening things up a bit with *Ghosts*, to facing those fears in *Sunset in ND*, to accepting the powers of nature and the universe in *Tree* and *Universal Conflict*, ending on a light note.

Running Order 2:

This begins with the story of the larger universe, implying that humans don't have as much control over life and death as we think we do, segueing into the inevitability of the life cycle, and ending with childhood innocence about death; by the final play, in which two children speculate on the death of a bug, the audience know what the children are just starting to figure out about the nature of life and death.

Running Order 3:

This is a darker consideration of life, death, and nature, ending with a note of hope in *Sunset*, in which the optimist contradicts the pessimist regarding what he knows he wants his life to be about.

Each of the examples above tells a subtly different overarching narrative story and colors your event in a slightly different way. This is one of the real joys of creating an evening of tiny plays. This extra narrative can provide audiences with an unseen road map between pieces, allowing them to enjoy the overall experience more fully. Your play order won't change the overall quality of what you have created, but like a well-seasoned recipe, it will ensure your audience tastes the work at its very best.

We hope these examples give you inspiration for enhancing the power of the storytelling for your event. Use the anthology section of this book to practice; choose your own series of 10 plays, experiment with the order of the stories, and reread them with each new arrangement. Or, better yet, bring the plays to your classroom and theatre company, and read them aloud in the different orders. How are the collective impressions different from running order to running order? What does the order of the plays say to different members of your group (we don't always hear the same story)? What themes emerge in one arrangement that are absent or different in another? How, if at all, does ending on "the sad and thoughtful play" as opposed to the "wild and irreverent" change your response to the overall set of 10 plays? Experiment, play, play some more, trust your instincts, and have fun.

Once you have chosen and rehearsed your plays, you will start to get a feel for the shape of the show and its overall emotional impact. The individual plays, when performed together, start to project a combined energy, and it will be this feeling, in conjunction with the suggestions above and below, that will help you decide the right running order for you.

Along with thematic connections, there are other practical and aesthetic considerations that you need to factor in. A few more thoughts for successful play ordering:

- Spread out your full-cast plays. There will probably be a small number of these plays, but they are your big production numbers, so use them wisely. Steve likes to start and finish with a full-cast piece. It gets all the actors on stage at the beginning of the show, which means nobody is waiting around in the dark and everybody is ready for their well-earned bow at the end. This can be especially useful for younger casts or if you are working with a group who have little or no previous acting experience. Everybody starts together with the same anticipation and nerves, and getting everyone on stage at the start of the show gets the nerves out of the way in the first few seconds. Steve likes to spread out the remaining full-cast pieces across the show, with one somewhere near the middle. Rose likes to slowly build up to full-cast pieces, mixing larger and larger-cast plays, until there is one play with all hands on deck that makes the audience suddenly realize how many actors they've actually been seeing. Then she likes to gently wind down thematically to plays about love or a sense of wonder, often ending on a smaller-cast play that captures the universal message of the festival that she would like to send the audience home with. Here, again, the choice is yours to make, and the actors you are working with, the material you are using, where you are performing, and many other elements, including your own excellent taste and creativity, will contribute to where you put which plays and why.

- Make sure your actors have a manageable backstage journey. Actors have to work very hard on and off stage in a one minute play festival. For many years, Gi60 UK was performed at the beautiful Viaduct Theatre in Halifax. This is a traverse stage with entrances on all four corners of the space. Crossing from one side of the stage to the other back stage is very difficult and quite a distance, so ensuring actors were able to make their next cue was essential. Gi60 US performs in a black box theatre that seats 120 with audiences on three sides and has large flats upstage, on which the play title, author, and author's location are projected. The actors have many options for crossovers, and they don't have long distances to cover for entrances/exits. However, because it's a smaller theatre, one has to be careful about placement of prop tables backstage, creating areas for hanging costume pieces so that they're not flung to the floor in between plays, creating a hazard for actors who are speeding toward their next entrance.

- Ensure the journey of your set and props is carefully considered. Gi60 UK uses a series of rehearsal blocks, and play choice can be affected by the "journey of the blocks." If a scene requires eight rehearsal blocks on stage and the following scene requires none, then perhaps these scenes shouldn't be placed next to each other, or perhaps the eight blocks can stay on stage for the scene that requires none as a backdrop. Gi60 US also uses cubes, but they are placed in specific patterns in different areas of the stage with little or no change between plays. Instead, the specific arrangement of the cubes determines whether a particular play will be "assigned" to that area. For example, the long cube at stage center becomes the area for plays set in cars or on park benches. Your venue and environment and the "set" pieces you use will play a large part in how you choose to set your festival.

- Try to avoid having the same actors in multiple consecutive scenes unless you have a good reason. It can be hard on the actors and can also become confusing for the audience. Try to give actors a minimum of one or two plays in between acting assignments so that they can catch their breath and prepare mentally, physically, and emotionally for their next play. This won't always be possible or practical, but think about your actors and their own personal journey through the festival.

- Start and finish strongly. Once your plays have been rehearsed, take a moment to consider what you have, and ask yourself a very honest question: how do I want to start and finish this show? This will connect back to your goals, which guided your play selection, and back to your experimentation with the running order and the overarching story of your festival/event/evening. When you have that sense of the zeitgeist/larger story, you can decide which of your plays feels like an appropriate "entrance" into that tale, and which play best puts a fine point on the end of the zeitgeist story. And maybe you don't want to end with the fine point, but conclude with an open question related to the larger story. Whatever your decision, be sure that the plays that represent your front door entrance and back door exit to the event are strongly written. And, make sure that your (or your associate's) directorial point of view on those plays is crafted so that those plays welcome the audience into the zeitgeist story, and then guide us out the door at the end with a goodie bag filled with what you want the audience to take home from your festival – besides potent memories of powerful stories.

What set, props, lighting, and [is that] sound will be needed?

I think that one of the great things about Gi60, things can go wrong. I have memories of broken props, forgotten lines, missed light cues, but in the end it doesn't matter. Things go wrong, life happens, but it's a great reminder that failure happens and that it's not the end of the world when it does. Fail big, succeed big.

(Adam Thomas Smith, Gi60 actor)

Set

Having worked out your structure, you are faced with the question of how to stage your event. You may have commissioned/devised a group of one minute plays placed in a specific locale that requires a unit set that you build and use, or you may be doing a site-specific event for the plays in which the audience travels from one room to the next. Most likely, you're producing a collection of plays that are set in different environments and "worlds." It's impractical to change realistic sets for every story when you're running 25–50 plays together, so keep it simple: blocks or cubes, chairs, or simple setups in assigned areas on stage that determine the placement of a play.

If you opt for the "permanent placement" version, remember what we've written previously about not having the same locale back to back in the running order. If you opt for cubes/blocks, and you move them in between plays, we suggest the Steve method: that is, don't try to hide or frantically rush through the movement; try to make it a part of the designed action. Whatever your choice, keep it simple, simple, simple. Trust that the audience's imaginations will fill in and build upon what the story and the actors provide without the need for 50 different sets.

Rose

Sometimes I crack up when reading elaborate stage or costuming directions in submitted plays. Playwrights that submit to Gi60 understand that their single play will be part of a larger festival of 49 other plays, yet others seem to write as if that script was the one and only play to be performed. Though I have absolutely no proof (because we don't save scripts that weren't chosen for production), and Steve can't recall, in 2005 there was a play submitted in which actors were meant to play hamsters scrambling for a way to escape their cage, and the stage directions read that "a giant hamster wheel is flown in from the grid above." I like to think of that as our equivalent of "Exit pursued by a bear ..." Now – bears, we have had onstage as characters, lest anyone think I have anything against hamsters in dramatic literature ....

Steve

My first short form event took place in a studio theatre, and I had a cast of about 12 people. Having a fixed cast size forced my next staging decision. With only one door in and out of the venue for cast and audience, it was clear that the actors would need to be in the space and "on stage" throughout the performance. The thought of actors passing among the audience and possibly bumping into each other as they fought to get on or off stage didn't seem very appealing. So, what to do with them when they were not on stage? With no budget for a set, we decided to simply place a row of chairs on either side of the playing area where the actors would remain when not on stage. The chairs were then used for all locations and set for the festival. We added a couple of extra chairs to make things a little easier, but apart from an easel on which we displayed the title of each play, that was the entire set. This simplicity of approach, which borrows from the Peking Opera idea that "all you need is two chairs and a table," has been key to the development of the Gi60 visual style. You may do things completely differently, but for me simplicity is the key. Let the words and the actors tell the story. A few chairs or some rehearsal blocks can become a rollercoaster or a starship, or a hospital or anything you need. I love working out how I can use these simple tools to create amazing worlds in which the actors can perform.

Props and costumes

Similarly to set pieces, a collection of plays with varied needs makes extensive props and costume pieces impractical. It's like the core principle of hiking in the wilderness; if you pack it in, you have to pack it out. And do it as if you're running from a grizzly bear. You may opt for no pieces whatsoever, or you may want to enhance the visual storytelling with a few carefully selected items. If so, some suggestions:

- Don't choose anything too elaborate, especially if the play is early in your running order. It sets up unreasonable expectations for the audience that the whole run of plays will be as realistic. For example, even if there's time and it's in your budget to put two actors in full Renaissance costumes, use simple collar ruffs instead. The audience will understand the reference, their imaginations will fill in the gaps, and you'll remain consistent with the theme of simplicity for your festival.

- Scarves and hats are easier to manage than a costume piece that needs to be put on, like a suit jacket or different shirt. Anything that can be mistakenly turned inside out, has buttons or zippers, or would take time to fix or manage while putting on takes time that you generally can't afford.

- If you choose to use hats and scarves in multiple plays, have enough in your stock so that actors don't have to work on "passing off" the item or having to set it in a specific place when they're done with it. However well meaning, that one scarf that Vera may need on stage left will invariably have been dropped on stage right when Louise finished her use of it.

- If you use simple props, absolutely no real liquid onstage, no matter how much your students or actors beg. With a run of multiple plays, there's no time to clean up a spill before the next play, and it creates hazards for all the plays yet to come. Same concept for "piles of papers" to represent a lawyer's case files or a busy office worker. You don't want the nightmare of a realistic pile of papers falling to the floor and scattering across the stage. Only what you absolutely need, and if it is being used as additional visual support, a file folder by itself communicates what you want – you don't need to see the many papers held within the folder to understand that.

- If your actors are wearing their own clothes, try to avoid logos and brand names, as these can be unhelpful and anachronistic. If a play is set in the 1920s and one of your actors is wearing a t-shirt proclaiming their love of Bruce Springsteen or Slayer, it won't give the impression you are trying to create. Block color on comfortable clothing with no logos is a pretty safe bet.

Projections

If you have the resources, projecting the title and author of each play will solve the problem of audiences scrambling for their programme (assuming you've created one) to see "what story is this?" If your festival is international or has gone beyond your local community for play submissions, the addition of the writer's location on the projection gives audiences an extra layer of information. This can also help viewers understand a writer's particular style, voice, or subject matter. It also serves as a reminder that the work being viewed may have travelled many thousands of miles and has been written by someone from a very different background and perspective. Universal truths are universal. Projections can also be useful for a play's special needs:

Rose

In Gi60 2016, we produced a one minute opera. In Klingon. The author, the amazing Walter Petryk, not only wrote The Great Tribble Hunt, or Kratok and Kezkhe: A Klingon Opera *– he created original music with Jackie Wilson, and he provided English subtitles for the Klingon text, which needs to be projected for the audiences.*

You can also take advantage of the projector and display photos of rehearsal or past festivals while the audience are arriving; a nice way to welcome them, and a reminder of all the hard work that went into creating the festival(s).

If you don't have the resources, or you're in a small classroom or studio, you can't beat good old-fashioned "titles on placards" or titles written on a flipchart pad where the pages can be turned.

Lighting and sound

These elements can be used to great effect and support your work, but they are not essential to the success of your event. We've seen one minute play festivals that are elaborately lit to enhance the filming of the plays, and we've seen outdoor one minute play festivals that had nothing but sunshine and some nearby sparrows for sound effects. Choose what best supports your goal and aesthetic, and then be consistent.

- As with props and lights, try to keep things simple. Are you underscoring or using recorded nature sounds to communicate environment? Can you achieve that with actors and imaginations?

- Are you filming your event? If so, be sure your light plot errs on the side of brightness that accommodates the camera instead of something dark or moodier that leans into the theatricality. It's a wonderful challenge for a lighting designer to find the balance. You don't want the audience to think they're attending a "live taping" of a show; it's live theatre. And, on the other hand, your viewers from far afield who can't attend and can only see your live stream or edited film want to be able to *see* the story.

- If you're using lights and projections, be sure that you can clearly read the projections along with the light cues. Designers will know how to balance for this, but many of you may be teachers or theatre practitioners trying to create it all on your own.

- If you're using a projector – and particularly if this is a school project or the equipment is being borrowed – be sure to test your equipment well in advance. Err on the side of making the projection large for audience members. Gi60 UK leaves the titles on throughout the performance, while Gi60

US removes the titles after about 10 seconds. Here again, your own aesthetic sense and practical considerations will determine your choices. Whatever you do, be consistent.

Steve

One of the key creative decisions I made when Gi60 started was that I didn't want anything to get in the way of the writing or the acting and that anybody, should they wish to do so, could put on a one minute theatre festival. The UK Edition of Gi60 has a single lighting state: "ON." We create a warm, general wash, we turn the lights on at the start of the 50 plays, and we turn them off at the end before the company bow. We have had some rare occasions when a blackout has been used, and on a couple of occasions we have added a simple lighting effect, but as a general rule it's "lights up" followed by "lights down" an hour later. For me, this is theatre at its purest; the audience can see everything – every scene change and every nuance of acting and movement.

Rose

For Gi60 US, we have established "areas" that our lighting designer knows will be primary locations that we'll return to again and again. They create cues for those areas along with a general wash for the many plays that use the whole stage. We never go to blackout until the end of the 50 plays; in between plays, the lights switch to a blue wash onstage. As soon as the light cue changes at the end of one play and we go to blue, we bring up the projection of the title and author of the next play. The "blues" also buy us adjustment time should an actor need it to set something for that next play. And yes, it buys that extra second of time for someone backstage to say to a flummoxed actor, "That's you! Get out there!"

If you use sound and have a setup, do you want to play pre-show music? Curtain call music? Do you have enough personnel to run lights, sound, and projections? If not, simplify. Sound can be one of the easiest things to be creative with.

Steve

I have always felt that sound created live by the actors is more interesting and dynamic (and fun) than simply recording effects. We have used an off-stage microphone, but generally all atmospheric sound is created by our cast. Over the years we have created the soundscapes of penguins on an ice cap, storms, aircraft, the rustle of wind through the trees, and even the inner workings of a spacecraft. We have also used live instrumentation, including guitar, ukulele, saxophone, and as previously mentioned a musical saw to add atmosphere to scenes. Once again, the decision to create the music "live" is a personal choice, and I could easily imagine a festival full of originally sourced and recorded sound. A collaboration between music students, acting students, and writing students could result in a festival full of sound.

The opportunity to add sound, complex lighting, video, augmented reality, and any emergent technology is really only limited by the creativity and resources of the team involved. However you choose to stage and structure your festival, at its heart is your reason for creating this festival: there is a script, a story, and the actors tasked with telling that story. You can fill the theatre with technology, costumes, and sets, or you can put some chairs in an empty space with a flipchart pad and an easel, but anybody who has a passion and a purpose, and who is prepared to put in the effort, can create a one minute theatre festival.

We've covered a lot of territory in this chapter, so in the spirit of compressing the coal to make the diamond, here's a small review of things to remember:

- Keep your goal and your audiences in mind. What is the purpose of this festival, and who is it for? How can you make it as positive and rich an experience as possible for all involved?

- Review your resources and available support teams before embarking on actively obtaining scripts and rehearsing them. This way, you can adjust the number of play selections to suit your specific needs.

- A one minute play takes a minimum of five minutes to read and to consider. Try not to underestimate how much time you'll need to review and consider the plays you'll need for your festival.

- If you accept open submissions, you're going to have a lot of reading to do. Remember that for an open call for one minute plays, you'll not only get a full range of experienced playwrights contributing, but you'll also get submissions from people who don't submit to any other festivals, and you'll (wonderfully!) get students and first-time writers.

- Keep your writers informed; make sure you are clear about your structure, your process, and your terms and conditions.

- Pace is important, and the changeover between plays is critical. A 15-second scene change might be quite acceptable in a full-length piece of theatre, but in a one minute play festival, it's a quarter of the show.

- Keep things simple. Remember Peking Opera, two chairs, and a table (and perhaps a pad on an easel).

- It's your festival, so take as much or as little from this book as you wish and then create something unique – oh, and have fun!

Most importantly, enjoy the process from beginning to end. You will work much harder than you imagine and you will be surprised, delighted, and possibly amazed by the plays and the players that form your particular festival.

PART TWO

CHAPTER FIVE
Anthology of one minute plays

Introduction

We hope you have found our guide to one minute plays helpful and perhaps, if we have done our job well, even inspiring. The next section of the book is for us the most important part and the reason we wanted to write the book in the first place. For many years we have been lucky enough to work with a global writing community who have submitted their tiny works of theatrical fiction to the Gi60 International One Minute Theatre festival. Each year it's a pleasure to open the inbox and see what has been delivered. Some writers have become part of the very bedrock of our festival, while others burn like comets, briefly but leaving an indelible impression. As we have said repeatedly throughout this book, a festival is nothing without its writers, and we are bursting with pride to share the brilliant, enigmatic, humorous, poignant, sad, funny, crazy, esoteric, and sometimes just plain silly work of our writers. What are you waiting for?

Quick guide to the anthology:

To make it easier to navigate the plays in the anthology we have broken them down into three very broad categories:

'U' (Universal Themes suitable for all),
'A' (Plays containing adult themes and or language)
'Y' (Plays that may particularly resonate with, or are suit for teenagers and young adults).

Within each section, the plays are categorized in the following way:

- By cast size (1, 2, 3 ,4 , 5 , 6+) lowest number to highest.
- Plays are alphabetized within their cast size by play title.

Each play has the 'category' and 'cast' listed at the top of the page. In addition, the year the play performed as part of the Gi60 One Minute festival is also listed i.e "Gi60 UK 2010." You can use this information together with the title to accurately search for the original production of the plays on the Gi60 YouTube channel.

Anthology contents

Actors and directors acknowledgements

All roles in plays included in this anthology were originally performed by the following actors in Gi60 UK, Gi60 US, G(hosts) in 60, and Gi60 #NextGen:

Oscar Allen
Fito Alvarado
Sergio Mauritz Ang
Luca Ansell
Mena Ansell
Sara Farrington
Sara Bahadori
Daley Barber-Allen
Anastasia Bell
Bryan Bencivenga
Martha Bennett
Lucie Novak
Meruan Bonilla
Kieran Borchard
Holly Bowman
Jasmine Bown
Keir Bown Hoyle
Bobby Brook
Hedley Brown
Bianca Bryan
Joe Bryant
Helen Buchanan
Robin Burch
Hannah Butterfield
Ally Callaghan
Sabrina Cataudella
Sofiya Cheyenne
Ugo Chukwu
Michael Colby Jones
JJ Condon
Gary Cowling
Fiona Criddle
Mathilde Davies
Justiin Davis
Joel Dean

Milly Dent
Chris Donovan
Daisy Dunning
Zachary Elliot-Hatton
Heather Ellis
Mack Exilus
Jack Farrar
Steven Fazzoleri
Rosa Fernandez
Will Fitzgerald
Ramona Floyd
Samantha Fontana
Madeline Frost
Michael Gaines
Ava Geffen
Christopher Gilkey
Samantha Gomesall
Marisela Gonzalez
Jonathan Hadley
Nealie Harmen-Cook
Jessica Hilton
Isabella Holy
Melanie Hopkins
Helen Huff
Vincent Ingrisano
Matt Johnson
Jaden Jordan
Lori Kee
Helen Kennedy
Vera Khodasevich
Verity Kirk
Samantha Kohlbrecher
Joanna Kozak
Larissa Laurel
Emily Lawrenson

David Ley
Matthew Lomax
Joan Lunoe
Andrew MacLarty
Brian Maloney
Roger Manix
Marcus Marsh
Christian Marte
Collin McConnell
Catleen McVey Kelly
Beth Metcalfe
Jessica Miley
Terril Miller
Lisa Moretta
Toby Morgan
Arielle Moses
George Mulryan
Sarah Mulryan
Jay Nickerson
Julie Orkis
Jim Osman
Jennifer Lyn Perez
Walter Petryk
Michael Pierre Louis
Shomari Pinnock
Cristina Pitter
Gareth Price-Bagurst
Katie Pritchard
Lucy Read
Harry Revell
Jose A. Rivera
Dave Robertson
Mickey Ryan
Tim Scoreby
Amy Sharp
Laura Sherwood
Anna Shotter
Alexandra Slater
Eugene Solfanelli
Darius Stone

David Storck
Conor Sullivan
Arthur Sutcliffe
Esther Sutton
Adam Thomas Smith
Micheal Thorne
Russ Thorne
Jordan Tucker
Andrew Wargo
Schylar Westbrook
Valerie Yelsukova
George Young
Heather Zoll

Plays included in this anthology were originally directed by:

Jan Ansell
Steve Ansell
Bobby Brook
Hedley Brown
Rose Burnett Bonczek
Michael Colby Jones
Mike Flanagan
Madeleine Frost
Sarah Good
Rebecca Guskin
Jonathan Hadley
Katherine Harte-DeCoux
Jessica Hilton
John Isgro
Julie Jensen
Vera Khodasevich
Roberta Loew
Anthony R. Ponzio
Peter Romano
Kirill Sheynerman
Eugene Solfanelli
David Storck

UNIVERSAL THEMES
Genre "U"

Category: U
Cast 1 F
Gi60 UK 2014

ONE CHARACTER PLAYS

AT THE END BUT NOT ALONE
By Harry Revell
York, UK

Setting

A young timid girl walks into the middle of the stage and remains there until the end. Alternatively, people could be placed lying around the floor of the stage, and as she speaks she could go over to some of them; they could be scared of her when she approaches, wide-eyed and helpless to move, but calm down and close their eyes when she comforts them as she describes in the speech.

GIRL

I don't get to talk to the people I have to meet. I see them lying there, all helpless and scared, and I see their eyes widen when they see me. Everyone knows who I am, and why I'm there, I think that's what scares them. They know that it means one thing. The ones in accidents I think are frightened the most because it's so sudden, they weren't ready. I like to sit next to these ones, stroke their head. I kiss them sometimes; try to give them a warm, safe feeling before they have to go. And then they do. I see it fade away, in their eyes. In their last moments, I like to think deep down they are comforted when they *see* me, because although it means the end, they are not facing it alone, and that's all I think they really want. So don't worry, because when the time comes, you won't be alone, I'll be there waiting for you, to stroke your head and kiss you for one last goodnight.

> (She blows a kiss into the audience, not as a joke, not as sarcasm, she does this to comfort the people she sees. She walks off stage without another word.)

END

Category: U
Cast: 1 M
Gi60 UK 2006

THE DAY I WAS SUPPOSED TO PLAY TENNIS WITH SAMUEL BECKETT
By Henry W. Kimmel
Atlanta, GA, USA

(Playwright's Note: In his youth, Samuel Beckett played tennis with a fair amount of aplomb.)

MAN

(Addressing an off-stage woman)

I'm supposed to play tennis with Samuel Beckett.

We were supposed to meet at eight in the morning, but now it's four in the afternoon – the next day.

I'd call him, but he tends to oversleep, and on the club ladder, he's more than a few rungs above me so it's considered proper etiquette to wait.

Normally, I wouldn't wait this long for a tennis game, but I hear our games are well suited.

We both like to camp out on the baseline and wait for the other guy to make a mistake.

We both like to win, but at the end of the day, all that matters is we've given each other our best shot.

In fact, people have been coming up to me all day – and night – saying how much I'll enjoy playing with Beckett, and I believe them – presuming he's going to come.
(Beat)

I know you think I'm nuts and wish I'd run off with you instead, but when a game is arranged with Samuel Beckett, you wait for as long as it takes, and even if it's dark, we'll turn on the lights, and even if the lights don't work, we can still sit and talk about the way we were going to play the game.

So, if you want to go without me, I'll understand, and if you never want to be with me again, I'll understand that, too.

Because he's going to come, you'll see, and when he does, it will be the greatest day in my life – except for the time I played golf with Walt Whitman, and we decided not to keep score.
(Man looks as off-stage woman walks off. Lights fade.)

END

Category: U
Cast: 1 Gender Neutral
Gi60 UK 2007

DEAREST ONE
By Jan Ansell
Holmfirth, UK

SANDRA KOLONGA

I am Miss sandra kolonga from Ivory Coast and I am contacting you because I need your help in the management of a sum of money that my dead father left for me before he died. This money is USD 4.5 million American Dollars and the money is in a security company here in Abidjan the capital city.

My father was a very rich cocoa farmer and he was poisoned by his business colleagues and now I want you to stand as my guardian and appointed beneficiary and receive the money in your country since I am only 19 years and without mother or father.

Please I will like you to reply to this email so that I will tell you all the information so that this money will be transferred to you so that you will get me papers to travel to your country to continue my education there.

I am waiting for your urgent reply and i will call you as soon as i hear from you. and send to you a copy of my picture so that you will know the person you are helping. email me at (sandrakolongao@yahoo.fr)

Thanks.

END

Category: U
Cast: 1 F
Gi60 UK 2006

ENGLEBERT
By Jessica Miley
Harrogate, UK

Setting

A woman searches for her cat.

Woman

Where's that darn, diddly cat gone now
        (She begins to search.)
Here, kitty, kitty, kitty, kitty, kitty, kitty, kitty, kitty, kitty
        (Pause)
Naughty cats get smacked
        (Pause)
Kitty, kitty, kitty
        (She continues until a minute has expired.)

END

Category: U
Cast Size: 1 Ghost
Gi60 US 2009, 2014, G(hosts) in 60 2010

THE GHOST LAMP
By Dwayne Yancey
Fincastle, VA, USA

NARRATOR
They say that theatres are haunted. That's why we set out the ghost lamp – although why ghosts need lamps I've never understood. But you know what I think? I think we're just afraid to cut off the light. Not out of some concern about the safety of whoever might stumble through the space in the middle of the night. But because no one wants the theatre to go dark. Not even the ghosts.

END

Category: U
Cast: 1 Gender Neutral
Gi60 US 2009

INSPIRATION I
(Based on a True Story)
By Andrew MacLarty
Queens, NY, USA

(CHARLIE sits in a lawn chair holding a half-deflated party balloon.)

CHARLIE

"Where be your gibes now? Your gambles? Your songs? Your flashes of merriment that were wont to set the table on a roar?"

(A slight laugh)

Did you know that once there was a truck driver who dreamt of flight? Of course you didn't. But there was, and I'm sure you want to know about him. This man dreamt *so badly* that he tied about 50 weather balloons to a lawn chair and lovingly dubbed it "Inspiration I." Lawn Chair Larry, they called him. He ascended 16,000 feet into the sky before he was ordered down. People laughed – of course – and they arrested him. But when police asked why he did it, he said: "A man just can't sit around." Well. Some people can. Not him though, poor guy shot himself right in the heart a few years later. Sad story. I guess there's nothing down here for some of us, you know?

Yes. You know.

END

Category: U
Cast: 1 (plus dean and staff if desired)
Gi60 US 2007 (Revised 2016)

REJECT[2]
By Stefan Lanfer
Boston, MA, USA

STEFAN

Dear Dean Estrup,

Thank you

for your recent letter,

rejecting my application

for a Masters of Fine Arts in Playwriting

at Brown University.

After careful consideration,

I regret to inform you

that I will be unable to accept your offer.

As you well know,

a decision to accept a rejection

requires meticulous evaluation

of the particulars of each offer,

in addition to the cumulative effect on the intended recipient –

namely its ability to disappoint

without utterly crushing the applicant's ambition.

While the majority of rejection letters that I have received

capably achieved this delicate balance,

yours, though discernibly sincere of intention,

was, in execution, a flagrant failure.

In consequence, though I do thank you for your interest

in stifling my career,

and wish you the best in your future attempts,

I cannot at this time accommodate your offer.

You may anticipate my arrival in September.

Sincerely,

Stefan Lanfer

Playwright

END

Category: U
Cast: 1 F
Gi60 US 2014

ROSE
By Karin Fazio Littlefield
Brooklyn, NY, USA

Setting

A kitchen. Present day. ROSE, a 45-year-old woman.

(ROSE, dressed casually and wearing an apron, is seated at the kitchen table rolling meatballs. On the table is a large metal bowl containing ground meat. There is a tray beside the bowl with several meatballs on it. She rolls one or two balls before speaking. She continues rolling meatballs throughout her monologue.)

ROSE

I am not so gifted as at one time seemed likely. Virginia Woolf. All beef. Most say to add pork or veal as if that makes it fancier. Here's a little known fact, veal doesn't add any flavor. And the pork nowadays is so lean. No, all beef. And of course spices and other things. Sauce. It's my mother's recipe. Well actually her mother's, and her mother's, and her mother's and so forth and so on. But each generation is supposed to add or change something. Make it their own. Kind of like having free will while keeping in line with a divine plan. I haven't. Made it my own, that is. It's not like I didn't try. I added shallots, oregano, increased the splashes of red wine to four. I switched the Parmesan cheese to Asiago. Once I even sunk so low as to sneak in some pork but it didn't work. They didn't like it. Wouldn't even eat it. So I make no mark. I add nothing. I change nothing. (She stares into the bowl. She takes great fistfuls of the meat and squeezes it between her hands. She takes a handful out and makes different shapes with the meat.) I suppose I could shape them different? Make patties? Or punch a little hole in them like a doughnut. Or make little meatball snowmen. Three meatballs high.

(She makes three meatballs and places one on top of each other.)

Kids would like it. I could be the lady up the street that makes those meatball snowmen. Sprinkle a little Parmesan for snow. Maybe oregano for the eyes and rosemary for the arms. Could be very cute.

(She uses her hand to squish the meatball snowman flat.)

But I am not that lady. I am not the lady that makes meatball snowmen. No. I'm the lady that makes no mark.

END

Category: U
Cast: 1 Gender Neutral or Ensemble
Gi60 UK 2015

THE SUCCESSFUL AUTHOR'S MORNING RITUAL
By Brandon M. Crose
Cambridge, MA, USA

Setting

A bed and a desk with computer on it.

This could also be performed with a NARRATOR/S reading the lines and SUCCESSFUL
AUTHOR pantomiming/reacting to them. AT RISE – SUCCESSFUL AUTHOR in bed, asleep.
Alarm goes off.

SUCCESSFUL AUTHOR

When you hear the alarm, do not shut it off. Do not tell yourself … that … you'll just do
better tomorrow …
(falls asleep)
(Reset. Alarm.)

SUCCESSFUL AUTHOR

When the alarm goes off, don't shut it off. Don't hit snooze.

Especially
(hits it)
don't
(hits it)
hit it
(hits it)
several
(hits it)
times …
(falls asleep)
(Reset. Alarm.)

SUCCESSFUL AUTHOR

Don't shut it off, don't hit snooze … Just get up! Don't check email or Facebook … Oh my
god, she did what …?!
(Reset. Alarm.)

SUCCESSFUL AUTHOR

Just get up! Don't check the phone at all! Go directly to the computer. (sits at desk) Don't
check email. Don't … check Facebook … E he he he …! Silly kittens.
(Reset. Alarm.)

SUCCESSFUL AUTHOR

Go directly to the computer. Disable internet! Open a Word doc. And ... write.
(not writing)

SUCCESSFUL AUTHOR

And ... write!
(still not writing)

Accept that writing is hard. Embrace the process.
(reaching for phone)

Absolutely do not check internet things on your phone because it's right there and so, so much easier than writing ...
(Reset. Alarm.)

SUCCESSFUL AUTHOR

Disable internet. Turn off the stupid phone. Engage with the blank page. Embrace the white oblivion. Rage against the void. Write something, anything. Anything at all! Write "poopy pants."
(writes)

Yessss. Poopy pants! You wrote those words. You will, I hope, delete them later, but that does not matter. This does: a moment ago you were just an aspiring writer, and now ... You're an author.
(getting ready for the day)

Is that a swagger in your step? Why, I think it is! Good for you. Bask in that victorious glow – you've earned it.
(energy begins to wane over the following)

Just remember: Eat well today. Get some exercise. Don't stay out too late with friends. Spend tonight preparing for tomorrow. Get to bed by ten at the latest, and tomorrow ...
(crawls into bed)
(Reset. Alarm.)

SUCCESSFUL AUTHOR

... Do it all over again.

END

Category: U
Cast: 1 Gender Neutral plus Ensemble
Gi60 UK 2015

WRITERS BLOCK
By Lucie Bezdickova
London, UK

Setting

Writer is sitting at the computer; typing. Facing the audience. Behind him his imagination comes to life. We see three people walk in and a fierce interrogation scene is set up with two cops threatening to beat up a prisoner, and at the moment of almost contact they all pause, looking expectantly at the writer.

WRITER

Ughhh NO!
(The three quickly leave the stage huddling as if ashamed of their existence. Writer starts typing again and again; we see his imagination come to life. We see two swordsmen come forth and start to duel; in the heat of the battle they suddenly pause, look at the writer with the same expectation as before.)

WRITER

Hmmm … NAH!
(And the two swordsmen leave in the same manner as the three before. Writer starts typing for the third time. And this time a creature crawls onto the stage slowly approaching two terrified scientists, and when it is about to pounce on them, it pauses.)

WRITER

No no … ahhh no!
(The three quickly leave. Writer quietly sits at the computer for a beat or two staring into it.)

WRITER

I've got nothing!
(Packs his computer and leaves.)

END

Category: U   **TWO CHARACTER PLAYS**
Cast: 1 F, 1 M
Gi60 US 2015

9/11 ANNIVERSARY
By Rhea MacCallum
Downey, CA, USA

Cast of Characters
JEFF: 60s, casual attire
SARAH: 30s–40s, casual attire

Setting
A park bench. New York City.
    (SARAH sits on a park bench. JEFF
    approaches, sits down at the opposite
    end.)

JEFF
Had to get away from the crowd.

SARAH
Me too.

JEFF
A little too much for me. I'm not
complaining, mind you. It's just more than
I can handle.

SARAH
I understand.

JEFF
If one more person tells me "never forget"
I'm gonna punch 'em in the face.

SARAH
As if we could. Forget.

JEFF
Exactly.
    (Pause)
On a day like today, it's good to be with
people.
    (Sarah shoots him a look.)

JEFF
Oh, I'm sorry. Did you want to be alone?
I could go.

SARAH
You're fine. It was all those people cryin' with
all them pictures I had to get away from.
I wear my picture on the inside.

JEFF
    (Nodding)
It was my son.

SARAH
Brother.

JEFF
First tower.

SARAH
Flight 11.

JEFF
Sorry.

SARAH
Me too.

JEFF
I miss him every day.

SARAH
Yeah.
    (She reaches her hand out, he takes it.)

LIGHTS OUT.
END

Category: U
Cast: 2 Gender Neutral, Ensemble
Gi60 UK 2008

ABOUT A PENGUIN
By Terry Collins
Harrogate, UK

Setting
The Antarctic. A Force 10 gale. A colony of
penguins huddle together against the cold.

PENGUIN 2
Going anywhere nice this year?

PENGUIN 1
Well, funny you should ask. I'm actually
thinking about Spain.

PENGUIN 2
Spain! I don't want to worry you, like, but has
anybody told you about the weather there?

PENGUIN 1
Not particularly. But it sounds like a nice place.

PENGUIN 2
Oh, it sounds nice in the brochures. But, what
they don't tell you is, they get the most
terrible weather.

PENGUIN 1
Oh, come on, it can't be that bad.

PENGUIN 2
I'm telling you. Even in winter, it never goes
below freezing. I wouldn't touch it with a
bargepole.

PENGUIN 1
Really? But how do the locals stand it?

PENGUIN 2
Search me! They must be tougher than us. If it
wasn't for that, I'd go myself. But don't let me
put you off.

PENGUIN 1
Oh, no, I couldn't stand that. There's always a
snag, isn't there?

PENGUIN 2
Me and some of the guys thought we'd hang
about here for a month or two, then pop over
to the coast and do some fishing. Why don't
you come with us?

PENGUIN 1
Ay, OK, thanks. I did that last year, actually. It
was good. East, west, home's best, eh?

PENGUIN 2
Yeah. When you think about it, this place
takes some beating.
        (They nod agreement.)

THE END

Category: Y
Cast: 2 Gender Neutral
Gi60 US 2014

ACE AND ME
By Alex Bernstein
Cranford, NJ, USA

Setting

JEFF walks his dog, ACE, late at night – the last walk before they turn in for the night. It's freezing out, almost zero degrees, and JEFF is shivering. ACE doesn't mind it quite so much, and pokes his nose around, not sure what he wants to do yet.

JEFF

Come on Ace it's freezing out here. Ace. Ace, please. Ace!
    (ACE finally looks at him, confused. Of course, they don't understand each other.)

ACE

What?

JEFF

Just pee!

ACE

What?

JEFF

Just – tinkle! Come on! Tinkle! Please.
    (ACE looks around a bit, wanders around. He doesn't pee.)

JEFF

Oh my god! Ace! Come on!
    (ACE looks at him.)

ACE

What? What do you want me to do?

JEFF

Please, Ace! You're killing me!

ACE

What do you want?

JEFF

Tinkle!

ACE

What?

                         JEFF
Tinkle!

                         ACE
What?

                         JEFF
Tinkle!

                         ACE
Come again?

                         JEFF
Ahhhh!

                         ACE
I have absolutely no idea what you're talking about.
        (JEFF jumps up and down, panicked.)

                         JEFF
Oh my god!

                         ACE
Can you just – hold that thought for one second?
        (ACE wanders over to the side and relieves himself. JEFF is ecstatic.)

                         JEFF
Yes! Yes! Good boy! I knew we understood each other!

                         ACE
What?
        (JEFF reaches into a pocket, leans down, and gives ACE a treat.)

                         JEFF
Here's your treat!

                         ACE
        (ecstatic)
Thank you! Thank you!

                         JEFF
You're such a good listener!

                         ACE
I'm confused, but I love you.

                         END

Category: U
Cast: 2 M
Gi60 US 2008

THE APTITUDE TEST
By Michele Markarian
Cambridge, MA, USA

A high-school career counselor, MR GREEN, is
seated at a table. A geeky male student enters.

MR GREEN
Come in! Let's see – are you James Gray?

JAMES
Yes.

MR GREEN
Well your aptitude test is very promising. Very.

JAMES
Wow. Thank you.

MR GREEN
Very promising indeed.

JAMES
Thanks.

MR GREEN
Tell me, James. What are your plans for after
high school?

JAMES
I thought I'd apply to Harvard, MIT, and
Stanford.

MR GREEN
Come again?

JAMES
I'd like to major in either math or economics.

MR GREEN
Uh huh. What made you decide on those
schools?

JAMES
They're the best, aren't they?

MR GREEN
If you think that that's the *best* use of your
abilities ....

JAMES
I got perfect SAT scores. I have a 4.0 GPA! I'm
first in the class, right?

MR GREEN
James, according to your aptitude test, you
are cut out for bigger and better things.

JAMES
Really? What could be better than Harvard,
MIT, or Stanford?

MR GREEN
To be honest –

JAMES
Is this about Yale? Does the test say that
I should apply to Yale, too?

MR GREEN
No –

JAMES
Because I can do that –

MR GREEN
James, this isn't about Yale. This is about a
higher calling. Your true purpose.

JAMES
Oh.

MR GREEN
I have two words for you: Clown College.

JAMES
What?

MR GREEN
Clown College.

JAMES
What's Clown College?

MR GREEN
James, according to your aptitude test, you have the makings of a great clown.

JAMES
You're joking.

MR GREEN
I've never been so serious about anything in my life.

JAMES
But — I can't be a clown! I'm a serious person! I can't even tell a joke.

MR GREEN
Let me read you the results of your test.

JAMES
No!

MR GREEN
"This individual has a comic genius that will convulse all he comes in contact with, particularly children."

JAMES
Are you crazy?

MR GREEN
"Enhanced with a round red nose, white face paint and brightly colored wig, this individual will have the potential for international recognition."

JAMES
Maybe they mean I'll teach math to university students? In a clown suit?

MR GREEN
No, James. (Pause) Let me show you the brochure for Clown College. It's located on 45 pastoral acres in Florida —

JAMES
I'm not going to Clown College! I'm going to an Ivy League school!

MR GREEN
Don't waste your talent on an Ivy League school —

JAMES
I can't listen to this nonsense. I'm not even funny!
        (He turns to leave and trips.)

MR GREEN
(Laughing hysterically)
Bravo, James! Brilliant pratfall! Hilarious!

JAMES
But I didn't do it on purpose!

MR GREEN
See what I mean? You're a natural! You don't even know you're funny!

JAMES
I guess — I never thought of myself as — do you really? Can I see that brochure?
        (MR GREEN shows JAMES brochure as lights fade.)

END

Category: U
Cast Size: 2 F
Gi60 US 2013

THE AUTHOR
By Jim MacNerland
Los Angeles, CA, USA

(A woman is going through some boxes. She smiles at various items. Another woman enters confidently with a newspaper.)

FIRST WOMAN
He's been dead a week and he's still front page news.

SECOND WOMAN
The world loved him.

FIRST WOMAN
The world loved his books.

SECOND WOMAN
They were so beautiful.

FIRST WOMAN
A lovely fantasy that's for sure.
(Looks about)
So, organizing this stuff?

SECOND WOMAN
So many boxes. Look at all this; original drafts, gifts from around the world.

FIRST WOMAN
Nice. It should get some good money.
(Slaps the paper)
He's hot right now.

SECOND WOMAN
We can't sell this! It's his legacy to us.

FIRST WOMAN
No, it's his legacy to the world. To us he left fear of the world.

SECOND WOMAN
What about Katharine? She started off in the ghetto and built a company with her one true love –

FIRST WOMAN
Katharine is a character in one of his books. Katharine didn't have a drunk father yelling at her or telling her what a lousy shit she was. And Katharine was allowed to date.

SECOND DATE
He just wanted the best for us.

FIRST WOMAN
He wanted the best for his Katharines, he wanted us to –. Listen, I get 50% of the estate. Price it out and give me half. You can keep his fantasies to live on. I want the reality of his cash.
(FIRST WOMAN begins to leave.)

SECOND WOMAN
Don't. We have to keep this together. It's all we have of him.

FIRST WOMAN
Then it's good that we get rid of it. Live our own lives for once.

SECOND WOMAN
This is my life. Here in these books.

FIRST WOMAN
Then I guess we'll have to see who lives the real fantasy. You and the books or me and the cash.
(FIRST WOMAN moves to the exit.)

FIRST WOMAN
I'll send an appraiser over tomorrow.
(FIRST WOMAN exits. SECOND WOMAN pulls the boxes to her.)

END

Category: U
Cast: 2 M
Gi60 UK 2007

BOMB DISPOSAL
By Clair Girvan
Devon, UK

Setting
COLONEL LENNARD and CORPORAL DARBY
are attempting to disarm a bomb.

DARBY
Thirty seconds, sir.

LENNARD
Ever seen one of these before, Darby?

DARBY
No, sir.

LENNARD
It seems pretty straightforward, but there's
something about it I don't quite like.

DARBY
What's that, sir?

LENNARD
Not sure. You get a nose for this sort of thing
after a while. Better go carefully.

DARBY
Yes, sir. Twenty seconds, sir.

LENNARD
OK. Hand me those.

DARBY
Sir. (Hands him the clippers.)

LENNARD
I think we can start with the red.
(Snips the wire. They breathe out
with relief.)

DARBY
More nerve-racking than you expect, sir.

LENNARD
How long left now, Darby?

DARBY
(very tense) Ten seconds, sir.

LENNARD
Right. As far as I can tell, it's this one. Say your
prayers, Darby.

DARBY
Already have, sir.

LENNARD
Good man. Here goes. (He snips the wire.)
Phew. Quite a simple one, after all.

DARBY
Er – sir – what's this little –

COMPLETE BLACKOUT

END

Category: U
Cast: 2 Gender Neutral
Gi60 UK 2007

CALL WAITING FOR GODOT
By Meron Langsner
New York, NY, USA

Setting
VLAD is on the phone. RAGS is watching him.
   (Silence)

RAGS
Any answer yet?

VLAD
Nothing yet.

RAGS
What are you listening to?

VLAD
A recording. Muzak.

RAGS
Let me listen.

VLAD
Why?

RAGS
It will pass the time.

VLAD
Very well.
   (He passes the receiver over.)

RAGS
The muzak is nice.

VLAD
It is.

RAGS
There is a recording.

VLAD
There is.

RAGS
With a message.

VLAD
Yes.

RAGS
It says that our call is very important to them.

VLAD
I should hope so.

RAGS
Godot Corporation believes in the highest
standard of customer service.

VLAD
That's reassuring.

RAGS
Operators are standing by! We are saved!

VLAD
Excellent!

RAGS
Our call will be answered in the order it was
received! Surely we were among the first.

VLAD
There must be many calls.

RAGS
Yes. Many.

VLAD

Let me listen! (He grabs the receiver and listens.) No!

RAGS

What has happened?

VLAD

Due to high volume of calls, we will not be answered. We should try again tomorrow.

RAGS

We should hang up.

VLAD

We should.
(They do not move.)

END

Category: U
Cast: 2 Gender Neutral
Gi60 UK 2009

CATS AND DOGS AND ...
By Greg Carraway
Atlanta, GA, USA

Setting
HANK and MARVIN stand on a sidewalk in front of HANK's house. JENNIFER walks up.

MARVIN
Here's the new girl. Ask her.

HANK
Are you a dog person or a cat person?

JENNIFER
Neither one.

HANK
Don't you like animals?

MARVIN
Don't you have a pet?

JENNIFER
I have a pet. She isn't a dog or a cat.

HANK
Well hypothetically, if you had a dog or a cat, which would it be?

JENNIFER
A cat, I guess.

HANK
See. There it is.

MARVIN
How many people have you asked? Three? That's a survey?

HANK
All three said cats, didn't they?

MARVIN
Look at our neighborhood. It's a cat-like neighborhood to begin with.

HANK
He thinks his dog is better than my cat because he's more human. You can train him to do stuff and he'll defend you from attack.

JENNIFER
That's human?

MARVIN
It's because he loves unconditionally.

JENNIFER
That's human?

HANK
Like my cat doesn't?

JENNIFER
Well what if it is true? That doesn't mean dogs make better pets.

MARVIN
What is your pet, then?

HANK
(to MARVIN)
See, she agrees with me. Dogs aren't ipso facto better just because they wear that goofy grin all the time. They're like having a two-year-old that never grows up.

JENNIFER
(to MARVIN)
A python.
(to both)
Who could eat both your dog and your cat.
(walking off, talking over her shoulder)
I just hope she doesn't slink out of bed one night and go looking for a snack.

END

Category: U
Cast: 2 Gender Neutral
Gi60 UK 2014

THE CHARITY COMMISSION
By Hedley Brown
Leeds, UK

A
Oh, hi! I wonder if you'd like to donate to a good cause? It's a charity for sick children which ....

B
Whoa! Whoa! Whoa! Hold your horses, Mother Teresa! Donate?

A
That's right.

B
Money?

A
Yes.

B
My money?

A
Err ... yeah.

B
What are you doing?

A
Sorry?

B
Look! If I'm going to give my money to a good cause – no matter how worthy it is – I want you to do something for it.

A
Oh, you mean like sponsoring me to do ... something?

B
Now you get the picture!

A
Okay ... So, would you sponsor me to ... er ... swim ... 50 lengths?

B
50?

A
Err ... 100?

B
Do you want my money?

A
... 10 miles!

B
Where?

A
The local pool? (B shakes head.) Reservoir? (B pulls face.) Canal?

B
Swim the English Channel!

A
... Err ... Okay.

B
Right! What are you wearing?

A
Swimming trunks? (B pulls face and shakes head.) Wetsuit?

B
(B shaking head) Oh dear, oh dear, oh dear.
Think of those poor sick children.

A
A kangaroo costume?

B
I like your style! But it's still too easy.

A
I could carry someone on my back?

B
Hmmmm? Do you know any celebrities?

A
I've got a friend who looks a bit like a fat
Bono.

B
That'll do! Soooo ...?

A
Will you sponsor me to swim the English
Channel, dressed as a kangaroo carrying a fat
Bono look-a-like on my back?

B
At night.

A
At night!

B
Of course I will, I like to help out when I can.
Put me down for 50p!

END

Category: U
Cast: 1 M 1 F
Gi60 US 2015

THE CHOICE
By Stephen Kaplan
Bogota, NJ, USA

Setting
An upscale department store. PHILIP faces the
audience. He holds two young girl's dresses,
one in each hand, and holds them up in front
of him as if looking in a mirror. A SALESLADY
enters.

SALESLADY
Can I help you?

PHILIP
(Frightened by her voice tries to hide
the dresses.)
No! I mean, no thank you.

SALESLADY
Are you looking for something particular?

PHILIP
Um, just a ... um, just a dress.

SALESLADY
I see.

PHILIP
Not for me. It's for my ... it's for my
daughter.

SALESLADY
OK. How old is she?

PHILIP
Eleven.

SALESLADY
Does she have a particular style that she likes?

PHILIP
(Beat)
I don't know.

SALESLADY
What does she tend to wear?

PHILIP
This is ... it's ...
(Beat)
It's her first one.

SALESLADY
(Smiling knowingly)
Tomboy?

PHILIP
No. She was a boy ... Is ... was ... I wanted
to buy a dress to show him ...
(Long beat as PHILIP looks down and
the SALESLADY looks at PHILIP)

SALESLADY
(Pointing at one of the dresses)
I like that one.

PHILIP
(Beat. Then looking up at the
SALESLADY)
Thank you.

END

Category: U
Cast: 2 Gender Neutral
Gi60 US 2012, 2014

CHOOSERS
By James McLindon
Northampton, MA, USA

Setting: The sidewalk outside a coffee shop in a city, today.

(A woman exits a coffee shop with a cup of coffee. She is a serious sort, but not necessarily a bad person. A homeless man panhandles. He is aggressive, but not threatening. His style should be funny and engaging, not accusatory.)

HOMELESS MAN
Yo, yo, can I have a quarter for some food?

WOMAN
I don't have any change.

HOMELESS MAN
You just got change, I can see it in your hand.

WOMAN
I can't give you anything, I'm sorry.
(She starts to leave.)

HOMELESS MAN
Why not?

WOMAN
Cuz most people who beg use the money for substance abuse, okay?

HOMELESS MAN
What, you took a survey?

WOMAN
The Times did this story —

HOMELESS MAN
Oh, yeah, the Times. That story that said you should give to food pantries instead.

WOMAN
Yeah, that one.

HOMELESS MAN
So, do you? Give to pantries?

WOMAN
(Pause; caught)
I just want to get a cup of coffee without being morally harassed.

HOMELESS MAN
Do you think Scrooge was morally harassed? Cuz I think of him more as an asshole.

WOMAN
I just want to be friggin' left alone, okay?

HOMELESS MAN
I just want to be friggin' given a quarter.

WOMAN
Will you drink it?

HOMELESS MAN
Look, if I drink it, it's on me. If you won't give me the chance, it's on you.
(She puts her change in her pocket.)

WOMAN
Morality's not that simple. I'm really sorry.
(She exits.)

HOMELESS MAN
Well, not nearly as sorry as I am.
(Spotting someone else)
Yo, yo, can I have a quarter, get something to eat?

END

Category: U
Cast: 2 Gender Neutral
Gi60 US 2012

CHRISTMAS TREE
By Hugh Cardiff
Dublin, Ireland

Background: in March 2012 a man's body was discovered in Waterford, Ireland, in a house on the main street in the town when a passer-by noticed the Christmas tree lights were still on in the front room.
 (JOHN and BRIAN are walking down a street. JOHN then glances in to a house window, then stops to have a better look.)

JOHN

Hey, look at this. This guy has still got his Christmas tree up. Can you see it?
 (They both peer in the front window.)

BRIAN

Some people just love Christmas.

JOHN

Whoever lives here is getting good value out of those fairy lights. Mine stopped working after two days.

BRIAN

Thank fuck they don't flash. Flashing fairy lights drive me insane.

JOHN

Do you think we should, y'know, give a knock?

BRIAN

What for?

JOHN

(shrugs) To see if everything's OK.

BRIAN

But it's none of our business. If they want to leave their Christmas tree up for 4 or 5 months after, who are we to criticize.

JOHN

Yeah, but no-one leaves a tree up for that long.
 (peers back in window)
I can imagine if you'd young kids they'd want a tree left up, but ... well, it doesn't look like any kids live here.

BRIAN

(shrugs) So what you gonna do? Knock on the door and demand they take down their tree.
Come on, we're wasting valuable drinking time.

(He walks on one or two steps.)

JOHN

But what if something's wrong? I mean, no-one leaves their tree up till May.

BRIAN

John, we're on the main street, in the middle of town. Thousands of people pass by this house
every day. Someone would have noticed the tree on, or would have noticed if there was a
problem.

(Pause)

JOHN

Or maybe people had the same conversation we're having. And no-one checked it out.

BRIAN

OK Columbo, you go investigate. I'll see you in O'Dwyers.

JOHN

Tell you what, I'll just give a quick knock.

BRIAN

And what if they answer?

(BRIAN continues on, exits. John gives a quick knock, he looks around, uncomfortably.
He looks in the window again.)

JOHN

Oh fuck it.

(He runs after BRIAN.)

END

Category: U
Cast: 2 Gender Neutral
Gi60 US 2013

CUMULONIMBUS
By John Levine
Berkeley, CA, USA

SANDY
Beautiful day. Not a cloud in the sky.

KAT
Yeah, but it's a little too ...

SANDY
Nice?

KAT
Unseasonably, yes.

SANDY
Still, what a day!

KAT
At what price?

SANDY
Can't you just this once enjoy today for today?

KAT
Not when I think about what it means for –

SANDY
Then don't think about it!
  (Pause)

SANDY
Now you've got me thinking about it.

KAT
I'm sorry. You're right. We should just enjoy the day. The sunshine, the warm breeze. Even if it is the dead of winter.
  (SANDY gasps.)

KAT
What is it?

SANDY
Is that ... a storm cloud?

KAT
Oh. No, I think that's just ...

SANDY
It's moving this way.

KAT
But it's not here yet. Let's just enjoy –

SANDY
I can't. Not with that ...

KAT
It's over there. Far away. And there's nothing we can do about it at this point.

SANDY
You're saying it's too late?

KAT
I'm saying ... I don't know.
  (They watch the approaching cloud.)

END

Category: U
Cast: 2 M
Gi60 UK 2011

CUTS
By Kieran Borchard
Harrogate, UK

Setting
We begin with JEFFERY sat onstage and BILL
off; JEFFERY is reading a newspaper
(preferably something like *The Guardian*, *The
Times*, *Washington Post*, etc.) in which all of the
Es have been meticulously cut out. Noticing
that something is amiss, JEFF's character is
naturally perturbed. After a long while gazing
at this paper, JEFFERY finally speaks.

JEFF
Wait a minut ...
        (It is at this moment that BILL, JEFF's
        friend, walks in.)

JEFF
Bill, do you notic anything diffrnt?

BILL
No, not rally Jff, things sm prtty normal to m
        (BILL seems rather undisturbed by this
        increasingly obvious lack of Es. Making
        himself welcome in JEFF's home, he
        takes off his jacket, revealing a Bruce
        Springsteen and The E Street shirt or
        some other band you can think of with
        an E as an integral part of their name.
        The E has been obviously removed/
        covered. JEFF jumps up in horror.)

JEFF
Bill! Your shirt!!

BILL
What about it?

JEFF
It's missing th lttr ' '!
        (JEFF is horrified that he can no longer
        pronounce the all-important vowel.)

BILL
Oooh, that? Thy got rid of it.

JEFF
What!?

BILL
Thy got rid of it.

JEFF
Why?

BILL
Budgt cuts. It wasn't conomically sound
anymor aftr the introduction of the nw lttr.

JEFF
It's a lttr! How can it b conomically sound?
... What nw lttr?

BILL
This
        (BILL unfurls a piece of paper with
        some absurd letter drawn upon it,
        perhaps an upside down 5 or a capital
        R with a smiley face in that holey bit,
        it's your decision really.)

JEFF
And how xactly do you pronounc this nw "lttr"?
        (BILL can make whatever noise he
        wants here but maybe for irony you
        could go for a sound that sounds kinda
        like an "eee" or "eh" sound.)

BILL (Making the sound)
Lik that.

JEFF
And what on arth will it b usd for?

BILL

That's the bauty of it, thr's no us yt, but thr's no doubt it'll b ky in the progrssion of the Nglish languag.

JEFF

So no words actually us it?

BILL

No.

JEFF

And w no longr hav the lttr ' '?
(Still attempting to pronounce the now lost vowel)

BILL

Nop, it's bn standing in the way of progrss too long!

JEFF (Exasperated)

This isn't progrss Bill, all w have now is a uslss nw lttr and thousands of words w can't vn say proprly anymor!

BILL

Now look hr! I'll have you know I'm awfully fond of the lttr (insert sound here). It rolls off the tongu asir.

JEFF

This is absurd. I'm going to put a stop to this.
(JEFFERY heads off to leave.)

BILL

Wait, that's the other thing. Cuts in grammar man you can't put a stop anymor. Just a comma.

END

Category: U
Cast: 2 M
Gi60 UK 2013

DAD AND SON
By Juan Ramirez, Jr
New York, NY, USA

(Lights fade up in a garage.)
(DAD, 45, SON, 18, are fixing the kitchen sink. DAD's hand reaches and he searches the floor. He comes out from underneath and bangs his head. Upset, he looks to the floor to see what he is looking for is not there.)

DAD
Where's the wrench?
(SON is daydreaming away staring at the floor.)

DAD
Hey, numbskull! Where's the wrench?!
(SON looks up at DAD. SON quickly walks over to a toolbox and looks inside it. DAD pushes SON away and searches in the toolbox. SON looks over at DAD's pocket.)

DAD
Carl, I asked you to do one thing! Just one thing!
(SON begins to speak but gets interrupted.)

DAD
No excuses! You gave your mother crap all week about the dishes! You didn't want to throw out the garbage!
(SON tries to speak again but gets interrupted.)

DAD
You got suspended for a week from school for low marks and now you can't focus on one simple thing!
(SON tries to speak again but gets interrupted.)

DAD
I'm done with your behavior! I'm done with your absent-mindedness! Now what do you have to say for yourself?

SON
It's in your pocket.
(DAD reaches into his pocket and pulls out the wrench.)

END

Category: U
Cast Size: 2 M
Gi60 US 2011, 2014

DEEP INTO OCTOBER
By Dwayne Yancey
Fincastle, VA, USA

Setting

On a sunny October afternoon, a grown man fantasizes that he's a Major League Baseball pitcher in the playoffs.

MAN

I am standing where I've always wanted to stand. For as long as I can remember, I have pictured myself here – on the mound – the air crisp – it's autumn – for the first time – the dreams of summer have turned to fall – and here I am playing deep – deep into October. This is where legends are made – and history is written in the blood of Curt Schilling's ankle. I have Don Larsen whispering in my ear – calling in the signs – and all the ghosts of Cooperstown cheering me on. Strike one – a fastball that rattles the leaves from the trees. Strike two – a curveball that arcs all the way from my days in Little League into the World Series. And now I look in for the sign – we're one pitch away – and here it comes – an entire season – an entire lifetime – riding on the spinning seams – because we're not just playing anymore – we're playing deep – deep into –
(A young boy enters.)

BOY

Mom says you need to come in now – we're almost ready to eat.

MAN

(Wanly, with a defeated air)
– October.
(Pause)
Tell her to wait a bit, OK? Let's play some catch.

BOY

But it's October.

MAN

That's the best time, son. That's the best time.
(He tosses the boy the ball and/or glove.)

END

Category: U
Cast: 1 F, 1 M
Gi60 UK 2009

DIGNITY AND LOVE: OINTMENT AND FLY
By Terry Collins
Harrogate, UK

A street. Enter ANNA pursued by TOM.

TOM
Can I carry your bags? Oh, go on.

ANNA
I haven't got a bag.

TOM
Well, shall I open doors for you?

ANNA
I've been opening doors all my life.

TOM
I could cut your grass.

ANNA
I haven't got grass. It's a concreted yard.

TOM
Does it need sweeping? Has it got a rotary
clothes drier? I could peg out your washing.
I would blow on it if there's no wind.

ANNA
I've got a tumble drier.

TOM
Well, I could change your light bulbs, take
out the rubbish, fetch your slippers.

ANNA
Like a dog?
(She moves away from him.)

TOM
I'd eat dog food. Bounce ideas off me then.
Bounce anything off me. Take up judo. You
can break my neck. Or just have me around to
punch when you've had a bad day. I could
hold your TV aerial so you get channel 5.
Shine a torch so your sundial works at night,
if you've got a sundial. I would be a bookend,
a paperweight, a doormat. You wouldn't have
to move your feet, I'd do the wiping. I could
be the thing you hang your coat on. The place
you park your phone. You could pluck my
eyebrows so's it didn't hurt. Get my teeth
filled. Practise brain surgery. I could breathe
for you when you can't be bothered, suck up
your bath water to save you pulling the plug,
stop a train for you with my foot. How about
a transplant? Have a kidney. Two kidneys!
(ANNA leaves, TOM shouts after her.)
I love you for Christ's sake.
(ANNA re-enters.)

ANNA
Well, why didn't you just say that?

TOM
I didn't want to sound stupid.
(They leave together.)

END

Category: U
Cast: 1 F, 1 M
Gi60 US 2014

A DOABLE RESOLUTION
By Rhea MacCallum
Downey, CA, USA

(A couple sits together. Sounds of the
New Year's Eve countdown)

MAN/WOMAN
3, 2, Happy New Year!
(They kiss.)

WOMAN
Gonna make any resolutions this year?

MAN
Never!
(She laughs.)
You?

WOMAN
Always!

MAN
You and your quirky resolutions.

WOMAN
Doable resolutions.

MAN
Right.

WOMAN
Why resolve to do the impossible just to give
up two days later. I prefer doable resolutions.

MAN
What was it this year, I mean, last year?

WOMAN
To give up peas. And you know what? I did it.
There were some fried rice moments that
almost got me, but I conquered them and
closed the year triumphant in my resolve to
go the year not eating a single pea.

MAN
So what's it going to be this year?

WOMAN
I think this year ... I resolve ... to have a baby.

MAN
Well, we have been trying, but with a three
month deadline for getting pregnant we're
gonna have to really be proactive about –

WOMAN
Oh, that's already done.

MAN
What?

WOMAN
Yep.

MAN
You're already?

WOMAN
Yep.

MAN
We're having a baby?!

WOMAN
That's what makes it a doable resolution.

MAN
Really?

WOMAN
Happy New Year, Daddy.
(They hug and kiss as ...)

END

Category: U
Cast: 2 Gender Neutral plus optional Ensemble
Gi60 UK 2013

EXAM
By Maude Lambert
York, UK

Setting

Boy in examination hall

TEACHER

This examination will take one hour and thirty minutes from the time I ask you to turn over your papers; please can I remind you to carefully read all the questions and instructions before answering. You may not talk, if you have any problems you must raise your hand and wait for the invigilator. All ready? Then please turn over your papers now.

STUDENT

Right this is it, the culmination of two years of hard study. I have read the books, attended the classes, carefully planned my revision study guide – over a three month period following the BBC Bite size guidance. I have attended the additional study workshops, quizzed my teacher. I am ready. In Mary Shelley's *Frankenstein* how does Shelley create sympathy for the Monster? Oh … don't panic, think … follow the guidance given.

(Pause)

Exam Checklist: handling the question

(Boy recites off wrote.)

Check that you have identified the direction words, the content words which identify the precise topic of the question, and any limiting words such as: *always, since, World War Two, in Australia*. OK … How … Sympathy … Monster (getting visibly stressed)

(Again off wrote)

What assumptions are present in the question? That I have read the book, taken it in, and can now answer this question. What stance/point of view have you adopted? That I have no idea …

(Again off wrote)

Have you used individuality in planning your answer? Will the examiner be able to distinguish your exam *favourably* from all the exams in the class? argh …. I know how to answer a question … I just know nothing about the subject!! All those weeks of creating colour co-ordinated tables, choosing a place in the house to revise where I wouldn't be distracted, making my family aware of the fact that I needed some peace and quiet. Switching revision between subjects to avoid becoming bored of a single topic. Looking for fresh sources of info other than class notes. Giving myself a "reward" after every revision session. Nothing extravagant, just a small treat to help you get back to your books. If only I had read the book!

TEACHER

Your time is now up.

END

Category: U
Cast: 1 F, 1 M
Gi60 US 2007

FAIL BETTER
By Jay Nickerson
New York, NY, USA

(A small New York apartment. Sarah is reading a newspaper at the table, a pile of bills nearby. Nathan enters, upset. Sarah doesn't look up from her newspaper until the last moment of the play.)

SARAH
(Lifts an envelope off the table and holds it in the air) The rent check bounced.

NATHAN
Great. Thanks. "Hey, welcome home. How did your audition go?"

SARAH
(Still reading) Sorry. Hi. How did your audition go?

NATHAN
I'm done. That's it. I quit. I'm never auditioning again.

SARAH
Shakespeare this time, wasn't it?

NATHAN
It's like panhandling in iambic pentameter. Auditioning has nothing to do with acting. Auditioning is to acting what pick-up lines are to sex. Being good at one doesn't mean you're good at the other.

SARAH
You're very good.

NATHAN
At which one, the ... ? No, that's not what I mean. I'm tired of begging to be allowed to practice my craft. I can't go on like this. It's like playing the lottery for a living. I'm not an actor, I'm a gambling addict. "Just one more audition. This one will hit." I've been doing this for how long ...?

SARAH
(Heard it before) Half your life.

NATHAN
... Half my life. And what do I have to show for it? Three off-Broadway shows, a handful of films, none of them released, and a grad school student loan that's been refinanced so many times, my kids will have to pay it off.

SARAH
You don't have any kids.

NATHAN
And there's a blessing. How could I look them in the face? I'm a complete failure.

SARAH
(Seeing something in the paper) Hey, here's a movie audition: (Sarah reads the ad and translates), "SAG Student Film Contract" – that means no pay – "award-winning young director" – that means he won some college prize as an undergrad – "chance to be a part of the creative process" – that means the screenplay's half written. "Prepare a one-minute comic monologue. Open auditions tomorrow and Friday, ten to five." Look at the character description.

NATHAN
(Coming over to look at the newspaper, reads) I am right for this. You know, this could really be the one. (Sarah looks up at him, skeptically.)

(BLACKOUT)

END

Category: U
Cast: 1 F, 1 M
Gi60 US 2012, 2014

FEBRUARY 15TH
By Robert Boatride
New York City, NY, USA

Characters
HER in fashionable grey. She is sitting
modestly reading something hardcover
and ironic
HIM pink shirted. He is cutting hearts out of
red paper, repeatedly

HIM
(Looking at her with sentiment)
Have I told you of my
Love at the sight of you sitting book in hand
On an evening when the stars above
Can't twinkle near as bright as you?

HER
(Never looking up from her reading)
No, I don't remember you saying that.
(Pause)

HIM
Did I mention, the happiness I feel
At having you near, through weeks and days
Through months and years ....

HER
(Interrupts)
No, you're not much for sharing emotion.
(She returns to reading. Pause)

HIM
In the twilight haze of early morning
As your sleeping visage rests on the pillow
next to mine
A ... Gladness opens through me ....

HER
(Interrupts)
When does that happen, Late Riser? I'm
always the one up first, brewing coffee,

cleaning out the cat's litter box, making lunch
for the kids.
(Pause)

HIM
You know .... I'm really trying here.

HER
You blew it, Sweetie. Today's February 15th,
yesterday was the day and there's no bringing
it back.

HIM
Make-upsies are possible in many areas of
human endeavor, Honey.
(HER puts down the book, looks at
him hard.)

HER
You got a box of chocolates over there?

HIM
(Pulling one out)
Right here; your favorite kind, see?

HER
(Standing)
Alright then. You know another word for
chocolate is forgiveness; don't you, Babe?

HIM
However we get there, Darling, high road or
low,
I'll go.

END

Category: U
Cast: 1 F, 1 M
Gi60 US 2005

FRAILTY, THY NAME IS WOE
By Paddy Gillard-Bentley
Kitchener, ON, Canada

Characters
OPHELIA: In love ... verges on madness.
THE GHOST OF HAMLET'S FATHER: A man
bent on revenge.
 (HAMLET'S FATHER'S GHOST watches
 OPHELIA enter.)

OPHELIA
Am I? Or not?

HAMLET'S FATHER'S GHOST
Ah, Ophelia ... a curious question. What was it
he said ... Within the madness of the mind to
suffer the slings and arrows of outrageous ....

OPHELIA
Love ... or to embrace a passion verily
unrequited.

HAMLET'S FATHER'S GHOST
Ah, there's the rub. Look, there comes your
love now.
 (OPHELIA begins to go to Hamlet. The
 GHOST grabs her arm.)

HAMLET'S FATHER'S GHOST
You will seem to my son, to be of more
translucent substance than a whispered breeze.

OPHELIA
But he could see you! He did swear upon his
own heart he spoke with you.

HAMLET'S FATHER'S GHOST
My intention is more essential than is thine.

OPHELIA
But I ...

HAMLET'S FATHER'S GHOST
(Monotonous)
Yes, I know ... when love speaks, the voice of
all the gods makes heaven drowsy with the
harmony .... etcetera, etcetera, etcetera. Love's
influence and qualities are inferior to that of
vengeance.

OPHELIA
I hoped, perchance he'd dream of me. But in
my sleep of death, what dreams may come
staring at love's eternal sky from beneath yon
icy river?

HAMLET'S FATHER'S GHOST
Good Gods, Ophelia. Frailty, thy name is wo ...

OPHELIA
Do not make blithe of my anguish!

HAMLET'S FATHER'S GHOST
Vengeance hath more power in death, than
has love.

OPHELIA
But his love for me had ...

HAMLET'S FATHER'S GHOST
Apparently been diminished by something
more fervent.

OPHELIA
We shall see, then, what is stronger in death.

HAMLET'S FATHER'S GHOST
Yes. Love ... or revenge?

END

Category: U
Cast: 1 F, 1 M
Gi60 US 2009

GHOST FLIGHTS
By Paul Barile
Chicago, IL, USA

(DANIEL is packing a bag. GLORIA is pacing and shining a St Christopher medal.)

GLORIA
What if your plane crashes?

DANIEL
That'll ruin the whole trip, won't it?

GLORIA
They go down you know. Those big metal monsters go down in cornfields and no one remembers the names of the people who were on the plane. Then they put up a plaque. They call them ghost flights.

DANIEL
Those who missed the plane remember where they were when they heard about the crash.

GLORIA
I hope that's you – the one who missed the flight.

DANIEL
I'll stand around the barbecue every Memorial Day and recount the story for our friends.

GLORIA
You were in the bathroom when you heard the final boarding call and you knew there was no way you were going to make it …

DANIEL
So I just figured I'll make the next flight so I headed over to the ticket counter to exchange my ticket.

GLORIA
That's when you felt the ground shake beneath your feet …

DANIEL
I smelled the smoke of the burning rubber and heard the sirens …

GLORIA
There was a young stewardess crying. An older guy – a skycap – tried to console her.

DANIEL
I tucked my ticket into my jacket and walked out of the airport and into a waiting taxi. When I got home, I saw you had been crying …

GLORIA
But now they're tears of joy because I see you didn't get on that plane.

DANIEL
Our friends will get sick of the story but every time a plane flies overhead …

GLORIA
They'll get a chill down their spine.

DANIEL
They'll tell their friends they know a guy who was almost on a ghost flight.

GLORIA
No one will believe them.

DANIEL
But it will be true. I'm going to call and see what time the next bus to Ann Arbor is?

GLORIA
Shall I put some coffee on?

END

Category: U
Cast: 1 F, 1 M, Ensemble of Warriors optional
Gi60 US 2016

THE GREAT TRIBBLE HUNT,
OR KRATOK AND KEZKHE: A KLINGON OPERA
Book and lyrics by Walter Petryk
Music composed by Jackie Wilson
Portland, OR, USA

*English translation runs on the projector throughout. English translation provided in italics.
*Musical timestamps provided in parentheses throughout in lieu of sheet music. Audio recording without lyrics can be provided by authors.

(0:00) Music starts.

General KRATOK, Commander of the Tribble Extermination Force of the Klingon Empire, stands on a rock addressing his specialized forces. His daughter KEZKHE stands next to him wearing a hooded cloak.

(0:07)

KRATOK

(spoken) qawlu' jawbe' joy'qang 'e' vIpIH tlhIngan wo' pong yIH 'oy'naQ 'oy'yaS!
(*No longer will the Klingon Empire be tormented by the Tribble scourge!*)
(sung) qaw qun DaHjaj!
(*History will remember this day!*)

(0:07)

KEZKHE

(sung) legh qun DaHjaj.
(*History will look down upon this day.*)

(0:19)

KRATOK

Qapla'!
(*Success!*)

(KRATOK raises his bat'leth and charges off stage.)
(0:22)

(KEZKHE, KRATOK's daughter, steps forward and removes her hood. She picks up a Tribble and caresses it.)

(0:25)

KEZKHE

(spoken) pagh batlh naDev tu'lu'.
(*There is no honor here.*)

(0:27)

(KRATOK re-enters and sees KEZKHE with the Tribble.)
(0:29) He chuckles.

(0:30)

KRATOK

(sung) je tun, puqwI'. Hegh rIntaH yIH!
(*You are too soft, my daughter. Death to the Tribbles!*)

(0:32)

KEZKHE

Qo' vIyaj!
(*You don't understand!*)

(0:34)

KRATOK

maHvaD muv, puqwI'; jIHvaD quvHa' SoH!
(*Join us, daughter; you dishonor me!*)

(0:36)

KEZKHE

Hoch tuHmoH maH pong.
(0:39) Qo'.
(*We are all dishonored by this. No.*)

(0:44) (Silence)

(0:45)

KRATOK

(spoken) vaj qaSjaj.
(*So be it.*)

(0:46)
(KRATOK raises his bat'leth and with a yell charges off stage. KEZKHE steps to center. Looking out where KRATOK and the warriors exited, she picks up the Tribble again and speaks an unheard warning.)

(0:53)

KEZKHE

(spoken) SuvwI' 'Iv jagh Hoch HoH vup.
(*Pity the warrior who slays all his foes.*)

(0:57)
(KEZKHE viciously rips the Tribble apart with her bare hands. She exits. Music fades.)

END

Category: U
Cast: 2 Gender Neutral
Gi60 US 2015

HAUNTED THEATRE
By Rosanne Manfredi, based on an idea by Rose Burnett Bonczek
Bay Shore, NY, USA

Characters
ARTISTIC DIRECTOR
MEDIUM

MEDIUM
Why am I here again?

ARTISTIC DIRECTOR
Well, you know that all theatres are haunted.
I mean, look at these photos – look at all the
orbs!

MEDIUM
Impressive.

ARTISTIC DIRECTOR
Anyway, we like having them around – live
and let live I always feel – so to speak. But
we've been having problems lately, missing
props, walls falling down. We need to know
what's going on.

MEDIUM
OK. Spirits of the … OK – hello. Hi Blanche.
Hello Elwood. Madame Arcati, a kindred
spirit – no pun intended. How wonderful.
    (Listens)
These aren't ghosts – in the regular sense. You
see, some of your actors imbue their
characters so completely with power and
intention that they remain on the stage when
the play ends. They're very happy here. This is
where they belong.

ARTISTIC DIRECTOR
Wow. But, I mean, what about the
disruptions?
    (Listens)

MEDIUM
Do you have a thespian who is overacting in
order to (listens intently) "make the unskilled
laugh"?

ARTISTIC DIRECTOR
Scott!!!!

MEDIUM
Yes, well, Hamlet really doesn't like that. Get
"Scott" to tone it down and the mischief will
stop.
Well, my work here is done. Goodbye, it was
nice to meet you.
    (to the spirits)
Goodbye, it was delightful to spend time with
you all.
    (Heads out. Stops.)
Oh, and they want me to tell you, they greatly
appreciate the light you leave on for them.

ARTISTIC DIRECTOR
(Looks around in wonder.)

END

Category: U
Cast: 2 F
Gi60 US 2015

THE HIDDEN STREAM
By Anna Shotter
Huddersfield, UK

A

I'm so lost. This is not where I wanted to be … is it? I don't even know where I wanted to be. But I thought I'd be somewhere different by now.
> (B appears quietly behind A.)

B

What do you see? Right here?

A

See? Well the hill sloping up away from me. The sky bluey grey and a bit cloudy. The road in the distance. The woods snaking down close to the valley. Glimpses of the stream in the sun though most of it is hidden.

B

Where does the stream go?

A

Go? You can't see where it goes. I don't know.

B

I do. Even when it is covered with brambles and barely visible on the landscape, I know where it is going and where it has been. I have seen it in full bloom and I have seen it clear as day. I have seen it covered in ice and snow. I saw it when it was but a trickle in the ground. I see it even in the dead of night – it is no less clear to me. It is a wild thing but I know where it will meet the sea.

A

(Getting upset) But I cannot see where it goes.

B

Do you trust me?
> (B holds hand out to A.)

END

Category: U
Cast: 2 M
Gi60 US 2007

IN AN HOUR
By Andreas Flourakis
Athens, Greece

(FATHER and SON at the beach)

FATHER
How did you find me?

SON
You always come here.

FATHER
What are you up to?

SON
You know. It's this afternoon, in an hour's time. That's why you left, isn't it?

FATHER
No, it isn't. I was fine, just sitting here and then you came along to … to do what?

SON
Take you with me. Come on dad, she was your mother after all.

FATHER
She just happened to churn me out of her belly.

SON
The dead should be forgiven for everything they've done.

FATHER
You have no idea what sort of a person she really was. I could tell you some things about that woman.

SON
I know all about her, dad.

FATHER
What d' you mean "know"?

SON
She told me everything some time ago.

FATHER
She obviously pulled the wool over your eyes, didn't she?

SON
The funeral is in an hour.

FATHER
I have no business at a stranger's funeral.

SON
She wanted to explain everything to you.

FATHER
It's too late now, anyway.

SON
There're still 55 minutes till the funeral. You should be there. Do it for yourself. Do it for me.

FATHER
Did she die peacefully?

SON
She passed away in her sleep.

FATHER
May God forgive her.

SON
May people forgive her too.

FATHER
Better get this straight first, I'm going to sit as far away as possible from all of them and I'm not going to cry.

SON
That's alright, dad. I'll be sitting right next to you.

END

Category: U
Cast: 1 F, 1 M
Gi60 UK 2011

LAST FIRST DATE
By Thomas J. Misuraca
Tarzana, CA, USA

Setting

A restaurant.

(LIGHTS UP on EVELYN seated at a table. BILL enters, glances around, finds EVELYN and takes a seat at her table.)

BILL

Evelyn?

EVELYN

Hi, Bill. Nice to meet you. We need to talk.

BILL

Yes. I can't wait to learn all about you.

EVELYN

This isn't working out.

BILL

You want to go to another restaurant?

EVELYN

It's not you, it's me.

BILL

Are you breaking up with me before our first date?

EVELYN

You deserve better.

BILL

Could you at least wait until after dinner? I'm starving.

EVELYN

See. You're too needy.

BILL

I thought it was you, not me?

EVELYN

It is. I'm just not that into you.

BILL

You don't even know me.

EVELYN

(rises to leave) We can still be friends.

BILL

I have enough friends.

EVELYN

This didn't have to end on a bitter note. But I understand.

(EVELYN exits, BILL sits, baffled.)

END

Category: U
Cast: 2 Gender Neutral
Gi60 UK 2007

LIFE EVERLASTING
By Terry Collins
Harrogate, UK

Setting

A mortuary. Bodies are lying on tables under sheets, including ALEPH and BETH. ALEPH pulls down her sheet and calls to BETH.

ALEPH

Psst! Psst!
     (BETH pulls down her sheet.)

BETH

What?

ALEPH

You been dead long?

BETH

About three days. How about you?

ALEPH

Four days. Boring, isn't it?
     (BETH nods agreement, and they return to being dead.)

END

Category: U
Cast: 2 M
Gi60 US 2015

LISTENING OFF BEAT
By Eugene Solfanelli
Brooklyn, NY, USA

Setting

DOCTOR's Office, Examination Room

Characters

DOCTOR: Mid- to late fifties
PATIENT/Mr Disperso: Late twenties (Disperso loosely translates to "I am lost" in Italian.)
Depicts possible edits if play runs long
        (DOCTOR walks in looking at PATIENT's chart.)

DOCTOR

So, Mr ... Disperso (checks chart). What brings you in?

PATIENT

I keep getting these ... palpitations.

DOCTOR

How often?

PATIENT

I don't know, 20 or 30 times a day.

DOCTOR

OK, describe how they feel.

PATIENT

Well everything's normal and then my heart starts pounding.

DOCTOR

(looking at chart) Well it says here that you've been to every heart specialist in the city. And all your test results are normal.

PATIENT

I know what I feel.

DOCTOR

I'm not discrediting how you feel. **But this here (taps files) says you're fine. **Tell you what, let's have a listen.
        (DOCTOR begins to listen with his stethoscope.)

                    PATIENT

Why do people die?

                    DOCTOR

What?

                    PATIENT

Why do people die?

                    DOCTOR

Did someone die, Mr Disperso?

                    PATIENT

My father. He had a heart attack. He was strong and healthy. Then, he was gone. Why?

                    DOCTOR

I'm sorry, I really can't say. Maybe if I can get his file, I could explain it to you ....

                    PATIENT

(cutting him off) That's not what I mean. I'm asking why!! Why do these things happen? Why are we good one moment and then a mess the next ... Why?

                    DOCTOR

I'm sorry. I can't speak to such things. Maybe if you spoke to a counselor or a priest.

                    PATIENT

They don't have the answers. No one knows anything.

                    DOCTOR

You're right, no one out there does. But you do.

                    PATIENT

What?

                    DOCTOR

The answers are within, Mr Disperso. You just need to listen with a little more clarity.
      (Gives him stethoscope)
Here, take this. You'll be able to hear more than I can.
      (Leaves room)

                    PATIENT

(Puts on stethoscope and listens to his heart)
H-h-hello??

                    END

Category: U
Cast: 2 Gender Neutral, Ensemble optional to play statues
Gi60 UK 2013

THE LOST ART
By Joel Dean
Harrogate, UK

Setting
An abandoned theatre. (Two archaeologists enter, one a young female in her twenties, FELICITY, shining a torch, the other an older male, PROFESSOR NIGEL, in his seventies, holding a map. They discover the rest of the cast on stage frozen in interesting positions, covered in dust and cobwebs.)

FELICITY
What is this place, Professor?

NIGEL
I believe this is the lost theatre of the Halifax Viaduct.

FELICITY
Theatre? What on Earth's that?

NIGEL
Oh, it was a building type of affair in which people used to watch plays, performances, and such like.

FELICITY
Plays? Performances? What strange words you speak, Professor!

NIGEL
Yes, it's now all lost to the winds of time sadly, but it was all once very popular. Little scenes would happen live before people's eyes. Empires would be conquered, loves would be sworn, and clowns would jest and caper 'till everyone's sides were well and truly split all in a single evening for a price of tuppence halfpenny. It was quite beautiful in its own way.

FELICITY
Not very efficient though. People indulging in emotions. Doesn't exactly get the work done.

NIGEL
Well, there was once this mad belief that work wasn't everything. (They laugh.) I know, stupid isn't it?

FELICITY
(Wondering through the frozen cast) What do you suppose this scene was?

NIGEL
Difficult to say my child. It's interesting though. Yes, very interesting and therefore lethal. I'll have it destroyed within a week.

FELICITY
Don't you think that's a bit of a shame?

NIGEL
Nonsense my child! We can't have things of interest distracting people from their work. I mean, someone might even try to revive this silly activity and that would be unthinkable.

FELICITY
Oh well. I suppose you know best Professor.

NIGEL
I do, I do and don't ever forget it. Come my child, let us venture forth to the Ministry of Destruction and report our findings.

END

Category: U
Cast: 1 F, 1 M
Gi60 UK 2010

LOVE AMONG MIDGES
By Terry Collins
Harrogate, UK

Setting
BILL has just led LISA to a special spot
overlooking the beautiful mountains of Skye.
But LISA is troubled by midges.

BILL
Well, this is it. Beautiful, isn't it?

LISA
Beautiful. But a lot of midges.
(She slaps a midge on her neck.)

BILL
You can probably guess why I've brought
you here.

LISA
Hang on, there's one!
(She slaps a midge on her arm.)

BILL
A beautiful place for a beautiful moment.

LISA
(She slaps a midge on her leg.)
Got you!

BILL
This is the exact spot where Dad proposed to
Mum.

LISA
There's one on your arm! (She smacks his
arm.)

BILL
Thank you! And his father before him.

LISA
Hold still!
(She smacks his bottom.)

BILL
My Granddad proposed to Grandma at this
very place. So, this won't come as any
surprise to you.
(He kneels.)

LISA
Stay like that!
(She slaps his face.)

BILL
Thanks! Darling, this is what I want to say …
(LISA slaps his face and neck several
times.)

LISA
I think that's most of them. Now what was it
you wanted to say?

BILL
Oh, never mind.

LISA
OK. Can we get out of here please?
(They leave.)

END

Category: U
Cast: 2 F
Gi60 US 2009

MAGGIE & MARY
By Alison Carr
Newcastle upon Tyne, England

(LIGHTS UP)
(Reveal MAGGIE AND MARY. They are dressed identically.)

MAGGIE

Morning.

MARY

Morning.

MAGGIE

Sleep?

MARY

Well. You?

MAGGIE

Yes. Dream?

MARY

Of you.

MAGGIE

Of course.

MARY

You?

MAGGIE

No.

MARY

No.

MAGGIE

Breakfast?

MARY

Yum.

MAGGIE

Toast. And tea.

MARY

Sugar?

MAGGIE

No.

MARY

Sweet enough?

MAGGIE

Slimming.

MARY

Work.

MAGGIE

Groan.

MARY

Typing.

MAGGIE

Yawn.

MARY

Filing.

MAGGIE

Lunch.

MARY

On the Common.

MAGGIE

North.

MARY

South.

MAGGIE

Meet in the middle. At the hole in the middle.
Like a doughnut.

MARY

For a doughnut?

MAGGIE

For a salad.

MARY

Slimming.

MAGGIE

Home.

MARY

Hot carriage.

MAGGIE

Musky.

MARY

Dirty.

MAGGIE

People.

MARY

(disdainful) Other people.

MAGGIE

(not) Other people.

MARY

Out into the fresh air.

MAGGIE

Fresh?

MARY

Out in to the air. A nice walk.

MAGGIE

A short walk. Build an appetite for

MARY

Dinner.

MAGGIE

Yum.

MARY

Your favourite –

MARY

Pork chop.
}

MAGGIE

Lamb chop.

DISCORD. THEY BOTH CORRECT
THEMSELVES AT THE SAME TIME.

MARY

Lamb chop.
}

MAGGIE

Pork chop.
FLUSTERED. EVENTUALLY –

MAGGIE

(a compromise) Chop.

MARY

(relieved) Chop.

MARY

Bed.

MAGGIE

At last.

MARY
All tucked up.

MAGGIE
Warm.

MARY
Comfy.

MAGGIE
Clean.

MARY
Safe.

MAGGIE
Good night.

MARY
Sleep tight.

BOTH
Don't let the bed bugs –
       (BLACKOUT)
       (LIGHTS UP. Same as opening of
       previous)

MAGGIE
Morning.

MARY
Morning.

MAGGIE
Sleep?

MARY
Well. You?

MAGGIE
Yes. Dream?

MARY
Of you.

MAGGIE
Of course.

MARY
You?

MAGGIE
Yes.

MARY
(surprised) Yes?

MAGGIE
Yes.

MARY
About?

MAGGIE
…

MARY
About?

MAGGIE
(just smiles and shrugs)

MARY
Sister?

MAGGIE
(mimicking her) Sister?

MARY
About?

MAGGIE
(lying) … You.

BLACKOUT.

END

Category: U
Cast Size: 1 F, 1 M
Gi60 US 2013

MIRROR, MIRROR ON THE WALL
By Anthony R. Ponzio
Los Angeles, CA, USA

Setting

LULA and NOEL stand in an empty apartment with only a mirror hanging on the wall. LULA is holding a taped cardboard box.

LULA

Well, this is the last of it.

NOEL

You sure you want to leave that mirror behind?

LULA

Yes, I'm sure. The girl moving in said she loved it and you have that long one on the bathroom door.
(He moves to exit and she follows but pauses. NOEL realizes she's not following.)

NOEL

How about one last look around?
(She protests but he leads her to the mirror.)

NOEL

I'm serious.
(He points into the mirror's reflection.)
Look right here, the window. Remember? You opened it in your sleep, and dropped the air conditioner out of it.
(Still pointing, he traces his finger in a line along another section of the mirror.)
And right here, that's where the mouse ran across your foot. And what happened there?
(Pointing to another section)

NOEL

In the corner?

LULA

You broke your toe on that rocking chair we found.
(Turning her from the mirror and taking her to another section in the room)

NOEL

And here?

LULA

This is where we kiss every morning. OK, I get it. Thank you.
(She kisses him quickly and EXITS. He follows, smiling into the mirror one last time before EXITING.)

END

Category: U
Cast: 2 Gender Neutral
Gi60 UK 2015

MY DAD'S A MARLIN
By J. F. Alberts
Palm Harbor, FL, USA

Setting
One actor is the HAWK, the other is a FISH.
The HAWK will be on the shoulders of the
FISH as if he were carrying the fish away. The
FISH will be moving in a slow pacing manner
from stage left to stage right while dialogue is
exchanged.

FISH
Am I going to be back soon?

HAWK
No.

FISH
But I have to be home before dinner.

HAWK
No.

FISH
(Pause) My dad's a marlin you know.

HAWK
That's fantastic ...

FISH
I'm serious ... if we go back now I think my
mom's making seaweed salad.

HAWK
No.

FISH
Yeah but –

HAWK
No.

FISH
There's some pretty hefty tuna in the part of
the lake ...

HAWK
Great.

FISH
(Pause) I knew UBER was a mistake, I should
have taken the bass.

END

Category: U
Cast: 1 F, 1 M
Gi60 UK 2008

NOT EVEN IF
By Amy Ignatow
Philadelphia, PA, USA

Setting
HAL is sitting on his front stoop. JANIE comes up to him.

JANIE

Hey, have you seen Sam?

HAL

The hoard got him.

JANIE

Which one?

HAL

Cyborgs.
    (JANIE shudders and sits next to him on the stoop, hugging her knees.)

HAL

I can't wait for them to come for me.

JANIE

You're kidding me.

HAL

I just hope it's the cyborgs and not the zombies. I mean, either way I'd be a mindless killing machine, but if I had the choice I think I'd rather kill people with lasers, you know?

JANIE

Why would you even think something like that?

HAL

How can you not think about it?
    (JANIE looks at him, disbelieving and aghast. HAL looks back at her eyerollingly, as if to say, Well, duh. JANIE responds by looking frustrated and aghast.)

HAL

Look, sooner or later we're going to be attacked by either zombies or cyborgs, and we'll either get eaten, or blown up, or turned into zombies or cyborgs. I don't know about you, but when all is said and done, I think that becoming a cyborg and serving the Great Cyborg Mother is probably the best option. I mean, lasers.

JANIE

We could be bitten by vampires.

HAL

Oh please. You can't even get more than 12 people to be fans of your band on Facebook. Like a vampire is going to bite you.

JANIE

Fine. But I still don't want to become a cyborg.

HAL

It's inevitable. I say we embrace it. Everyone else has.

JANIE

That's just not true. Jerry hasn't.

HAL

The zombies got him on Tuesday. Didn't you hear?

JANIE

This is awful. I don't want to die, and I don't want to be a zombie, and I don't want to serve the Great Cyborg Mother! I want to live. There are too many things I haven't done yet. I've never had sushi. I've never been to Paris. I once smoked pot but I just got a little dizzy, and I've never been in love –

HAL

(Grabbing a hold of JANIE)
Hey. Hey. Calm down.
(Breathes deeply with her, puts his hand gently on the side of her face and looks deeply into her eyes)
I'll do you.
(He kisses her, and it kind of looks like he's just sort of mashing his face into hers. They separate. It's super awkward.)

JANIE

So ... lasers?

HAL

(Resignedly)
Lasers.

.JANIE

It could be worse.

END

Category: U
Cast: 1 F, 1 M
Gi60 US 2011, 2014

NOTHING
By Kevin Clyne
Babylon, NY, USA

HIM
I don't understand. What are you mad about?

HER
(Clearly mad)
Nothing!

HIM
Nobody's mad about "nothing." It's about your birthday, right?

HER
What do you think?

HIM
You're mad because I didn't get you anything?

HER
Duh!

HIM
But that's what you said, you said not to get you anything.

HER
No I didn't!

HIM
I asked you what you wanted and you said "nothing."

HER
I said I didn't want anything. I didn't say don't get me anything.

HIM
Isn't that the same thing?

HER
No!

HIM
What's the difference?

HER
Just because I said I didn't want anything, doesn't mean I didn't want anything.

HIM
I'm not a mind reader.

HER
I don't want you to read my mind. I just want you to know what I'm thinking without me telling you.

HIM
That's pretty much the definition of a mind reader ... look, I don't get it.

HER
Exactly, you got me nothing.

HIM
(Confused)
Well ... what can I do to make it up to you?

HER
Nothing.

HIM
Right.

END

Category: U
Cast: 1 F, 1 M
Gi60 US 2013

OH BABY!
By Jennifer Provenza
Sacramento, CA, USA

SHE

Guess what? My mom said she would take the baby tonight.

HE

You know what this means? Oh my God. Do you know how long it's been?

SHE

It's been since before the baby.

HE

Yeah. That's a long time.

SHE

I know.

HE

You know what? Let's open that bottle of Champagne we've been saving.

SHE

And we can eat by candlelight!

HE

And then we'll take a hot bubble bath together, and I'll rub your shoulders with some oil.

SHE

Yeah? I'd like that.

HE

And you know what will happen next, don't you?

SHE

Oh yes. We'll go into the bedroom.

HE

That's right. We'll go into the bedroom.

SHE

And then? What will we do then? Tell me.

HE

We'll get into bed.

SHE

Yes! And then …

HE

And then …

SHE

Oh, God.

HE

Yes!

SHE

It's going to feel incredible …

HE

It's going to be amazing …

SHE

We're going to do it …

HE

That's right. We're going to …

SHE

Oh, God, say it!

HE

We'll sleep.

SHE

Yes! Yes! We'll sleep! Oh my God, we'll sleep ALL. NIGHT. LONG.

END

Category: U
Cast: 1 F, 1 M
Gi60 UK 2007

ON THE WAY DOWN
By Dwayne Yancey
Fincastle, VA, USA

Setting

In the dark, from off stage, we hear a male voice shout.

MALE VOICE

Go! Go! Go! Go!

(LIGHTS UP. Two women, in skydiving outfits, are on stage. To simulate the dive, they should be on their stomachs, with their arms outstretched. ONE speaks to the audience; TWO smiles throughout – because of the rushing wind, she can't hear what ONE is saying.)

ONE

You know, Hollywood has it all wrong.

In the movies, whenever two people parachute out of an airplane, you see them carrying on entire conversations all the way down.

That's impossible, of course.

Oh, you can talk, all right.

It's just that no one can hear you.

The wind is way too loud.

So that means my friend Lucy there can't me hear me say that I know all about her and my boyfriend.

She can't hear me when I tell her exactly what I think of her.

Or that when I checked her 'chute in the pre-jump checklist, I cut the cord.

In a few seconds, she'll try to deploy her 'chute and wonder why it's not working.

She'll think it's just a malfunction. She's trained for those thousands of times.

That's when she'll try to activate the reserve chute.

She can't hear me tell her I cut that one, too.

Too bad.

I wish I could tell her how much I hate her guts and how I hope she dies a horrible, gruesome death.

I wonder if she'll figure it out?

END

Category: U
Cast: 1 F, 1 M
Gi60 US 2006, 2014

ONLINE SENIOR DATE
By Laurel A. Lockhart
New York, NY, USA

Setting
Computer room of a senior center, BOB and
BETTY are side by side at the computers.

BOB
How did you make out yesterday?

BETTY
We had lunch at EJ's.

BOB
Very nice. You and "Forever Young Fred"
going out again?

BETTY
Don't think so, he's a little "too young" for
me.

BOB
Too young, huh.

BETTY
How about you, any hits?

BOB
Two so far, today.

BETTY
Great.

BOB
Not so great, one is from Germany and the
other is from Minneapolis.

BETTY
You need someone just around the corner.

BOB
Don't I know it.

BETTY
Your new picture is great.

BOB
Thanks, my son took it.

BETTY
Would he take one for me?

BOB
Why not, he's coming over Sunday afternoon.

BETTY
I could make my famous apple cake.

BOB
Is it a date?

BETTY
It's a date.

END

Category: U
Cast: 1 F, 1 M (1 non-speaking)
Gi60 US 2016

PIT STOP
By Allie Costa
Studio City, CA, USA

(LIGHTS UP: CARVER stands outside of a convenience store bathroom, staring at the closed door.)

CARVER
(Under his breath) C'mon, c'mon ...
(JINN, lost in her thoughts, walks up and grabs the door handle.)

CARVER
It's occupied.

JINN
(snapping out of it, stepping back) Oh.

CARVER
And there's a line.

JINN
Right. Sorry.

CARVER
It's okay. I won't take long. Not like some people!
(This is said pointedly, loudly, at the door. A beat passes; the door remains closed. CARVER exhales and looks at JINN.)

CARVER
Sorry. I'm just – I get kinda cranky when I –

JINN
– have to pee?
(JINN's frankness catches CARVER off-guard.)

CARVER
I was gonna say when I've had a long drive. Don't get me wrong, she's a good truck, but after being trapped in her for hours, I really gotta – (catching himself) stretch my legs.

JINN
You a truck driver, or ...?

CARVER
Surfer. Well, businessman, technically. I own a shop. But I prefer the ocean to the office.

JINN
Who wouldn't?

CARVER
Right? (Pause) You from here?

JINN
What?

CARVER
Dakota County. You from here?

JINN
Born and raised. Far from the ocean, huh?

CARVER
Way too far. No offense. But hopefully the good people at the Summertime Shoppe decide to sell my wares.

JINN
Oh my god, I used to work there in the summer!

CARVER
Small world.

JINN
Small town.

(She fidgets with the flimsy plastic convenience store bag in her hand. The bag tears, and a small cardboard box drops to the ground. CARVER and JINN both go to retrieve it; CARVER gets to it first. As he picks it up, he realizes it's a pregnancy test.)

                    CARVER
(Handing it over carefully) Here you go.

                    JINN
Thanks.
          (They stand.)

                    CARVER
A public bathroom's gotta be crawlin' with –
It's probably gross in there. (gently) Maybe
you should do that at home.

                    JINN
(simply) Can't.
          (The bathroom door opens; someone
          exits wordlessly. JINN looks at
          CARVER.)

                    JINN
Aren't you gonna –? (gestures to door)

                    CARVER
          (shakes head, swoops arm toward
          door)
Ladies first.

                    JINN
Thanks.
          (JINN enters the bathroom. The door
          clicks shut. CARVER exhales)

                    END

Category: U
Cast: 2 M
Gi60 US 2009, 2014

PLATO'S CAVE
By Mark Harvey Levine
Pasadena, CA, USA

Setting
ANDY and GARY are watching TV on a ratty old couch.

GARY
Did you ever wonder if this is all there is?

ANDY
This show?

GARY
No, reality. All of reality. Did you ever wonder if there's more to it?

ANDY
No.

GARY
I mean, sometimes I wonder if this is all a dream, or something. Maybe I'm really lying in a hospital somewhere, in a coma, and this is all a vast hallucination. And all I need to do is wake up, and I'll be greeted by my wife and three children.

ANDY
You have a wife and three children?

GARY
Here, I don't. But maybe I do, out there ... or up there. In real reality.

ANDY
Am I still your roommate there?

GARY
I don't think my wife would like that.

ANDY
I'm starting not to like her.

GARY
Hey, that's my wife you're talking about.

ANDY
Yeah, but she's got too much control over you. You've got to make your own decisions.

GARY
How can I make my own decisions? I'm lying in a coma.

ANDY
Well, then, wake the hell up and leave me alone. I'm trying to watch this.

GARY
Today the checkout lady at the grocery store asked me if I was comfortable.

ANDY
Why would she say that?

GARY
Exactly! Why would she say that? She wouldn't. But a nurse might.

ANDY
A nurse.

GARY
I think a nurse said that, in my hospital room, and for a moment it broke through my ... my vegetative state ... and like in a dream I put it in the mouth of the checkout lady.

ANDY
So none of this is real? The TV ... our apartment ... the city ...?

GARY
Not really ... it's like Plato's cave.

ANDY
Play-dough? I love the smell of Play-dough.

GARY
Plato. Plato. The Philosopher. He imagined that we are all ... like ... these people, sitting in a cave. With our backs to the opening. We see light flicker on the back wall, and think that's reality. But then someone turns around, goes outside, and realizes there's the sun and people and that's what's making all the shadows. And that the sun and the people are the real reality. You know what I mean?

ANDY
I'm just going to change your IV now.

GARY
What?

ANDY
(Annoyed, repeating)
I'm just going to watch TV now.
(He does. The lights flicker on ANDY's face. GARY stares at him.)

END

Category: U
Cast: 2 M
G(hosts) in 60 2010

READY FOR SCIENCE
By Julian Kaufman
Woodford Green, UK

A haunted castle. The laboratory.

PROF
Igor!
    (Enter Igor)

IGOR
Master, my name isn't Igor.

PROF
Silence! Have you warmed up the positron machine?

IGOR
Is that the one with the flashing lights and the sparky wires?

PROF
Yes.

IGOR
Then I've warmed it up.

PROF
Have you charged the electron gun?

IGOR
I think so, master.

PROF
Have you dipped the telemask lens in acid?

IGOR
Yes, master.

PROF
Did you wear the dainty gloves for that purpose while you did so?

IGOR
Of course, master.

PROF
Did you oil the sticky, gritty gears of the slidy slippy machine?

IGOR
Yes, I oiled the sticky, gritty gears of the slidy slippy machine.

PROF
Have you primed the zombies?

IGOR
Zombies primed.

PROF
Did you switch the red danger, danger, lights on in the external danger chamber?

IGOR
All red and glowy, master.

PROF
Have you prepared my anti-radiation suit?

IGOR
Yes master, with a pink carnation in the toxic gas outflow vent just as you like.

PROF
Did you put a banana in Mr Bunty's cage?

IGOR
Master, I don't think Mr Bunty likes me …

PROF
Did you put a banana in his cage!

IGOR

Yes, master.

PROF

Have you de-wormed the cat?

IGOR

Yes, master.

PROF

Did you take that pie out of the oven?

IGOR

Yes, master. It's on the window sill cooling as we speak.

PROF

Did you remember to stop the milk?

IGOR

I left a note for milky.

PROF

Did you set the video to record "Top 100 Insane Scientists" on Channel 5?

IGOR

Yes, master.

PROF

Did you put plenty of newspaper down on the floor, remember what happened last time?

IGOR

Yes, master, this time there will be no spillages.

PROF

Did you phone my mother and tell her I was in the lab and not to call under any circumstances?

IGOR

I left a message on her machine.

PROF

Good. Did you get me a glass of water? Tepid not cold? Bottled not tap? Still not sparkling?

IGOR

It's by the petri-dish of worms, master.

PROF

Ah.
    (Pause)

PROF

Then, Igor, then …

IGOR

Yes, master?

PROF

We are ready for Science!
    (Demonic chord. Musical bubbling)

END

Category: U
Cast: 1 F, 1 M
Gi60 US 2014

REALITY VISION
By Julia Lederer
Toronto, ON, Canada

Setting

Outside. A woman sits in a plastic chair on one side of the stage slowly eating popcorn, staring intently off into the distance. A man enters in her sight line. He has a lawn mower or a rake – something to do yard work. He begins. She stares. She chokes on some popcorn. The man looks over –

WOMAN

I'm fine. Don't break the fourth wall.

MAN

Huh?

WOMAN

Nothing, nothing. Go about your day.
        (She eats more popcorn.)

MAN

OK, what do you – this is getting weird.

WOMAN

My cable's out. I'm just watching reality. Instead of reality television.

MAN

You can't.

WOMAN

Why not? You should try it. Better than TV, more pure.

MAN

Fine.
        (Man exits. He comes back with his own chair and popcorn. The two sit across from one another and stare at each other, eating popcorn.)

WOMAN

Interesting plot twist. Never could've written this.

MAN

Welcome to the future.
        (They sit and munch and stare at one another.)

END

Category: U
Cast: 1 F, 1 M
Gi60 US 2014

RETURNS
By Tom Valentine Gelo
Dallas, TX, USA

Setting
LIGHTS UP. A small baby boutique. The walls are adorned with strollers, toys, baby clothing, etc. Various racks of newborn products stand throughout the store.
(WOMAN stands behind the cash register stage right.)
(MAN enters from stage left, pushing a large box.)

WOMAN

Can I help you, sir?

MAN

Um. Yeah. I bought this cradle here a couple weeks ago. I, uh … I just need to return it.

WOMAN

Okay. Was there an issue with it?

MAN

No. I mean uh … it's unopened. I just … I was hoping I could return it.
(Beat)

WOMAN

Oh. Okay. I can do that for you, sir. Would you like cash or store credit?
(MAN removes a small pair of baby's socks from the rack next to him. He turns them over in his hands, examining their weight, their size, the soft material they are sewn from. He is absorbed for a moment.)
… Sir?
(The MAN snaps out of his trance and places the socks back on the rack.)

MAN

Oh … um … cash. Please.

END

Category: U
Cast: 1 F, 1 M
Gi60 UK 2010

ROLLERCOASTER OF LOVE … SAY WHAT?!
By Brian Palermo
Santa Monica, CA, USA

Setting
ANDY and STEPH are in a rollercoaster car.
This is established by sound f/x and their
body language; leaning steeply backwards on
the uphill. They're really enjoying
themselves.)

ANDY
Today has been so much fun. I love
amusement parks, Steph.
(She takes this in, then decides to
share.)

STEPH
And I love you, Andy.
(This first time admission comes just
as the coaster car reaches its peak.
ANDY's shock registers exactly in the
breathless moment before the car
plunges down the first big hill. They
rattle and shake in the coaster. He
clutches the handlebar in fear, she
holds her arms over her head in
abandon.)

ANDY
Oh, god, oh, god, oh god!! It's too fast!!!

STEPH
Just enjoy it!

ANDY
I can't enjoy it, I'm too nervous about what's
ahead!
(The coaster levels out.)

STEPH
It's too late now, we're in the middle of it.
Let's just hope it doesn't fly off the tracks!

(As ANDY takes in STEPH'S line, they
speed into a massive turn. The actors
lean viciously to the right.)

ANDY
Aaaaahhh, I'm scared!!

STEPH
You're the one who wanted to do this!
(They viciously lean left.)

ANDY
Whoa! I thought I did but now I just want to
be in the Fun House!

STEPH
You can't have both, silly!
(Lean right)

ANDY
I want out! I want out! I want out!!
(They jostle back to centre position and
shake and rattle towards the end of the
ride.)

STEPH
Gosh, calm down. It's done, it's finished.

ANDY
Ugh, now I'm all dizzy and beat up and
unsatisfied.

STEPH
Me too.
(Beat)

ANDY
Can we do it again?

END

Category: U
Cast: 1 M, 1 Gender Neutral
Gi60 US 2015

SAVING INGE
By Loy Webb
Chicago, IL, USA

(AT RISE: CHARLIE (twenties: woman or man) is sitting on her couch reading a book on the life of William Inge. WILLIAM INGE is on the other side of the couch smoking a cigarette.)

CHARLIE

What could I have done to save you?

INGE

You couldn't. It happened in 73. You weren't born then.

CHARLIE

But if I were? You were on Broadway. Won a Pulitzer. People hail you as one of the greatest playwrights of our time, for Christ sake.

INGE

For 15 years I never had a hit. The day before I did it, one of my scripts was returned with the notation – "We don't accept unsolicited manuscripts." So in the grander scheme of things, what does William Inge really mean?

CHARLIE

You can't base success on external validation, Mr Inge. That's as fickle as the weather. Success is measured by doing something bigger than yourself. And you did that by illuminating the lives of people from small towns everyone else deemed insignificant. That's what makes you a legend. Not the Pulitzer. Not Broadway. That.

INGE

If only you realize these sorts of things while you're alive.

CHARLIE

Would that have saved you?

INGE

Quite possibly.

END

Category: U
Cast: 1 F, 1 M
Gi60 UK 2009

SEVEN
By Allie Costa
Studio City, CA, USA

(KATHRYN, a teenager, crosses the stage. VINCENT, a boy the same age, run-walks after her and "accidentally" bumps into her.)

VINCENT
Hey!

KATHRYN
Oh. Hi.

VINCENT
So ... I'll pick you up around 7?

KATHRYN
How many times do I have to turn you down before you realize I don't want to go out with you?

VINCENT
How many times do I have to ask you out before you realize I'm perfect for you?

KATHRYN
You are annoyingly persistent.

VINCENT
Thank you.

KATHRYN
Are you trying to wear me down? Make me so sick of you that I'll say yes just to shut you up?

VINCENT
No. (Beat) Maybe. (shrugs) I'm just waiting for you to accept the obvious. People don't always see what's right in front of them.

KATHRYN
I see a boy I barely know.

VINCENT
At least you acknowledge my existence.

KATHRYN
Well, you – (she searches for a word) – trouble mine!

VINCENT
Don't be cruel.

KATHRYN
Don't sing Elvis Presley.

VINCENT
Sing him what?

KATHRYN
You can't sing him any – Stop that!

VINCENT
Stop what?

KATHRYN
Stop tricking me into talking to you.

VINCENT
I promise you one thing.

KATHRYN
What's that?

VINCENT
I promise not to sing Elvis songs on our first date.

KATHRYN
(walking away) Good – (spins on her heel)
WHAT?

VINCENT
Maybe on the second.

KATHRYN
There will be no second date. There will be
no first date.

VINCENT
Should we skip dating altogether and go
straight to the engagement period?

KATHRYN
I'm going to be late for class.

VINCENT
I'll see you at lunch!

KATHRYN
Please don't.
        (She exits. He calls after her.)

VINCENT
Then … I'll pick you up around 7?

END

Category: U
Cast: 2 Gender Neutral
Gi60 UK 2015

SHOES
By Edgar Chisholm
Bloomfield, NJ, USA

STORE CLERK

May I help you?

CUSTOMER

I'm here to return this.
    (shoes removed from bag)

STORE CLERK

Infant shoes? Brought online or in store?

CUSTOMER

In store.

STORE CLERK

These are our premium best quality newborn shoes. A bit pricey, but you won't find them anywhere for less – even online. These are amongst our hottest sellers. They've got wings … that means they're flying off the shelves.
    (THE STORE CLERK flashes a smile.)

CUSTOMER

    (Acknowledges)
Oh.

STORE CLERK

No scuff marks or abrasions – at this age why would there be? However, Department of Health regulations require I ask – Were they ever worn?

CUSTOMER

No.

STORE CLERK

    (STORE CLERK prepares to fill out e-form.)
May I inquire as to the reason for your dissatisfaction?
    (CUSTOMER is non-responsive.)
Store Policy – It can't be left blank …

CUSTOMER

    (CUSTOMER pauses …)
Not needed.

END

Category: U
Cast: 1 F, 1 M
Gi60 US 2010, 2014

SHOP ... 'til you drop
By Joan Lunoe
Bronx, NY, USA

Characters

JOHNNY NUBUCK – 1940s film noir detective in the style of Sam Spade
MYSTERIOUS LADY – desperate femme fatale

JN

The name's Johnny Nubuck. I work the lunch hour shift out of the Payless at Broadway and
95th. It was a cold, gray Monday when she walked into the store with all the forced bravado of
a glossy patent kitten heel sling back with bonded leather uppers and an exposed front zipper.

ML

I'm looking for something casual for evening wear in a faux suede upper, peep toe, adjustable
strap with a 4 inch wrapped heel!!
　　(She pulls a gun.)

JN

Easy, angel ...

ML

All right Johnny. I'm givin' you one last chance. Are you going to take these back for a full
refund or are you gonna force me to plug you full of more holes than a year old pair of crocs?

JN

I reached for her gun. We struggled. And as I explained to her that we only accept returns for
store credit, I shut her up by showing her the latest leatherette ankle boot with functional side
zipper direct from our "man" in the Mauritius Islands.

ML

I hate you! I love them! I hate you! I love them! Oh Johnny, why is it I never could resist you
when you give me the boot??

JN

Because precious, it's the stuff that dreams are made of. There are a million shoe stories in the
Naked City. This has been one pair.

END

Category: U
Cast: 2 Gender Neutral
Gi60 UK 2006

THE SHORTEST ZOMBIE PLAY EVER WRITTEN
By Christopher White
Costa Mesa, CA, USA

Setting

Wreckage.

BOB

Jerry! Are you alive!?

JERRY

(hoarsely)
No.

END

Category: U
Cast: 1 F, 1 M
Gi60 UK 2012

SILENCE IS GOLDEN
By Jim MacNerland
Los Angeles, CA, USA

Setting

Park

(A man is sitting waiting for someone. She is late. As he waits, he is saddened and then he begins to relive past slights in his mind, becoming agitated and then angry. He stands up with a huff and then sits down with a sigh. He decides to get up and leaves with determination. As he walks away he sees her and stops. She stands apologetic. He melts. She looks at him wondering whether he'll continue to leave. He smiles and opens his arms. She comes over and they hug. They break and she sighs.)

The woman signs "I'm sorry, I'm late."

He takes a finger, places it over his lips as if to say "Quiet." He signs "I love you."

She smiles and signs "I love you, too."

(They look into each other's eyes and then hug, as the lights fade.)

END

Category: U
Cast Size: 1 F, 1 M
Gi60 US 2012

SOULMATING
By Ivy Vale
New York, NY, USA

Setting

A waiting area.

JENNY

I'm here for the commercial. My agent wouldn't say which website it's for. He thought it
might make me nervous. I'm thinking Google, Facebook, Amazon … a biggy. Do I seem
nervous to you?
        (A man, BEN, is sitting and doesn't look up. He's reading what appears to be a script.
        JENNY leans over to sneak a peek.)

JENNY

Is that for this or …

BEN

Listen, I don't mean to be a jerk or anything, but I'm trying to go over my lines.

JENNY

Sorry. Understood.
        (They both go back to minding their own business. JENNY breaks the silence.)

JENNY

Twitter?

BEN

Soulmating dot com. It's supposed to be the next big online dating site.

JENNY

But they use real couples in those ads. Don't they?

BEN

Let me guess. You're from a small Midwestern town and came to New York to make it in show
business …

JENNY

They're not selling deodorant —they're mating souls. Can't they find two people who have
actually met and liked each other enough to go on TV and say so? Oh my God. I'm depressed
now. Fake couples peddling fake love. I know enough real couples pretending to be happy.
Soulmating. Really? This is why I'm still single.

BEN

I'm Ben, by the way.

END

Category: U
Cast: 1 F, 1 M
Gi60 US 2011

SPYING (VARIATIONS)
By Sara Farrington
Brooklyn, NY, USA

(SPYING led to a full-length play titled MICKEY & SAGE)

Characters
MICKEY, nine-year-old boy
SAGE, nine-year-old girl
(MICKEY and SAGE peer over SAGE's
fence, spying on their neighbor, Mr
Cohen.)
(A moment of dumbstruck silence as
the kids stare out, into the audience,
bewildered by what they're seeing.)

SAGE
Mickey?

MICKEY
Yeah?

SAGE
What's Mr Cohen doing?

MICKEY
Well, Sage, Mr Cohen appears, in fact, to be
... naked ... and ... I guess I'd call that
prancing about his living room.

SAGE
Yeah. That's what I'd call that too.

MICKEY
So I'd say Mr Cohen's either doing that, I
mean, prancing around naked, I mean,
without his typical attire of pleated khakis
and a canary colored polo shirt ... or ... that
Mr Cohen is just ... rehearsing a play.

SAGE
I'm sure he's just rehearsing a play.
(Beat)

SAGE
Mickey?

MICKEY
Yeah?

SAGE
Our Town has a scene like that?

MICKEY
What?

SAGE
Well that's what the community playhouse is
doing this year, Our Town. Granted, I may not
be as familiar with the play as I should be, but
I don't remember a scene where a man
prances around naked.

MICKEY
Oh yeah it's in there.

SAGE
(reassured) Oh.
(Beat)

SAGE
Do you think he knows his curtain's a bit
open?

MICKEY
Doubtful.
(Beat)

MICKEY
For a larger man, he can move.

SAGE
He can.
(The two kids recoil in horror.)

MICKEY
What's he doing now?

SAGE
It appears he's … rubbing his belly against
the TV, his … back … to us.

MICKEY
He must really love TV.

SAGE
(agreeing) Really.
        (Beat)

SAGE
TV –
        (SAGE looks at her watch.)

SAGE
Hey Mickey! It's 4 o'clock! Transformers!
        (MICKEY and SAGE leap off the fence
        and rush off stage, quickly, so they
        don't miss their show.)

END

Category: U
Cast: 1 F, 1 M
Gi60 US 2015

SUDDEN DEATH
By Nancy Brewka-Clark
Beverly, MA, USA

RYAN
(Enters stage left with foil-covered plate)
Hey, babe.

OLIVIA
Ryan, you're late. People will be coming any minute now. I've already fired up the grille. Did you remember the ice?

RYAN
(Hands her plate)
Coach wanted me to work on my slap shot. He thinks I can turn pro.

OLIVIA
You're in a rink. An ice rink. Ice all around you. And you forget to get ice.

RYAN
(Grins)
No I didn't.

OLIVIA
Well, where is it?

RYAN
On the plate.
(OLIVIA rips off foil to reveal a pile of pucks.)
Surprise! Happy birthday!

OLIVIA
(Crumples foil, throws it down)
First you're late. Then, no ice. Now, no hamburgers. Just pucks.

RYAN
(Pointing at plate)
There's ice there, too.

OLIVIA
Were you wearing your helmet?

RYAN
Yes! Just, oh – Olivia – marry me!

OLIVIA
Some proposal! Some birthday!
(Hurls plate, pucks to ground)

RYAN
Olivia, I meant diamonds. Two carats.
(OLIVIA falls to her knees, scrabbling through pucks as RYAN delivers mock play-by-play.)
Icing – offside – delayed penalty –
(OLIVIA triumphantly dons ring.)
And – he scores!

END

Category: U
Cast: 2 M
Gi60 US 2011

SUNSET IN NORTH DAKOTA
By Dwayne Yancey
Fincastle, VA, USA

Setting

Two baseball players are in the dugout during a minor league game somewhere in North Dakota. Both are near the end of their careers. Player ONE is pessimistic; player TWO is optimistic.

ONE

Do you see what I see?

TWO

I dunno. What do you see?

ONE

I see the sun going down.

TWO

Yep. Happens every day. Kinda pretty tonight, though. All red and everything.

ONE

No. I mean this is it. It's over.

TWO

What are you talking about? It's only the fourth inning. We still got time to come back. Only down a few runs.

ONE

Not that. I meant – everything. Everything we've ever worked for. From T-ball to Little League to high school – this is how it ends, doesn't it? Sitting in a dugout in a minor league stadium in the middle of North Dakota watching the sun go down. So this is what it's like – watching the sunset of our careers.

TWO

I think you're just in a slump. You'll break out of it.

ONE

Look out there. Don't you see it? The stadium's practically empty. We're not even in a real farm system anymore. We're out here in some independent league – just hoping against hope somebody will notice – but let's face it – it's over – we're never gonna get to the show.

TWO

So that's what you see, huh?

ONE

Yep.

TWO

You know what I see?

ONE

What's that?

TWO

I see a right field fence that's only 305 feet down the line. That's what I see.
> (TWO puts on his batting helmet, takes a bat and exits; ONE looks at the sunset as the lights fade.)

END

Category: U
Cast: 1 F, 1 M
Gi60 UK 2013

THE THINGS THEY DON'T TELL US
By C.J. Ehrlich
London, UK

Setting
A bus stop in a grey, undisclosed location.
Man and woman stand back to back.

MAN
Pardon me. Do you have the time?

WOMAN
It's four thirty. But my watch has only one
hand.

MAN
What a lovely timepiece. Would you take fifty
groschen?

WOMAN
You're Agent 73? But – but – Wait. Where is
the package?

MAN
Agent 51!? Who knew you were a woman!
The package escaped. Broke out of his bonds,
shot 10 agents, and fled. Our entire cell,
gone! I'm the only one left.

WOMAN
Escape? Months to capture him, smuggle him
over the frontier, loosen him up with a little
torture – well, a lot of torture. And you lost
him. Who pays for this blunder?

MAN
But I have the location of the plutonium!
Unless he lied.

WOMAN
Give it to me. This is terrible! I'm phoning
Minsky now.

MAN
Ay, the things they don't tell us! Wait. Who's
Minsky?

WOMAN
Minsky is the head of my cell.
(She makes a quiet phone call.)

MAN
All this secrecy – unbelievable. We're like
blind mice in a dark maze, snuffling and
running without dignity or cheeses. We're all
phantoms! For what? For the Motherland?

WOMAN
I have some good news and some bad news.
The bad news is (she points a gun at him)
Minsky says to make an example of you.

MAN
What's the good news?

WOMAN
The bus is coming. I can give you a head start.

MAN
That is good news. And the bad news for you
is, I'll be late for dinner, dearest. Very late,
I guess.

WOMAN
Run, darling. See you on the frontier? They
kiss. He runs. She aims.

END

Category: U
Cast: 1 F, 1 M
Gi60 US 2016

UNIVERSAL CONFLICT
By Matthew Konkel
Milwaukee, WI, USA

Setting

Before time. Before space.
    (SHE comes in with her hands cupped tightly, laughing.)

SHE

Yes. Yes. Yes! It's mine. It's mine.
    (HE enters, chasing after her. They are playful and childlike.)

HE

Give it back.

SHE

No way. I've got the universe now and I am not giving it up.

HE

Give. It. Back. The universe is mine.

SHE

Sorry, it's my universe now. You tripped over it.

HE

So? I still found it first. That gives me rights.

SHE

I say the universe belongs to whoever knows how to care for it. You're a reckless klutz.

HE

I'm not a – What's a klutz?
    (HE reaches, SHE eludes. HE falls.)

HE

It needs to be ruled in the proper direction.

SHE

I have no desire to watch you make a fool of yourself.

HE

Please. Please give it back. I must control the universe.
    (SHE laughs.)

SHE

You can't control the universe. You have to let it free.

HE

Let it free? You're crazy! Give me the universe or I'll take it.

SHE

The universe can't be acquired violently.
 (HE approaches her, gingerly.)
It needs nurturing. It needs caution and mutual consideration.
 (His hands are now cupped over hers. SHE smiles and opens her hands. HE tries to take
 the universe but her hands are empty.)

HE

Where is it?! Where is the universe?!
 (SHE points to her lips. They meet for a revolutionary kiss. The universe escapes from
 their lips.)

HE

NO –! What have you done?
 (They watch the universe expand.)

SHE

It's beautiful.

HE

It's horrific.

SHE

It's glorious.

HE

You have no idea what you've done.

SHE

What *we've* done. And neither do you. Doesn't that feel good?

HE

It does.
 (They stare at one another as lights fade to BLACKOUT.)

END

Category: U
Cast: 1 F, 1 M
Gi60 US 2009

THE UNWELCOME MAT
By Stacey Lane
Miamisburg, OH, USA

Setting
A dirty old doormat that reads "Welcome."
A doorstep (a bare stage).
>   (AT RISE, MAT sits center. A large
>   doormat that reads "Welcome" is laid
>   across his lap. HEIDI enters.)

MAT
Welcome! So glad you could come! Make yourself at home! Mi casa es su casa! Please wipe your feet on me.
>   (She does.)
Oh great! Heels!
>   (HEIDI mimes ringing the doorbell.
>   A doorbell chimes.)
So, you're just going to ignore me, huh?

HEIDI
I don't normally talk to doormats.

MAT
Oh. So you think I'm beneath you?

HEIDI
Well, I am standing –

MAT
And you're just going to walk right over me without a second glance?!

HEIDI
Isn't that what you're there for?

MAT
No. I'm here to make you feel welcome. To make you feel appreciated and loved.

HEIDI
Thanks.

MAT
Because he doesn't want to do it himself. He doesn't like you. You've worn out your welcome.

HEIDI
But I've just arrived.

MAT
And he wishes you hadn't.

HEIDI
But he invited me.

MAT
No, you invited yourself and he didn't stop you. Notice, he's not rushing to answer the door.

HEIDI
It's been less than a minute.

MAT
He came a lot quicker when that unbelievably hot girl rang the doorbell late last night.

HEIDI
What? You mean …
>   (HEIDI runs off, crying.)

MAT
You're welcome.

END

Category: U
Cast: 2 Gender Neutral
Gi60 UK 2008

VALE OF TEARS
By M. Rigney Ryan
Queens, NY, USA

MAN
I saw a red-eyed vireo today.

WOMAN
How did the job search go?

MAN
He was building a nest haphazardly on the limb of a tree.

WOMAN
Did you follow up on any of the leads Laura sent you?

MAN
He had some yarn in his beak.

WOMAN
I hope you did because we need the income. Soon.

MAN
The female was nowhere in sight.

WOMAN
I still don't think you realize how dire our situation is.

MAN
He was trusting that she would be there.

WOMAN
If you're not going to be serious about this, I can't stay.

MAN
He continued his feckless effort to make things comfortable in the nest.

WOMAN
Are you even listening to me?

MAN
A storm came in, but the vireo continued his casual pace.

WOMAN
You're just never going to change.

MAN
He was dropping twigs and other nest materials and would go back and retrieve them.

WOMAN
I can't live like this. I can't trust you.

MAN
A gust came and knocked the nest out of the tree.

WOMAN
Goodbye.

MAN
When the vireo fought through the wind only to see his shelter had vanished. He sat. Bewildered.

END

Category: U
Cast: 1 F, 1 M
Gi60 UK 2005

A VOLUME OF SILENCE
By Joe Bryant
London, UK

A MAN and a WOMAN sit next to each other on a sofa, facing the audience. She is leaning into him, and he has an arm around her shoulders in a casual, comfortable embrace. His eyes are closed and he is the picture of contentment. The woman addresses the audience; the man does not hear her.

WOMAN

He looks so ... content. We've been sitting here in silence for a while now and it's such a contrast to his nervous chatter back when this was so new and exciting. But now, look at him; relaxed, secure ... happy.

That's why this is so difficult. I know, now, past the flirting and the giggling, past the blushes and the awkward stares, I know now that he's not my future. The way he looks at the world; I can never be like that.

And we've been sitting like this for a while now. It's a silence begging to be broken, and I know, I KNOW how he's going to break it, and I'm not ready, but this time, for the first time, I don't think I can –

(The MAN opens his eyes and looks at her. She remains facing the audience.)

MAN

I love you.
(She looks at him, for a beat, and then away.)

END

Category: U
Cast: 2 F
Gi60 US 2011

WAVE FAREWELL
By Hugh Cardiff
Dublin, Ireland

Time
1950s, 1960s

Characters
ANNE, BRENDA, females in their twenties.
(Two friends are leaning over a wall,
with their backs to the audience,
watching a friend emigrate by boat, in
the harbour down below. They might
have baskets beside them on the
ground to give an indication of the
period.)

ANNE
Do you think he'll ever be back?

BRENDA
No.

ANNE
Why not?

BRENDA
It's too far. Would you spend four weeks on a
boat coming back to this place?

ANNE
(shrugs) I'd come back if I was homesick.

BRENDA
He'll be homesick now, for the next month or
two. He's not going to be homesick next year.

ANNE
How do you know! You've never been outside
the country.

BRENDA
I'm not saying he'll never come back. (Beat)
He might come back, in 10 or 15 years. With
wife and children (looks at ANNE, laughs).

ANNE
Oh don't say that! (Beat) Do you think he'll
marry an American woman?

BRENDA
I don't know. Maybe he'll send the money for
you.
(ANNE looks at BRENDA for a
moment)

BRENDA
Did you love him?

ANNE
(shrugs) He was alright. Actually, considering
the quality around here, he was pretty good.
(They both laugh.)

BRENDA
So if he offered to send you money for the
boat fare, you wouldn't take it?

ANNE
Ah no, I'm not saying that. I probably would
accept it, but before I'd marry him, I'd have a
good look around New York first, to see what
the talent was like over there.

BRENDA
Well it's bound to be better than this dump.

ANNE
Hey I think he's looking up at us!

BRENDA
No he's too far, he won't be able to make us
out. (ANNE starts waving, then puts her arm
down, as the man didn't wave back.) You see,
I told you.

ANNE
He's as blind as a bat.

BRENDA
But it could be anyone, all the lads are
wearing black jackets. Not a bit of colour
amongst the lot of them.

ANNE
Do you think he'll think of me much?

BRENDA
I don't know. It depends what the talent in
New York is like.
        (She puts her arm around ANNE's
        waist.)
Only joking. You'll be able to tell by the

amount he writes. If he writes every week
you know he's lonely.

ANNE
I hope he writes every week. But I hope he
doesn't expect me to write back. I've got my
own life to lead.

BRENDA
Absolutely. (Pause) Did you love him?

ANNE
(nonchalantly) Ah no, I wouldn't go that
far. It's not as if I'm going to miss him. (Beat)
Well I'll miss him a little, for the first few
weeks. (Excited) Oh look he's waving to us!
        (The two wave, ANNE more
        vigorously than BRENDA.)
You see, I told you he could see us!

END

Category: U
Cast: 2 M
Gi60 US 2012, 2014

WELCOME HOME
By Bill Grabowski
Huntington Station, NY, USA

JOE is outside, with a camera (real or implied), taking photos of his former home, smiling and nodding. MAN (implied inside house – perhaps on top of ladder – implying upper window, sits on top turned away not noticing).

JOE

(Moving slowly, taking photos)

MAN

(Turns, noticing someone taking photos of his house, somewhat upset – lifts up imaginary window with a grunt)
Uh … yo … 'cuse me.
(Motions to him)
Can I help you pal?

JOE

(Fumbling a bit)
Oh. Yeah …. Sorry …. Hi. Just taking a few shots of the house if that's OK. I … um … used to live here. About 40 years ago. Actually was born here – in this house – in that room where you're sitting. Haven't been back to Queens in years. Sorry. Didn't mean to be a …

MAN

(Interrupts)
Hold on. Wait. I'm coming down.
(Climbs down from ladder (house) and moves toward him.)
Sure – no biggie. Just wondering you understand. Kinda spooked me a bit, you understand.

JOE

Of course. That window.
(Points up)
I just found an old family photo of it. Big banner hanging in that window said – "Welcome Home Joe." For my uncle – coming home from WW II. Lived with us – I was named after him. Kinda made me wanna see if I could get here and see the place again. My uncle's still around. It'll mean a lot to him. He's not all there now – but smiles when he talks about the house.

MAN

Ya wanna come inside?

JOE

Oh gee, no. Thanks. Better go. Been here long enough.
(Turns to leave but turns back)

Oh, yeah. Funny. Gotta apologize … for the door.
> (Points to implied front door)

… For some absurd reason my parents took the front door from your house when they moved years ago. Found it buried in the garage after they passed away. Couldn't figure out why. Guess they needed something – to hold as a memory. Funny too. I'm an artist. I made a sculpture with it. So it still lives. I guess they knew I'd need it someday. Forty years later.

MAN

That is funny.
> (Smiling)

I've been through four doors in the last 30 years. None of the darn things seemed to fit right …. There's the answer ….
> (He nods.)

JOE

Thanks again. Gotta run. Gotta get the train back.
> (Starts to walk away at a good pace)

MAN

Hey Joe.
> (JOE doesn't hear – keeps walking.)

Joe!
> (JOE turns back to him.)

Welcome Home!

END

Category: U
Cast: 1 F, 1 M
Gi60 US 2007

WELL BREAD & LOAFING AROUND
By Paddy Gillard-Bentley
Kitchener, ON, Canada

ADAM: Witty, charming man in his twenties.
JULIE: Serious, broody, a comparable age to
fall for him.

Setting
ADAM is behind the counter of some fast
food place or sandwich shop, or bakery. JULIE
enters wearing a nametag from a company.

ADAM
Let me guess … whole wheat. Cream cheese
… (looks at her name tag) … Julie?

JULIE
(frowning and covering her nametag) Rye
with Caraway. Just butter.

ADAM
(like the Dragnet guy) Just the flax, Ma'am.
(She ignores this. He tries again.)

ADAM
Anything else you knead?

JULIE
No. Are you aware that puns are the refuge of
an uninventive mind?

ADAM
No. Are you aware that women who seem a
little crusty are usually sexually frustrated?

JULIE
(stares) Why do you do that?

ADAM
I don't know … I think it's ingrained.
(She groans.)

ADAM
Are you eating here, or shall I baguette for you?

JULIE
I'm taking it with me! You know, you might
try reading something other than the Sunday
funnies. Something like literature.
(He gives her a bag with her order
inside.)

ADAM
Something like literature?
(She gives him money.)

ADAM
Thanks for the dough. Like Shakespeare?

JULIE
(taking her change from him) Exactly like
Shakespeare.
(She begins walking away.)

ADAM
(yelling after her) But soft!
(She stops.)

ADAM
(overtly dramatic) What light rye through
yonder window bakes.
(She turns, shaking her head, trying
not to laugh.)

ADAM
It is the yeast and Julie yet is the pun.
(She cannot help a smirk, and as she
exits.)

ADAM
OH YEAH! She'll be back.

END

Category: U
Cast: 2 M
Gi60 UK 2010

WHAT IS IT GOOD FOR?
By Steve Ansell
Holmfirth, UK

Setting
A war room

SIR
Ah, morning Jenkins, are the men ready?

JENKINS
Yes Sir! Fighting fit and ready for action.

SIR
Right.

JENKINS
Shall I give the order Sir?

SIR
Yes! Er … No.

JENKINS
SIR?

SIR
I was thinking why don't we try something
different this time?

JENKINS
Such as?

SIR
Not fighting.

JENKINS
I'm not with you SIR?

SIR
Well it's always the same isn't it: you get them
ready, I give the order and then we attack.
Then there's that nasty bit in the middle with
the bodies and the crying families. I just
thought maybe we'd do something different
this time.

JENKINS
It would free up some time for my
needlepoint SIR.

SIR
Exactly, so pop over to the enemy, wave a
white flag, and tell them we've surrendered.
(Pause)
Ah, JENKINS, that was fast. Report.

JENKINS
I offered our surrender to the invading horde
as ordered SIR.

SIR
And …

JENKINS
They refused to accept on the grounds that
they have surrendered to us.

SIR
Surrendered to us!

JENKINS
Yes SIR.

SIR
How dare they, we surrendered to them. It's
an outrage! Gather the men, give the order to
attack and show no mercy.

JENKINS
Yes Sir!

END

Category: U
Cast: 2 F
Gi60 US 2014

WINTER COAT
By Hugh Cardiff
Dublin, Ireland

Setting
A woman tries to reclaim her coat from a second-hand charity shop. She enters, holding another jacket in a plastic bag.

WOMAN
(embarrassed) Oh hello. I was just passing … the coat in the window, it hasn't sold?

ASSISTANT
No dear. (smiling) If it was sold it wouldn't be in the window.

WOMAN
It's a very good coat.

ASSISTANT
(looks towards the coat) Yes, Ralph Lauren.

WOMAN
(quietly, to herself) And no-one wanted it.

ASSISTANT
It will sell soon enough.

WOMAN
It's my coat. I donated it a few months ago.

ASSISTANT
Oh really. That was very kind of you, thank you so much.

WOMAN
(Beat) I'd like to have it back.

ASSISTANT
Pardon?

WOMAN
I didn't think I'd need the coat, but now I do. It's a good winter coat. Normally I'd get a new coat … when the new season's stock arrived.

ASSISTANT
(rolling eyes) As you do.

WOMAN
Well, I like … liked to keep up with the fashion, y'know.

ASSISTANT
It looks very warm. Would you like to try it on?

WOMAN
Why would I try it? I know it fits me perfectly.

ASSISTANT
(sarcastic) Oh of course, because it's yours.

WOMAN
May I have it back?

ASSISTANT
We can't be giving clothes away; anyone could come in and say "oh that's my jacket, I need it back." Why did you give it away in the first place? Didn't you know winter was coming?

WOMAN
Yes, I did know … but I wasn't expecting this kind of winter. (Pause. They eye each other up.) I could give you a men's jacket in return. Leather. He forgot to take it.

ASSISTANT
(sigh) OK. We don't normally do this, it's not our policy, but I can see you're determined.

WOMAN
(Beat, nods, sadly) That's what he said too.

END

Category: U
Cast: 1 F, 1 M
Gi60 US 2015

YOU'RE THE ONLY ONE OF YOU I'VE GOT
By Aurora Stewart de Peña
Toronto, ON, Canada

(MICKEY sits and reads.)

MICKEY
You're wearing that?

SAMANTHA
What?

MICKEY
That black dress?

SAMANTHA
Dad.

MICKEY
What?

SAMANTHA
I'm a fully functioning adult.

MICKEY
What's the best low-rate Visa card?

SAMANTHA
I –

MICKEY
Your three-year-old vomits on your boss,
what do you do?

SAMANTHA
Soda water?

MICKEY
Who was president in 1831?

SAMANTHA
Elijah … Florgenson?

MICKEY
Elijah Florgenson. Fully functioning adult,
huh?

SAMANTHA
Dad, I'm just meeting Aiesha for dinner. It's
so tame. And there's nothing wrong with this
dress. I love you, but you don't get to tell me
what to wear.

MICKEY
You're – You look beautiful.

SAMANTHA
Thank you.

MICKEY
But you'll blend right into the night.

SAMANTHA
I'll blend into the night?

MICKEY
(Holding out a roll of fluorescent
protective tape)
Here.
(He unravels some, begins to approach
SAMANTHA with the intention of
covering her black dress in bright
fluorescent tape.)
(SAMANTHA tries to bat him away.)

SAMANTHA
Where did you get that – Oh my god, stop!

MICKEY
What about a white bike helmet?!
I think we've still got one that belonged to
your mom –

SAMANTHA
Oh my god, how old do you think I am?
(MICKEY stops. He looks at
SAMANTHA. He sees her, actually.)

MICKEY
About seven and a half.
(Father and daughter look at each
other. They hug.)

SAMANTHA
I won't stay out too late, okay?

MICKEY
Okay.
(Exit SAMANTHA. MICKEY looks at
where she was.)

MICKEY
(Yelling after her) Text when you get to the
restaurant please!

END

Category: U
Cast:1 F, 1 M
Gi60 UK 2013

ZOMBIE SPEED DATING
By Ron Burch
Los Angeles, CA, USA

Setting

DREW, a zombie, sits at a table. He's ghostly white, with streaks of blood on his face and clothes. His clothes are in tatters. A bell dings, and AMBER, a cute gal with a name tag, hurries over and sits at the table.

AMBER

(speaking quickly) Hi, my name is Amber. I know we have to hurry since this is speed dating, but I always find it hard to collect myself. I'm 29 and I'm a dental hygienist. Which is not what I always wanted to do but sometimes life takes you in funny directions and you end up where you end up. Not that I want to work in dentistry all my life, I mean, it's kind of depressing, looking in wet, dirty mouths all the time, and you'd be surprised how people don't even floss or brush because they're coming to the dentist so they think they can skip it that day. So, anyway, what's your name?

DREW

Uhhhhhhh.

AMBER

Uhhhh what?

DREW

Uhhhhhh.

AMBER

Is that your first name or last name?
		(DREW looks around for a name tag
		and holds it up.)

AMBER

Oh, your name is Drew.

DREW

Uhhhhhhhh.

AMBER

So tell me about yourself, Drew. Are you looking for a serious relationship or just dating? Are you religious? What do you like to do for fun?

Do you work all the time or would you like to spend time with people? Do you have any pets? How do you spend your time?

DREW

Eeeaaaatttt pppeeeeooopppllleee.

AMBER

(still perky) Okay, it was great meeting you.
		(AMBER starts to leave.)

DREW

(sadly to himself) Aaaalllooonnnneee.
		(AMBER sees him and turns back.)

AMBER

When you say eat people, would that include me?

DREW

Noooooooooooooo.

AMBER

Okay, call me.
		(She gives him her number and exits.)

DREW

Scccooorreeeeeee.

END

Category: U   **THREE CHARACTER PLAYS**
Cast: 2 F, 1 M
Gi60 US 2013

ALIEN ABDUCTION
By Thomas J. Misuraca
Tarzana, CA, USA

Characters
ERNIE: forties, truck driver. MARGO: sixties,
waitress. ABIGAIL: thirties, waitress.

Setting
The Little Griddle diner; table and counter.

Time
Morning.
>(LIGHTS UP on ERNIE, at table, reading
>newspaper. MARGO brings his
>breakfast. ABIGAIL, at counter, fills
>catsup.)

ERNIE
Two more alien abductions last night.

MARGO
Were there now, love?

ERNIE
Says there was a drive-by shooting in the city
around 11. Killed two little girls, age 10.

MARGO
That's terrible. My granddaughter's 10.

ERNIE
Little girls should be in bed at 11 o'clock. I'm
sure they were, and aliens beamed them up
through the roof.

MARGO
Did they now, love?

ERNIE
Yeah. But the FBI forces the media to make up
these other stories. Keeps people scared of
humans, not aliens.

MARGO
Can't believe everything you read. I'll get you
a refill.
>(MARGO joins ABIGAIL at the counter.)

ABIGAIL
What conspiracy is he on this morning?

MARGO
Aliens.

ABIGAIL
Illegal or space?

MARGO
Space.

ABIGAIL
Poor guy. He's a sweety, but obviously insane.

MARGO
I dunno. Maybe it's better thinking aliens are
to blame for all the horrors of the world, not
your neighbors.
>(ABIGAIL shrugs. MARGO picks up a
>coffee pot. She returns to ERNIE's table
>and refills his cup.)

MARGO
Tell me more about these alien abductions,
love. (LIGHTS FADE.)

END

Category: U
Cast: 1 F, 2 M, plus Ensemble
Gi60 UK 2014

BMG, BLG, BGGB
(boy meets girl, boy loses girl, boy gets girl back)
By Chris Widney
New York, NY, USA

Setting

AT RISE: A BOY and GIRL enter from opposite sides of an empty stage surrounded by their camps. Eyes meet.

BOY

Glance.

GIRL

Glance.

BOY'S CAMP

(to BOY) Cautionary turn.

GIRL'S CAMP

(to GIRL) Redirection.

BOY

(toward GIRL) Sneaky diversion.

GIRL

(toward BOY) Isolation.
(They use histrionics to distract the camps, then find themselves alone and smitten.)

BOY AND GIRL

Fireworks.

ANTAGONIST

(from girl's camp, entering)
Spoiler!

BOY

Antagonist.

ANTAGONIST

Weighty exposition.
(The rival camps return and square off.)

GIRL

Complications.

BOY'S CAMP

Outrage.

GIRL'S CAMP

Anger.

GIRL

Rising tension.

BOY'S CAMP

Call to arms!

ANTAGONIST

(stepping up to the boy)
Unavoidable conflict requiring clearly decisive act.

BOY

Indecision. Doubt.

GIRL

Disappointment.

ANTAGONIST

(reclaiming the girl)
Triumph.

BOY

… Surprising and inspired flurry!

BOY'S AND GIRL'S CAMPS
Battle! Struggle! Violence! Danger!

ANTAGONIST
(besting the boy)
Impossible odds.

BOY
Miraculous reversal!
(The boy counters and could finish the
ANTAGONIST, but he doesn't; instead
he turns to the camps.) Idealism. Call
for peace and understanding.

GIRL
Renewed and heightened interest.

BOY'S AND GIRL'S CAMPS
(bonding)
Harmony.
(The BOY and GIRL kiss, then everyone
stares dreamily into the distance.)

ALL
Denouement.

END

Category: U
Cast: 1 F, 2 M
Gi60 US 2013, 2014

THE CREDIT CARD APPLICATION
By David MacGregor
Howell, MI, USA

(A YOUNG MAN stands holding an unopened envelope. Behind him stand his MOTHER AND FATHER.)

YOUNG MAN
(To audience) People sometimes ask me why I am the way I am. This is why.
(YOUNG MAN begins opening envelope.)

FATHER
What's that?

YOUNG MAN
It's a credit card application.

FATHER
To you? Who would send you a credit card application?

YOUNG MAN
A credit card company.

MOTHER
It's a credit card company.

FATHER
I know it's a credit card company. But who would send him a credit card application? He doesn't have a job.

MOTHER
They do that these days.

FATHER
It makes no sense. How is somebody with no job going to pay off a credit card?

YOUNG MAN
It's just an application.

FATHER
To you? What the hell are they thinking? How are you supposed to pay it off? Where did they get your name? I mean, there you go. You want to see what's wrong with this country? That's it right there! Somebody sending my son a credit card application!

MOTHER
It's just an application.

FATHER
To somebody who can't pay it off! Oh my God! It's a travesty! It is. A joke. One giant cosmic joke. Somebody sending my son a credit card application. You know what? I give up! I do! What's the point? There is no point in living! Not in this world. JUST SHOOT ME IN THE FACE!!!

YOUNG MAN
(to audience) And that's why I am the way I am.

END

Category: U
Cast: 1 F, 1 M, 1 bus driver
Gi60 US 2015

THE FIRST STEP
By Kat Ramsburg
New York, NY, USA

Setting

A NYC Airporter Bus that has just arrived from Newark and sits underneath Port Authority on 41st.

Time

Pretty much every day in New York.
(The BUS DRIVER haphazardly pulls suitcases from under the bus. CALLIE stands on the last step of the bus before stepping foot in NYC for the first time. NICK scoots around CALLIE in order to exit.)

BUS DRIVER

Lady, get off the bus. Your bag is over here.

CALLIE

Thank you! I'm – It's just – (She goes to take the step but pulls her foot back on to the bus.)

NICK

First time in NYC?

CALLIE

Yes! But I've seen every movie.

NICK

(finds this humorous) Oh … okay.

CALLIE

When I step off this bus, that's it. My first step in New York City. Everything begins.

BUS DRIVER

Come on lady.

NICK

(To the Driver) Give her a second. This is a big deal.

CALLIE

You're making fun of me.

NICK

I wouldn't dare.

CALLIE

I guess I always imagined my first step would be in Times Square. Where are we?

NICK

Underneath Port Authority.

CALLIE

Do you remember your first step in NYC?

NICK

I was born here, so no.

CALLIE

How sad. You never got to dream of living here.

NICK

Sure.

CALLIE

You never got to have your first step!

NICK

I guess not.

CALLIE

I guess it doesn't really matter if it was just going to be here, with all of this pigeon poop.

NICK

NYC is already making you bitter.

CALLIE

Not bitter. Just …

NICK

You know Times Square is just tourists and creepy giant Elmo's with fleas right?

CALLIE

I read that. I refuse to believe it.
    (NICK considers this.)

NICK

Fine. Okay. Come here. Get on.
    (NICK turns and offers CALLIE his back.)

CALLIE

You're serious?

NICK

This city is going to crush your dreams eventually. But I'm not going to let it start today.
    (CALLIE climbs on NICK's back. He grabs the two suitcases with his free hands and begins to slowly walk out of the tunnel.)

END

Category: U
Cast: 2 F, 1 M
Gi60 UK 2012

GRTC
By Irene Ziegler
Richmond, VA, USA

Setting
A train

FEMALE VO
Welcome to GRTC. Please have your GO PASS
ready.
>   (WOMAN sits next to BOY.)

FEMALE VO
The next stop is Cary and Robinson.

BOY
(Imitating the announcer-like tone of
the VO)
"Cary and Robinson."

WOMAN
Which one is your stop?

BOY
None. I don't live on the bus route.

WOMAN
You don't? Where do you get off, then?

BOY
I don't. I just ride it.

WOMAN
Why?

BOY
Because it talks.

WOMAN
Ooooh, you like that it talks.

BOY
Yes ma'am. I like the voice.

WOMAN
It's nice, isn't it? I can't see so good, so I like
it announces the next stop.

BOY
Yes, ma'am. It's my mother.

WOMAN
What's your mother, dear?

BOY
The voice.

WOMAN
You mean it sounds like your mother?

BOY
No ma'am. It's my mother.

WOMAN
The bus is your mother?

BOY
No ma'am. Just the voice.

WOMAN
Oh, I see. Scared me there for a second.

BOY
She's dead.

WOMAN
Who is?

BOY
My mother.

WOMAN
I see. So you —

BOY
Ride the bus. Yes ma'am.

FEMALE VO
Cary and Robinson. Next stop, Belvedere.
I love you, Evan.
(The woman bugs. Did she just hear
that? The BOY smiles at the woman.)

END

Category: U
Cast Size: 1 F, 2 M
Gi60 US 2015

HOLDING ON, HALLOWEEN
By Patrick Gabridge
Brookline, MA, USA

(RANDY at the door in a Halloween costume, with a bag)

RANDY

Trick or treat!
(No response)
Trick or treat!
(GERALD answers the door)
Trick or treat!

GERALD

Hi, Randy.

LINDA
(From inside)
Is that Randy?

RANDY

Trick or treat?

GERALD

It's fine, Linda. I've got it.

LINDA

Close the door. For Christ's sake, it's January.

RANDY

Hi, Gerald. Trick or treat.

LINDA

He's too old, anyway. Tell him Halloween is over and it's freezing outside. Donna is not coming back. Tell him to grow up.

GERALD

So. Uh. Randy. You know, we all miss her.
(RANDY holds up his bag)

RANDY

One more time?
(GERALD takes a piece of candy out of his pocket and puts it in RANDY's bag)

GERALD

Happy Halloween.

RANDY

Thanks. See you tomorrow.
(RANDY exits.)

END

Category: U
Cast: 1 F, 2 M, plus Ensemble
Gi60 UK 2015

THE IMPORTANCE OF MARKET RESEARCH
By Dan Morra
Middletown, PA, USA

Setting
An artist is at an easel painting a picture which the audience cannot see. Three observers are behind him striking thoughtful poses. The artist stands back with an air of finality, then turns to them.

OBSERVER #1
I like it, I really do; but the hair ....

ARTIST
What's wrong with the hair?

OBSERVER #1
(while looking at a hand-held
electronic device)
The color. All our research indicates the public prefers blondes.

ARTIST
But –

OBSERVER #2
Yes, and background is rather mundane. People want more vivid images and vibrant colors.

OBSERVER #1
The clothing is rather non-descript, wouldn't you say?

OBSERVER #3
I agree. It is well done but I don't see it having much commercial appeal, especially in view of her expression.

OBSERVER #2
Yes, yes. The smile isn't really a smile at all.

OBSERVER #1
What do you call this work?

ARTIST
Mona Lisa.
(The observers cringe.)

OBSERVER #3
Not an especially catchy title, is it?
(The artist storms off.)

OBSERVER #2
(to his compatriots)
Temperamental and not responsive to consumer preferences. I'm afraid he'll never be very successful.

END

Category: U
Cast: 2 F, 1 M
Gi60 US 2013

IS JIM DEAD?
By Nancy Brewka-Clark
Beverly, MA, USA

(Set in upscale urban restaurant, AT RISE, JANE, who is JOAN'S literary agent and JIM, JOAN'S publisher, are seated at the table, drinks in front of them, when JOAN stalks in stage left.)

JANE
Ah, here's our favorite mystery writer now.

JIM
(half stands, raises glass)
Good to see you, Joan. Here's to the new book. Love it.
(drinks)

JOAN
(sits)
Then why'd you rip its guts out?

JIM
Think of it as more like liposuction.
(puts down half-full glass)

JANE
Book No. 1 was longer, yes. But No. 17's punchier. I'm your agent, Joanie. Trust me. People think in bytes now.

JOAN
You bite. If it weren't for that series, you'd've starved to death. You, too, Jim. Your publishing career would be dead.

JIM
Hey, the series has been around so long, half your readers are –

JOAN
(points stage right)
Oh, look – isn't that Daniel Radcliffe?

(When JANE and JIM twist around to look, JOAN passes clenched hand over their glasses.)

JANE
(settling back down)
What did you just do?

JOAN
Who, me?

JANE
(As JIM picks up drink)
Don't drink that.

JIM
Why not?

JANE
She's put something in it.

JOAN
(jumps to feet)
Oh, really, this is ridiculous. I write murder novels. I don't actually murder people.
(She stalks toward stage left, turns.)
And No. 17 will top the best seller list. Guaranteed.
(exits stage left)

JIM
(staring at drink)
She wouldn't –

JANE
Of course not.
(as JIM gulps it down)
But if she did, what great PR.
(BLACKOUT)

END

Category: U
Cast: 1 F, 2 M
Gi60 UK 2015

LOVING AND LEAVING
By Matthew Konkel
Milwaukee, WI, USA

Setting
Backyard of a suburban home. AT RISE,
HAROLD and MIKE, two leaves, have just
fallen from their tree. Wind howls throughout
the scene.

HAROLD
Ow.

MIKE
Oof.
    (They shake and quiver in the wind.)

MIKE
Whew. That's quite a fall, huh?

HAROLD
Sure is.

MIKE
Get it? We're leaves and we just like fell from
the tree. Fall.

HAROLD
It's very clever.
    (MIKE laughs as he dances around
    circles, pushed by the wind.)

MIKE
That is some breeze! I love being a leaf!

HAROLD
Come back here. Help me. I gotta get back up
there.
    (MIKE comes back to HAROLD, they
    both shake in place.)

MIKE
Back up? Why?

HAROLD
My wife is still up there.

MIKE
Really? Well, she'll be down eventually.

HAROLD
Not everybody falls. The women are the
strong ones, y'know? Throw me into the
wind. Maybe I can float back up.
    (MIKE tries to throw HAROLD up but
    he floats back down.)

MIKE
It's no good. We are grounded. We can't stay
here, though. The rake. Or worse, the mower.
You don't want that either. Chopped up into
little bits and spit out.
    (They struggle to hold their place in
    the strong wind.)

HAROLD
This is horrible.

MIKE
It's getting windier. Just try and enjoy the
ride.

HAROLD
I can't. I gotta hang on.

MIKE
Suit yourself. Whoaooooa. Ohhhh. I gotta
rustle outta here. I'll see you over by the

fence. Maybe I'll see you in the spring.
(MIKE rolls and shakes out. HAROLD hangs
on to whatever he can.)

HAROLD
Must not let go.
(MAUDE, another leaf, rolls in next to
HAROLD.)

MAUDE
Harold?

HAROLD
Maude. What happened to you?

MAUDE
I must have dropped over there.

HAROLD
Thank goodness we found one another.

MAUDE
I guess this is it then, Harold. What do you
say? One last tumble?

HAROLD
Sure. Why not?
(They embrace and roll out together as
one leaf unit. BLACKOUT.)

END

Category: U
Cast: 3 F
Gi60 US 2015

THE LYE
By Sandra Hosking
Newman Lake, WA, USA

(Three women stand over a casket.)

JANICE
There were many times I wished she were dead.

PATTY
You got your wish.

JANICE
Not like this.

MO
Be careful what you wish for.

JANICE
Every time I asked a question, she'd glare at me like I was an alien from outer space.

PATTY
I got that look a few times.

MO
That's not really a reason to wish someone dead.

JANICE
Then there was the time I saw her at Chili's.

PATTY
What's special about that?

JANICE
With my husband. She was feeding him a fajita.

PATTY
She sat on my Benny's lap.

MO
I tried to get her to sleep with my husband.

PATTY
I guess she had to draw the line somewhere.

JANICE
But that's not the worst of it.

PATTY
No?

JANICE
Poured lye in my tea.

MO
No!

JANICE
On Bridge Tuesday.

PATTY
With everyone around?

JANICE
You girls hadn't arrived yet.

PATTY
She could've killed you! Why didn't you report her?

JANICE
Who would believe it?

MO
What did you do?

JANICE
Switched cups when she wasn't looking.
   (Pause)

PATTY and MO
Oh.
   (They look at the casket.)

END

Category: U
Cast: 1 F, 2 M
Gi60 UK 2013

OTHERWISE DON'T PUT IT THERE
By Vic Allen
Otley, UK

Setting
Two well-dressed men in a room stare up at gun hanging on the wall.

BREZHNEV
(With gravitas) You know what I am thinking? I am thinking that the great Russian writer
Chekhov once said: "If in the first act you have hung a pistol on the wall, then in the following
one it should be fired. Otherwise don't put it there." Do you see the comparison? Here we are
in the first act, and what do we have hanging on "the wall" between our two countries?
Nuclear weapons!

NIXON
Yes. Yes. But you forget that the great AMERICAN writer F. Scott Fitzgerald once said: "There are
no second acts in American lives." And if there's no second act, then the pistol doesn't have to
be fired!

BREZHNEV
(Laughs politely. Then stops suddenly) No. I don't understand. Why is there no second act?

NIXON
(Uncomfortably) Probably because the "pistol" gets fired in the first act …
    (A door opens.)

CO-ORDINATOR
Gentlemen. The Strategic Arms Limitation Talks are ready to begin!

END

Category: U
Cast: 1 F, 2 M
Gi60 US 2013

OUTER SPACE BEATS HOLLYWOOD EVERY TIME
By Corey Pajka
Brooklyn, NY, USA

Characters
ARTHUR: male, twenties
ISAAC: Arthur's friend, twenties
SALLY: Isaac's girlfriend, twenties

Time
Present day. Evening.

Place
ISAAC and SALLY's backyard in the Arizona desert.

Setting
The backyard is suggested only by the placement of a reclining lawn chair at center and maybe a few additional set pieces or props at the discretion of the director. Natural noise is all we hear. The lights should slowly rise to half at the top suggesting dusk or early evening. A small light somewhere suggests a porch light, which is "switched off" by an actor during the play. The setting should seem peaceful and serene, but in a way that could be overlooked if one did not stop to pay attention.
    (Lights rise slowly to half. A young man named ARTHUR is seated in a reclining lawn chair at center stage. He is totally relaxed, sipping a beer, and staring towards the ceiling. He is transfixed by whatever he is looking at. A porch light is switched on somewhere, casting a dim light on the space. ARTHUR is alone for a moment until his friend, ISAAC, enters.)

ISAAC
Hey, Arthur? Arthur?

ARTHUR
Hmm?

ISAAC
We're gonna fire up the movie in a minute. You wanna watch?

ARTHUR
Turn off the light.

ISAAC
Huh?

ARTHUR
The porch light. Turn it off.

ISAAC
Why?

ARTHUR
Come here, and I'll show you.
    (ISAAC turns off the light. It is now almost completely dark on stage, save for the twilight glow on the actors. It is an ethereal sight. ISAAC crosses to ARTHUR.)

ARTHUR
Now look up.

ISAAC
Wow.

ARTHUR
How long have you lived here?

ISAAC
Two years.

ARTHUR
How often do you stop to look at this?

ISAAC
Uh, not very. I guess I take it for granted.

ARTHUR
It's amazing. The light from these stars left them millions upon millions of years ago, and it's just now arriving here for us to enjoy. They go on forever. They'll be here long after we go. A visual extravaganza – and it'll always be here. Outer space beats Hollywood every time.

ISAAC
I'll say.
(A brief pause. After a moment, Arthur's girlfriend, SALLY. enters.)

SALLY
Hey, guys. Do you want to watch the movie?

ISAAC
Hey, honey. Come here and look at this.
(Sally joins ARTHUR and ISAAC. She looks up.)

SALLY
Oh wow …

ISAAC
Wow …

ARTHUR
Wow …
(ARTHUR sips his beer. The three look up in utter fascination as the lights very slowly fade to black.)

END

Category: U
Cast: 1 F, 2 M
Gi60 UK 2007

PANDORA
By Jose A. Rivera
Buffalo, NY, USA

Characters
Pandora
Epimetheus
Boy

Setting
PANDORA is sitting on chair. There is a table in front of her. A golden box is on the table. EPIMETHEUS stands next to her.

EPIMETHEUS
Now I'm going to leave this with you. Don't open it. You got that, whatever you do don't open the box.

PANDORA
Why not?

EPIMETHEUS
Because I said so. Just watch over it. Don't let anyone touch it or open it. Especially you. Got it?

PANDORA
What's in it?

EPIMETHEUS
Don't worry about that, just don't open it.

PANDORA
Yeah but –

EPIMETHEUS
Look, just don't open it.

PANDORA
What's –

EPIMETHEUS
Just don't open the box.

PANDORA
OK but –

EPIMETHEUS
DON'T OPEN IT.

PANDORA
I mean but –

EPIMETHEUS
PANDORA. DON'T EVER OPEN THE BOX.

PANDORA
How long do I have to watch it for?

EPIMETHEUS
Forever.

PANDORA
FORE –

EPIMETHEUS
DON'T OPEN IT!

PANDORA
OK, fine!

EPIMETHEUS
Good. (Begins to leave) Pandora, if you open that box, very bad things are going to happen.
        (Exits)
        (PANDORA sits by herself and looks at the box. She then turns her attention elsewhere. A young BOY enters.)

BOY
Hey! What's in the box?

PANDORA
I don't know.

BOY
Why don't you open it?

PANDORA
OK.

(Opens the box. EPIMETHEUS runs back on stage.)

EPIMETHEUS
Aw come on!!! I said don't open it!!!

END

Category: U
Cast: 3 Gender Neutral
Gi60 UK 2008

SLAM POETRY
By Dwayne Yancey
Fincastle, VA, USA

Setting

A scene reminiscent of a bad wrestling match, First Man is pounding Second Man onto the floor in every conceivable way. Throughout, First Man is reciting poetry – one word – followed by a slam and a grunt – at a time.)

FIRST MAN

Roses – are – red – violets – are – blue – and – in – the – morning – you – will – be – too.
(FIRST MAN slams SECOND MAN on the ground and exults triumphantly. The moderator enters.)

MODERATOR

Uh, thanks for coming out and taking part tonight, guys, but, uh, that's not really what we mean by a poetry slam.

END

Category: U
Cast: 1 F, 2 M
Gi60 US 2007

STAR JASMINE
By Diane Lefer
Los Angeles, CA, USA
(Adapted from Lefer's short story of the same name first published in *In Posse*)

(GREGORY and HEATHER enter on
bicycles. He crosses and almost exits.
She stops her bike and stands beside it.
As the play continues, the lights begin
to fade.)

HEATHER
Gregory, wait! That building! Pacific View. It's
where that man lived.
    (He walks his bike back to her and looks.)

GREGORY
Oh, yeah. "He was a very quiet man. He paid
his rent on time."

HEATHER
"Pacific View." You'd need a telescope on the
roof to see the ocean from here.
    (Enter MAN from direction of Pacific
View apartments.)

MAN
Aren't you people tired of gawking?

GREGORY
We weren't doing anything.
    (They regard each other. Then:)

HEATHER
Did you know the guy?

MAN
I did. And I can tell you, as I once heard a
priest say in a similar context, he was better
than the worst thing he did. (Beat as he
regards them) I can't get you into his

apartment, but if you come in, I can walk
you past his door.

HEATHER
I don't have a morbid curiosity.

MAN
My own apartment has the same layout.
If you'd like.

GREGORY
No thanks.
    (He mounts bike, ready to go.)
    (MAN puts hand on handlebar to
detain him.)

MAN
If you're not here to gawk, take a moment
and appreciate. Star jasmine.

HEATHER
Yeah, smells great.

MAN
Star jasmine and motion sensor lights. I come
home after dark and walk down this street
and it's like a red carpet being rolled out.
I walk along and the lights come on one after
another. Magic. I love it here. I've been here
almost a year. (Beat) When the police came,
I didn't know it was for him.
    (MAN exits back into building but first
he stops, turns, and waves.)

HEATHER
What do you think he did?

GREGORY
What makes you think he did anything?
(Beat) Let's get out of here.
> (Lights are now very dim, fading to
> black.)

HEATHER
Wait. Let's walk. Like he said.
> (She walks her bicycle and as she
> moves, lights go on ahead of her, one
> by one, and one by one they go dark
> behind her. This continues until she
> exits and we go to BLACKOUT.)

END

Category: U
Cast: 1 F, 2 M
Gi60 US 2016

THE STRUGGLE
By Janice Kennedy
Los Angeles, CA, USA

(LIGHTS UP on a table and two chairs in the center of a bare stage. DEATH enters. He's wearing a plaid suit, huge shoes, and a drooping daisy in his lapel. He also sports a bulbous fake nose and is wearing a fuzzy red wig. DEATH is, in short, a clown. He holds up a sign that reads:)

"I AM DEATH"
(He holds up another sign as he mimes a big belly laugh. It reads:)

"I WANNA HOLD YOUR HAND"
(LIFE enters. He's wearing the kind of silken robe boxers wear before a fight. He hops around, jabbing at the air. LIFE takes off his robe and turns around. On his back is a sign that reads:)

"I AM LIFE"
(He gives the audience a "thumbs up." DEATH sits at the table and motions for LIFE to join him. DEATH leans in, puts his elbow in the center of the table, and raises his hand, as an arm wrestler would. DEATH wiggles his fingers at LIFE, who cannot resist. LIFE sits down, places his arm next to DEATH's, and clasps the hand of his foe. From off:)

A VOICE
Begin.
(The struggle is ferocious and the two competitors well met. But, in the end, DEATH forces the hand of LIFE. With a resounding THUD, it is over. DEATH stands, looking at the motionless body of LIFE. He mimes crocodile tears and pulls out another sign. It reads:)

"I ALWAYS WIN"
(DEATH mimes laughing so hard he can hardly stand up. He takes the daisy out of his lapel, throws it on the table, and exits. A voluptuous WOMAN enters carrying a small flowerpot and watering can. She goes to LIFE. The WOMAN puts the drooping daisy in the flowerpot and puts the pot into one of LIFE's outstretched hands. In the other, she places the watering can, then guides that hand as it waters the pot. Miraculously, the withered daisy revives, and with it, LIFE as well. He places the flowerpot in the center of the table as he speaks.)

LIFE
Hope! I thought you'd never get here.
(HOPE smiles and helps LIFE to his feet. He is wobbly, but she steadies him. LIFE exits with HOPE. A light on the flowerpot narrows to a single focused spot before BLACKOUT.)

END

Category: U
Cast: 2 F, 1 M
Gi60 US 2016

TAG
By Mark Harvey Levine
Pasadena, CA, USA

Setting
On the street. ERIN approaches a couple, LAUREL and ANDY. She taps LAUREL hard with her hand.

ERIN
Tag! You're it! Ha!

ANDY
Hey!

ERIN
Twenty-seven years I've been waiting to do that. Twenty. Seven. Years.

ANDY
Who are you?

ERIN
Who am I? I'm it, that's who I am. I'm IT.

LAUREL
I have no idea what you're –

ERIN
Shaffer Elementary School?

LAUREL
Oh my God ... you're ... Erin? Erin Dolan? Wow! How have you been?

ERIN
How have I been? How have I *been*?! I've been it, that's how I've been!

LAUREL
You keep saying that, but I don't –

ERIN
Last day of school. Last day of fifth grade. *Recess?*

ANDY
Are you talking about ... tag?

ERIN
Yes! Tag! On the playground! On the last day of school! I can't believe you don't remember this!

LAUREL
Erin, that was ... a long time ago ...

ERIN
Really? I remember it like it was yesterday. We were playing tag. And you tagged me. Like you always did. And I was "it." Again. Like I always was. And then recess was over. And then school was over. And in middle school I tried to start up the game of tag again. But you said, no, tag was for babies. And I've been "it" for twenty-seven years!

ANDY
... Wow.

ERIN
My whole adult life, I've been "it." It's become the metaphor for my existence. Always reaching out to people, looking for a little touch, a simple connection, chasing after them, and everyone running away from me. Like I'm a pariah. Who has to go to her fifth choice college because all the other ones rejected

her? I'm it! Who has her husband leave her
for an optometrist with a limp? I'm it! Well,
I'm not it any more! You're it now! AND I
CALL NO BACKSIES!

ANDY

"No backsies"?

LAUREL

Apparently I can't tag her right back.

ERIN

Who's this? Your husband? Of course. Of
course. I bet you've had a perfect, wonderful
life. Gorgeous house, beautiful blonde
children.

LAUREL

No, Erin, I haven't had a perfect life. I've had
troubles, like anyone else. And we've just got
a little apartment. But you're right. It is
wonderful. We've got one kid – he's brunette,
actually, if that's okay – and he's great. We've
got a happy life. I grew up, Erin. I left the
playground a long time ago. I made my own
choices. I don't blame anyone for the bad
things that happen in my life. But y'know,
I do thank someone for the good stuff. Andy,
if there's any reason for all the happiness in
my life, well you're it.

(She touches him gently on the
shoulder.)

ANDY

(to ERIN) And it's not too late for you. You're
still young. Grab the reins of your
life. Nothing is holding you back. No school-
yard game has cursed you. You're in charge of
your own destiny. Starting today. Starting right
now. There's only one captain of your
ship. And you're it.

(He touches ERIN gently on the arm.)

LAUREL

Good luck, Erin. I really do wish you all the
best.

(ANDY and LAUREL walk off. ERIN
stands there for a moment and then it
dawns on her what just happened.)

ERIN

NOOOOOO!!!

LAUREL AND ANDY

(as they run off)

NO BACKSIES!

END

Category: U
Cast: 2 F, 1 M
Gi60 UK 2010

THE TANTALIZING GARDENIA
By Tom Carrozza
New York, NY, USA

(RISE on an exterior train platform at midnight. Doggedly entering with suitcases and a glittering sign that reads "The Tantalizing Gardenia" are The Tantalizing Gardenia and her manic sidekick Thumbs, both having seen much better days. Under their coats, a glimpse of their dazzling costumes can be seen. It is both comic and tragic to see them schlepp across the stage apparently defeated. They sit on a bench.)

GARDENIA
I hate to say it, Thumbs, but I think we hit the end of our careers in show business. We ain't the hit we used to be.

THUMBS
Did you see them faces in the first row? Not one smiled. Not one laugh. We might as well have been playing at the morgue.

GARDENIA
I'm kinda scared. The stage is all I know. You take that away and all I am is a very strange lady who thinks she can sing.

THUMBS
You're a star, Gardenia, and don't you forget it.

GARDENIA
Even stars die when they're time is up, Thumbs. I gave my entire life to it, and where has it gotten me? Here, on another train platform speeding out of town in the middle of the night. No, kid. This is it. I know the end when I smell it – and pal, I smell it.

THUMBS
Maybe you're right. My eyes are going. My back too. We're probably just fooling ourselves thinking we're as good as we used to be. Sad, ain't it? After all these years.

GARDENIA
(crumbling a bit) Sure is. We had fun while it lasted, didn't we.

THUMBS
Yep. No one gave 'em what-for like we did.
        (A very plain WOMAN enters wearing a heavy coat and carrying a small suitcase. After a moment, she notices Gardenia and Thumbs, and slowly approaches them and eventually sits down nearby.)

WOMAN

Oh, my word, I don't believe this. You're The Tantalizing Gardenia, aren't you! And you're the guy next to her on the piano, uhh, Thumbs, right? I cannot believe I'm seeing you here again like this, it must be the hand of God. I just saw your show tonight, at The Pickwick, and you were marvelous. To tell you the truth, the other acts didn't do much for me, but you two made my night! I hope you don't mind me saying so. I came to town, you see, to close my sister's house. She passed on last Summer and, well, I'm the only one left to get things done. Had to clear out her house and get it on the market and whatnot, and today was the last of it. It was very sad for me, but it had to be done, and it was, but I wasn't feeling very good at all. And my ticket wasn't for the 12:33 and I had a few hours to kill by myself. And that's when I passed The Pickwick, saw the sign, and went inside. I was sitting way way way up at the top of the balcony, but I'm telling you right now, the minute you two came on stage it was like you were in my lap, ha-haa! You just lit up the place! And I really needed that. Especially today. My, when you slid off your piano stool, I never laughed so hard in my life! And you, with those high notes – absolutely inspirational. What a gift. I always wanted to be a singer, or at least take lessons, but you know how life is. I can't tell you how glad I am to meet you like this, and let you know how talented you both are. Just wonderful. How lucky I am to bump into you like this! ...

(Without turning away from the WOMAN, GARDENIA and THUMBS quietly reach out to each other and hold hands as she rambles. Gardenia wipes a little tear from her eye. They both continue to listen intently.)

END

Category: U
Cast: 1 F, 2 M
Gi60 US 2013, 2014

THE THING THAT RINGS
By Michele Markarian
Cambridge, MA, USA

Setting
Three people are sitting in an office,
headphones on, listening to music, typing.
None of them face each other.
>   (A telephone rings. One by one, they
>   stop typing.)

DEIRDRE
(Taking headphone out of ear)
Dude, is that your music?

JOHN
(Continues typing)

DEIRDRE
I said, Dude, is that your music?

JOHN
(Takes headphone out of ear)
What?

DEIRDRE
That noise. Is that your music?

JOHN
I thought it was yours.
>   (They stare at JIM. JIM stops typing and
>   takes off headphones.)

JIM
What?

JOHN
You hear that?

JIM
What is it?

DEIRDRE
Maybe some kind of fire drill?
>   (THEY get up and start to look around
>   the room. They stop at the phone and
>   stare.)

JIM
It's coming from that thing.

DEIRDRE
Oh my God!

JOHN
What?

DEIRDRE
It's – it's – one of those things you pick up
and someone talks on the other end. Like on
Mad Men.

JOHN
I don't watch it.

JIM
Oh. Yes! I've heard of these!
>   (JIM looks at DEIRDRE.)
Pick it up.

DEIRDRE
What? No way! You pick it up!

JOHN
I'm not touching that thing.
>   (He puts on his headphones and starts
>   typing.)

JIM
You!

DEIRDRE
No, you!

JIM
You!

DEIRDRE
What if someone's on the other end?

JIM
Just do it.

DEIRDRE
What do I say?

JOHN
(Takes off headphones)
Make that thing shut up, will you? I can't hear my music with that ringing!

JIM
Go 'head.
(He points his cell phone at DEIRDRE.)

DEIRDRE
(Picks up phone)
Don Draper's office.

JIM
Cool! (Snaps DEIRDRE'S picture)

JOHN
Who's Don Draper?

DEIRDRE
(Holding phone)
They hung up.

JOHN
Good riddance.

JIM
I know, right? Who uses these things, anyway?
(JIM is pressing buttons into his phone.)

DEIRDRE
What are you doing?

JIM
Posting the shot of you holding that thing.
(He shows her the picture.)

DEIRDRE
Cool! Totally retro!
(DEIRDRE and JIM look at each other and stare.)

JIM
Your eyes. They're blue. I never noticed it before.
(DEIRDRE and JIM hold their gaze.)

JOHN
You're freaking me out.
(The telephone starts to ring again. They break free, and one by one, put their headphones back on, ignoring the phone. All three resume typing and texting as lights fade.)

END

Category: U
Cast: 3 Gender Neutral
Gi60 UK 2014

THREE TREES TALKING
By Dwayne Yancey
Fincastle, VA, USA

Setting
Three trees – or actors with arms outstretched – are in the woods, talking.

TREE ONE
So if you were a human, what kind of human would you be?

TREE TWO
What the hell kind of question is that?

TREE ONE
I don't know. People ask each other – "if you were a tree, what kind of tree would you be?"

TREE TWO
And that's a stupid question, too.

TREE ONE
Really?

TREE TWO
What human wants to be a tree?

TREE ONE
I don't know. But if they did, wouldn't it be interesting to know what kind of tree they wanted to be?

TREE TWO
Not to me.

TREE ONE
Oh. (Pause) Well, I think if I were a human, I'd want to be a travel agent.

TREE TWO
A travel agent?

TREE ONE
Just think – you get to move around. You get to see what's on the other side of that hill. Or the other side of that tree. Or the other side of anything!

TREE TWO

Has somebody been spraying pesticides around here – because you're sure acting like you've sucked up some chemicals in your root system.

TREE ONE

I'm just curious, that's all. Aren't you curious?

TREE TWO

I'm deciduous. That's what I am.

TREE ONE

Or a truck driver. Or a cross country runner. Or – oh, wait, get this – a pilot.

TREE TWO

A pilot?

TREE ONE

So I could fly overhead and look down and see everything. Wouldn't that be something?

TREE TWO

Oh, that'd be something all right.

TREE ONE

I think about a lot of things. What it'd be like to be a basketball player or cowboy – or an astronaut. An astronaut! They really get to travel!

TREE TWO

You are one strange tree.

TREE ONE

(to TREE THREE) What about you? If you were a human, what kind of human would you be?
      (TREE THREE glowers, pauses, then says)

TREE THREE

A lumberjack.

END

Category: U
Cast: 3 F
Gi60 US 2012

TRES SORS
By Helen Huff
New York, NY, USA

Act I
(Three girls/young women sitting in a quilt circle, sewing)

DICTATORIA
Ok, Scaridia Felinina, you take red. Dramatika, you have blue.

SCARIDIA FELININA
Oo, I don't want red! It's too loud and scary.

DRAMATIKA
Oh, I want red! It's so real.

DICTATORIA
No, everyone stays with their color! Now, stop it!

DRAMATIKA
Well, who died and made you Quilt Queen?

DICTATORIA
I'm the oldest, so what I say goes – like it or lump it.
    (Pause)
And watch your stitches. They're uneven.

DRAMATIKA
No, they're not.

DICTATORIA
Yes, they are.

DRAMATIKA
No, they're not.

DICTATORIA
Yes, they are.

SCARIDIA FELININA
Kumbaya, my lord, kumbaya ...
    (BLACKOUT)

Act II
(Three older women sitting in a quilt circle, sewing)

Scene 1
DICTATORIA
You've got chocolate all over the quilt! What is wrong with you?

DRAMATIKA
Out, out damn'd spot!
    (Beat)
Frankly, my dear, I don't give a damn!
    (Beat)
After all, tomorrow is another day!
    (Beat)
Life is like a box of chocolates – and I was looking for the ones with nuts.

DICTATORIA
Nuts?! It's a box of assorted creams! Creams!! CREAMS!!!

SCARIDIA FELININA
Kumbaya, my lord, kumbaya ...

DICTATORIA and DRAMATIKA
Oh, shut up!!
    (Lights dim – LIGHTS UP)

Scene 2
SCARIDIA FELININA
    (Gasp)
A stitch dropped!

(DICTATORIA and DRAMATIKA rush over to SCARIDIA FELININA, feverishly stitch for several seconds, stop.)

SCARIDIA FELININA

There's a hole.

DICTATORIA

Yes, there is. And always will be.
(Lights dim –DICTATORIA and DRAMATIKA return to their spots.)

Act III

(Three old women sitting in a quilt circle, sewing)

Scene 1

SCARIDIA FELININA

Ohhhh, look and see. She's beautiful, isn't she?

DRAMATIKA

Oh, she is – she looks just like you
(Pause)
used to.

DICTATORIA

Look at them all – they're all so beautiful.
(The women take a moment to take in the beauty of their work.)
(Lights dim – LIGHTS UP)

Scene 3

(Three contented women sitting in a quilt circle, sewing)
(Several beats of silence – DICTATORIA freezes in mid-action of raising her thread.)

DICTATORIA

Oh. Well. That's it.
(Beat – DRAMATIKA and SCARIDIA FELININA lean into DICTATORIA and cut her thread.)

END

Category: U
Cast: 2 F, 2 M
Gi60 US 2013

FOUR CHARACTER PLAYS

BORSCHT
By Anthony R. Ponzio
Los Angeles, CA, USA

(GRACE and NICK ENTER. She is fumbling with keys, mail, and work stuff (legal pads, stack of papers, brief case, etc.)

GRACE

Thanks again for letting me in. I'll figure out which keys are which sooner or later.

NICK

No problem, that stupid lock is finicky anyway. But if you need help again, whatever you do, don't ring 1A. (Motions to an apartment door) The old man is, well, a couple sandwiches short of a picnic.
(NICK exits as GRACE is still trying to get herself in order. EARNEST, from apartment 1A, enters, startling GRACE. He is whacking the floor with a broom.)

EARNEST

Get out of here you cats! Stop stealing all my lemons! (Spotting GRACE, dropping the broom) Mary! Oh, Mary, you've come.

GRACE

Um, I'm not Mary. My name is Grace.

EARNEST

Mother made borscht. The beets are as ripe as an autumn sunrise. I wrote you so many letters, but the cats kept licking all my stamps.
(From 1A, EVELYN (EARNEST's wife) enters.)

EVELYN

(Pulling him toward the apartment) Earnest, leave the girl alone please. (To GRACE) Hello dear, welcome to the building.

EARNEST

(To EVELYN) Do you see? Mary's come back. She's here for your borscht.
(He stops at the door.)
Mary, I waited for your letters. Why didn't you write? Was it the cats? (EVELYN takes his shoulder and gently brings him inside.)

EVELYN

Say goodbye Earnest.
(They exit. GRACE is left alone to recover.)

EARNEST

(From inside the door) Look at that cat, it's the size of a pig. Where's my broom?
(GRACE moves to leave but after a moment, picks up the broom and knocks on the door of 1A.)

END

Category: U
Cast: 4 Gender Neutral
Gi60 UK 2013

FOUR
By Ramona Floyd
New York, NY, USA

SPRING

(Skipping or dancing in … youthful and giggling) Bursting, birthing, blossoming. I am Spring
Break-ing in through frozen faces that sit silent and dead-white in too much darkness. …
(continues dancing)

SUMMER

(Slinking or sliding in …) Sssssultry and somnolent, I'm the Summ o' your watermelon
dreams. Hot lips and cool shade melt away the prissy little bulbs, all pale and spent in the
shadow of my skyscraping sunflowers. … (continues dancing)

FALL

(Floating or twirling in …) Blazing back drafts of Charlie brown, red, and orange color-blind
your sorry slip 'n' slide yellow. I'm Falling back to school and into the sweet acrid smell of
smoke and memories. … (continues dancing)

WINTER

(Marching in …) Definite. Infinite. Nite-time stories explain what goes bump and grinds away
faith in the harvest, the sun, and the bloom. In cold contest, I win terms of endearment
whispered as an ice breaker to silence in snow. Huddled and shivering together in darkness,
you forget to kill each other.

SPRING

Aaaand …. we're back. Bursting, birthing, blossoming. (giggling) What else can I do. There are
only four.

END

Category: U
Cast: 1 F, 3 M
Gi60 UK 2007

"J'ADOUBE"
By Vic Allen
Otley, UK

(Three people, dressed in black, stand facing the wings on a chequered stage. A bored woman stands directly in front of a distracted man. The third man is young, handsome, and stands a distance away. He looks apprehensive. A fourth person enters from the direction the three are staring towards. He is wearing white clothes and rides as if on a horse. He "gallops" alongside the isolated person, then turns suddenly and strikes him violently with a sword. The man falls to the floor screaming, but the horseman continues to thrash him. The man and woman standing in line look on impassively. As the assault continues, the woman sighs, pulls out a mirrored compact, and distractedly starts to dab her eyebrow with a moistened finger.)

ROOK
(i.e. the man behind the woman): He's such a drama queen!
(They both look at the "horseman," who is now standing with a leg atop his vanquished foe.)

PAWN
(i.e. the woman in front of the man) Who? Mike?
(Mike, the trampled victim, moans. The "horseman" kicks him again several times.)

ROOK
No – whatsisname, you know, the Knight. He doesn't have to be so theatrical. It's "human chess," not a zombie movie.

PAWN
Well … The audience love it.

ROOK
That doesn't mean that he isn't a prat.

PAWN
Okay, you're right. Dave from accounts IS a prat. But at least he's a horse and not … not … "the king's rook's pawn." I'm sick to death of all the boss's stupid charities. You're okay. You're a castle. You'll be whizzing up and down the board, soon. I'll be stuck here like a lettuce all game.
(MIKE – the "taken pawn" – gets up, unharmed, and walks off stage smiling.)

ROOK
We don't say "horse," we say "knight." And we don't say "castle," we say "rook." (The pawn gives him a threatening look. The rook simpers and hastens to continue.)
But I don't get it? Why did she "take" Mike – I mean the King's Pawn – anyway? It's weakened her whole defense.

PAWN
Oh come on! You can't be that simple!

ROOK
(Looks perplexedly around the board) No. I still don't get it. Why didn't she take the Queen's Knight's Pawn? She's weakened her center … her husband's bound to win the endgame now.

PAWN
Which one is the Queen's Knight's Pawn?

ROOK

Er … Bill from computing.

PAWN

Oh yeh … Fat, bald, sweaty Bill. You really don't get it, do you?

ROOK

(Smugly) Oh, I think it's YOU that doesn't get it. It'll take a while, but the "boss's little wifey" is sure to lose now!

PAWN

God. Men are stupid.

ROOK

No, no, no. That's a typical woman. Acting on impulse without any thought for the consequences.

PAWN

You think so, brainiac? So tell me, what happens to Mike now?

ROOK

Who? Oh, the King's Pawn? Well, he's taken. He's off the board. Surely you understand that?! He has to go and sit in the wife's box for the rest of the game.

PAWN

Yeh? I mean, like "Durr!" (The rook looks uncomprehending.) The wife COULD have taken the thingumybob prawn, namely boring Bill from computing, who's got breath like a fish-eating dog. But instead she took Mike from sales. Young, succulent Mike. Firm as an ironing board. A smart dresser and,

rumour has it, a QUICK dresser too! (The pawn checks her eyebrow again in the mirror.) … I know who I'd prefer to climb into MY box.
(Dave, the "Knight," raises his hand to acknowledge an instruction from his "player" and gallops off stage.)

ROOK

(Watching Dave, preoccupied) Gosh that's deep.

PAWN

Oh you get it now? She's had her eye on Mike for a while, I reckon.

ROOK

(Not hearing her) Yes. The husband's moved Dave to the Queen's Side. That's very subtle.

PAWN

(With a sigh) Subtle, you think?

ROOK

Oh yes. The husband's definitely going to have a mate in the end.

PAWN

I think you'll find it will be exactly the opposite!

ROOK

(Belatedly hears the PAWN's remark and shakes his head pityingly.)
Women! They'll never understand strategy …

END

Category: U
Cast: 4 Gender Neutral
Gi60 US 2015

MAYBE
By Peter Hsieh
San Jose, CA, USA

Characters

JIMMY
MORGAN
ANGEL 1
ANGEL 2

> (Bare stage. Lights come up on JIMMY and MORGAN, music and dream-like ambience plays in the background, two ANGELS fly around them.)

MORGAN

Tall and lanky, with dirty blonde hair and a movie star face.

JIMMY

Red lips, pretty smile, and eyes that are like plasma cannons.
> (Everyone inhales and exhales.)

ANGEL 1

Maybe …

ANGEL 2

… just maybe …
> (Everyone inhales and exhales.)

JIMMY

Would you like to go out to dinner this Tuesday?

MORGAN

Tuesday's perfect. I'll see you then.
> (ANGELS 1 and 2 inhale and exhale. JIMMY and MORGAN sit down on the ground next, facing each other, and have an imaginary conversation as if they were on a date; we can't hear them.)

ANGEL 1

Maybe he'll be the one –

ANGEL 2

– to sweep her off her feet –

ANGEL 1

– like a gust of Neptune wind.

> ANGEL 2

And maybe she'll be the one –

> ANGEL 1

– to rock his world –

> ANGEL 2

– like an anvil dropped from the tallest building.

> ANGEL 1

… and Maybe …

> ANGEL 2

… just maybe …
>> (ANGELS 1 and 2 fly away to the edges of the stage, while JIMMY and MORGAN start to speak.)

> JIMMY

Hey, I had a lot of fun tonight.

> MORGAN

Me too.

> JIMMY

Maybe uh …

> ANGEL 1

And Maybe …

> ANGEL 2

… just maybe …

> MORGAN

Yes?

> JIMMY

Maybe you'd like to do this again sometime.

> MORGAN

I'd love to.
>> (Lights fade as ANGELS 1 and 2 inhale and exhale.)

> END

Category: U
Cast: 2 F, 2 M
Gi60 UK 2008

PIRATE'S DAY
By Rose Burnett Bonczek
Brooklyn, NY, USA

(MATT's room. His sister HANNAH is packing his duffle – he is about to leave for college. HANNAH is doing all the activity. MATT, unsettled, is trying to get her attention.)

HANNAH
There. That's your duffle bag done.

MATT
Oh, thanks. Hannah, will you ...

JASMINE
(entering in pirate garb)
Arrrr! It's Pirate Day!!

MATT
Jaz, not now. Why don't you sit a minute ...

JASMINE
Pirates don't sit, they Arrrgue!! (She runs out.)

HANNAH
Right. I'll call the cab and make sure they're on their way.

MATT
But Hannah ...?
    (She exits; ZACH enters carrying a box.)

ZACH
Oh. Still here? Just wanted to start moving my stuff in.

MATT
What?? Of course I'm bloody well still here. And I'm only off to university, not to the moon ...

ZACH
Don't worry, I'll put all your stuff in the closet. (turns to exit)

MATT
Zach, aren't you even going to ...?

JASMINE
(Entering, swinging a sword)
Arrrr! Take that, and that!

MATT
I don't want to play pirates, I just want to ...

HANNAH
(re-entering)
Cab's about five minutes away. I'll take your duffle out front.

MATT
Stop!!! (They do.) I'm leaving. I'm leaving. Don't you care? Are you going to miss me? Even a little?
    (ZACH, HANNAH, and JAZ look at one another. They go to the box ZACH has brought in, and open it. They remove pirate hats/or eye patches and put them on. JAZ takes out the best pirate hat, and places it on MATT's head. They have prepared for this ceremony. JAZ steps back.)

HANNAH
Your crew is ready, sir!
(ZACH, HANNAH, and JAZ snap a
salute.)

MATT
What ...?

JASMINE
Our captain is our compass.

ZACH
You know, I could be captain for a ...

HANNAH
(elbowing ZACH in the side)
Crew awaiting orders, Captain ... Matt.

(Pause. MATT finally draws himself up,
returns the salute.)

MATT
Your orders are ... set a course for London. As
soon as you can. Will you come at half-term?
Please?

HANNAH, JASMINE, AND ZACH
Aye, aye, Captain!
(He firmly places the hat on his head,
returns the salute, picks up his duffle,
and slings it over his shoulder like a
practiced seaman. Exits.)

END

Category: U
Cast: 2 F, 2 M
Gi60 US 2013

STAGE FRIGHT
By Michael Flanagan
Cortlandt Manor, NY, USA

Setting
JANE is in the kitchen making dinner. She seems annoyed at the whole prospect. She shouldn't have to do this. MATT, her husband, walks in the front door, home from work.

MATT
Honey, I'm home!
   (Drops off his work stuff on the table, sits and starts to take off his shoes.)

JANE
   (As soon as she hears MATT, she pretends to be happy: singing to herself, relaxed – as if she now loves to cook.)

JANE
   (From kitchen)
Hi honey! Welcome home! Dinner will be ready in about five minutes. Will you go up and get the kids?

MATT
   (Mid-shoe-untie)
Uh, sure.
   (Over his shoulder toward upstairs)
KIDS! DINNER!
   (Jane starts from the volume.)

JANE
   (Sarcastic)
Thanks, honey.

MATT
No problem.
   (Puts on his slippers. Ready for dinner, MATT stands up and looks out at the audience. He freezes, eyes wide with horror.)
   (The kids, BEVERLY and CHASE, enter, ready for dinner.)

CHASE AND BEVERLY
Hi Dad!
   (They freeze, staring out at the audience, also in horror.)

BEVERLY
Dad, what's going on?
   (MATT is too terrified to speak.)

JANE
Kids, can you set the table?
   (No answer)
Kids?
   (She turns and enters the living room, carrying her salad bowl, sees everyone frozen in fear.)
What's going on –
   (She looks at the audience, screams, drops salad bowl.)

MATT
Honey, don't move. I think they see us.

JANE
Who ... who are they?

CHASE
Ghosts?

BEVERLY
   (To CHASE)
Ghosts? Are you kidding? The walls are gone!

MATT

Sssh!

BEVERLY

And the ceiling. What are those lights?

CHASE

Were we abducted by aliens?

MATT

Kids, stop it! Everybody, slowly back out of
the room.
(They all back away. They notice the
audience react.)

JANE

(Standing near an audience member,
but backing away)
I think they can see us!
(Audience reacts.)
They definitely can see us!
(She runs backstage, into what would
be another room of the house.)
Matt! It's dark in here!

MATT

In the sun room? Jane?
(No answer)
Jane!
(Runs off stage. The noise of hitting a
wall, dropping something)

CHASE

Oh yeah, definitely aliens.
(To audience)
We come in peace!

(If audience laughs, Chase reacts almost
proudly.)

BEVERLY

Shut up, Chase!

CHASE

You shut up!
(To audience)
Take her first!
(Pushes BEVERLY toward audience. She
screams, runs off. The sound of her
running stops abruptly once she exits.)

(CHASE is alone on stage)

CHASE

Exit family, pursued by boredom!
(Audience laughs. Chase reacts to
laughter.)
My family, man, I tell you. My parents may
look nice, but they really hate each other.
They just express malice gently. I was twelve
years old before I knew that "you ungrateful
bastard" wasn't a compliment! And my sister,
Beverly? Her cell phone tumor is on our
family plan!
(Audience reacts.)
I like you guys.
(Pulls a chair center stage, sits.)
Now take my girlfriend, Please.
(Audience reacts, he stops them.)
No, my girlfriend's name is actually Please.
(Audience laughs.)
But seriously …

END

Category: U
Cast: 1 Hooligan, 1 Scalawag,
    1 Ruffian, and 2 police officers
Gi60 US 2010, 2014

FIVE CHARACTER PLAYS

HOOLIGAN AND SCALAWAG
By Ramona Floyd
New York, NY, USA

(HOOLIGAN and SCALAWAG rush
into the police station.)

HOOLIGAN   SCALAWAG
The jig is up.   Uncle!

HOOLIGAN
(Holding out his wrists for the cuffs)
You got us, copper.

SCALAWAG
(Follows HOOLIGAN's lead)
Throw us up and lock away the key.

SGT O'SARGE
Alright. Take it easy, now. What seems to be
the trouble here?

HOOLIGAN
We're Hooligans!

SCALAWAG
Well, actually I'm a scalawag – he's a
hooligan.

HOOLIGAN
Yeah. And we been on the lam long
enough, see.

SCALAWAG
Yeah. Enough, and that's plenty.

HOOLIGAN
We're ready for the hoosegow.

SCALAWAG
Yeah, we're ready for the big house, the
caboose, the jug, the pen …

HOOLIGAN
(To SCALAWAG)
Aw, shut yer trap.

SCALAWAG
… the can …

HOOLIGAN
(Makes to hit SCALAWAG)

SCALAWAG
    (Pause)
Stir.

SGT O'SARGE
Well now … just what exactly might yer
crime be, then?

HOOLIGAN
I told ya already, Buttons, we're hooligans.

SCALAWAG
Well, actually I'm a scalawag – he's a

HOOLIGAN
Clam up, I say!

SCALAWAG
… hooligan.

SGT O'SARGE
What've ya done to break the law, then?

HOOLIGAN   SGT O'SARGE
(Starts to answer) …   other than bein'
                      hooligans.

SCALAWAG   SGT O'SARGE
(Starts to answer)   … and
                      scalawags.

HOOLIGAN
(Dumbfounded … searching for a crime)
Well, let's see now. Well, there was that dustbin we knocked over last month.

SCALAWAG
Yeah. The dustbin. We just knocked it over … and left it there … didn't pick it up.

SGT O'SARGE
(Had enough)
You're wasting my time. Beat it, will ya.
(At this point two policemen bring in a dangerous criminal to be booked.)

HOOLIGAN
We skipped and ran outside the train station. And, and … we laughed at an ugly girl behind her back.

SCALAWAG
Snickered really.

SGT O'SARGE
(Ignoring them now. To the new criminal)

SCALAWAG
Well now … just what exactly might yer crime be, then?

RUFFIAN
I'm a ruffian.

END

Category: U
Cast: 3 F, 2 M
Gi60 US 2010, 2014

OLD ITALIANS IN LAWN CHAIRS
By Tom Carrozza
New York, NY, USA

Setting
Rise on a yard where five old Italians are sitting in lawn chairs: JOSEPHINE, NELLA, JOHNNY, PHILOMENA, and PIPPO. Birds are chirping.

JOHNNY
ehem.

PIPPO
Huh?

JOSEPHINE
ehem.

PIPPO
Oh.

JOHNNY
Eh?

JOSEPHINE
Oh.

JOHNNY
Oh.

PHILOMENA
Ahh!

PIPPO
Wha?

NELLA
Uhh.

PHILOMENA
Ahh!

JOHNNY
Wha?

JOSEPHINE
Hmm.

PIPPO
Wha? Wha?

NELLA
Ha.

JOSEPHINE
Ha?

NELLA
Uh-huh.

PHILOMENA
Aahh!

JOHNNY
Uhh?

PHILOMENA
Ahh!

PIPPO
Ah.

NELLA
Oh. Ah.

JOSEPHINE
(Sarcastically)
Oh. Ah.
(There is a pause in which all sit and blink for a while. Then …)

JOHNNY

ehem.

PIPPO

Huh?

JOSEPHINE

ehem.

PIPPO

Oh.

JOHNNY

Eh?

JOSEPHINE

Oh.

JOHNNY

Oh.

END

Category: U
Cast: 5 M
Gi60 UK 2016

WE THREE KINGS ON THE ORIENT ARE
By Liam Ashmore and Ellice Price
Leeds, UK

Setting
A train carriage. The Three Kings (CASPER, MELCHIOR, and BALTHAZAR) are sitting talking. There is one other man on stage, hiding his face with a newspaper he is reading. The background sound of a train moving is heard.

CASPER
Well I do say, it is a good job that we took the Orient Express, it would have taken us 12 days if we went with Balthazar's idea of camels. What were you thinking?

BALTHAZAR
I'm sorry, just thought it would have been more fun, plus the tour guide that wanted to sell them to us was a lovely chap.

MELCHIOR
Luckily at this rate we'll be in Bethlehem by Christmas Eve.
 (CASPER and BALTHAZAR look at
 MELCHIOR, confused.)

CASPER
Christmas Eve … What's that?

MELCHIOR
I … Don't … Know ….
 (They all scream in panic.)

BALTHAZAR
And what's this thing we're sat on?

MELCHIOR
I don't know.
 (They all scream in panic.)

CASPER
What's going on?
 (A woman's scream is heard off stage.
 A man in a trench coat enters the stage
 with a fine moustache. POIROT.)

POIROT
There has been a murder, and I have discovered that the suspect was you!
 (In a Belgian accent)
 (Points to the man with the newspaper.
 The man with the newspaper lowers
 the paper.)

THE THREE KINGS
King Herod!!
 (They all scream in panic.)

END

Category: U   **SIX CHARACTER PLAYS**
Cast: 5 Gender Neutral, Ensemble optional
Gi60 UK 2007

ANGRY DANCING
By Bruce Shearer
Melbourne, Australia

Setting
Five people are standing in a small suburban hall. RAWL speaks to the other four.

RAWL
Good afternoon and welcome to Angry Dancing.
I'm so glad you're here and you'll never regret it.
        (The other four shuffle around at this statement and several look toward the door.)
You'll be amazed at what this will open up and release in all of us. This is certainly a special day.
        (RAWL holds out his hand to the four participants.)
I'm Rawl and you are?

HARV
Harv.

LURRA
Lurra.

ESME
Esme.

SLYD
Slyd.

RAWL
It's great to meet you and it's great for you to meet me!
We're going to harness our anger and let it speak through our hands and feet. We're going to
dance into the positive. What are we going to do?

ALL (Slowly)
We're going to dance into the positive.

RAWL
That's right people. Now I want you all to think of a personal issue, something that's been
burning inside you and you just haven't known what to do with it. Have you got something?

ALL
Yeah.

RAWL

Now take those feelings of anger, fury, jealousy, or whatever and start to turn them into dance.
> (RAWL starts to stomp around the hall in a strange dance.)

That pain and anger is the fuel, so let's burn it up. Consume your grief in the movement.
> (Awkwardly the group starts to move, each in a distinct personal kind of way. RAWL
> weaves his way through them shouting encouragement.)

Don't think about it! Dance with your feelings! Let it all blow up and out in the dance!

LURRA

I hate this. My therapist's got no idea.

RAWL

Put it in the dance.

SLYD

I don't want to be here. It's just crap.

RAWL

Use it, use it.

ESME

You're full of it and this is ridiculous.

HARV

That's right you're a weirdo!

RAWL

Are you angry?

ALL (shouting)

You bet we are.

RAWL

Then you're where you ought to be. If you're uncomfortable, awkward, sad, or sorry, let me
see it in the dance. Expel those feelings, dance them into oblivion.
> (LURRA, SLYD, ESME, and HARV are getting caught up in the dance and RAWL is with
> them all the way. He provokes them with his body, silently steaming them up with weird
> and wacky grins and grimaces.)

RAWL

If you never do it again, you'll never forget what happens today. If you're wrapped up in your
issues, let's bid them goodbye. Take my hands. Yes, grab hold of someone, and let's just go for it.
> (LURRA, SLYD, ESME, and HARV awkwardly, along with RAWL, hold hands, and RAWL
> commences an offbeat out-of-step can which is somehow compelling.)

This is Angry Dancing, you've hit it, and we've made it HAPPEN!

END

Category: U
Cast: 5 Gender Neutral
Gi60 UK 2015

TOO MANY HEROES
By David Ley
Leeds, UK

Setting
A villain sneaks on stage, looking all evil and
such. Suddenly, SUPERHERO 1 appears.

SUPERHERO 1
Not so fast, evildoer!

VILLAIN
Not again.

SUPERHERO 1
This time, I will defeat you in the name of ...
(SUPERHERO 2 appears.)

SUPERHERO 2
Stop in the name of justice!

SUPERHERO 1
Whoa, whoa, wait a minute. I've got this
covered, we don't need you here.

SUPERHERO 2
What? But he's my arch enemy!

SUPERHERO 1
No he isn't! He's my nemesis!

VILLAIN
Well, this is awkward.

SUPERHERO 2
Quiet, you.

SUPERHERO 1
Look, I was here first, so ...
(SUPERHERO 3 enters.)

SUPERHERO 3
Never fear! I am here to save the day!

SUPERHERO 1
Oh, come on! How many superheroes are in
this city?

VILLAIN
Look, I'm sure we can come to some kind of
arrangement.

SUPERHERO 2
You stay out of this.
(SUPERHERO 4 appears.)

SUPERHERO 4
I am vengeance! I am justice!

SUPERHERO 2
What are you doing here?

SUPERHERO 3
You aren't even from this city.

SUPERHERO 4
All my villains are in jail. What am I supposed
to do, sit around waiting for them to break
out again?

SUPERHERO 3
It's what the rest of us do!

SUPERHERO 1
OK, fine, we'll team to take this guy down,
but in future we should really organize this
stuff better.

SUPERHERO 2
Actually, I think he's gone.
(They turn and see that the villain has
indeed left.)

SUPERHERO 3
Rude.

END

Category: U
Cast Size: 3 F, 3 M
Gi60 US 2015

THE BENCH
By Olivia Arieti
Torre del Lago, Puccini, Italy

Setting
A garden bench.
> (LARRY and JOE bring in the bench
> and place it in the garden.)

LARRY
Good thing you've come down to give me a
hand, Joe.

JOE
Can't see why you brought it here, Larry,
everyone's so unfriendly in the building.

LARRY
Give folks a chance.

JOE
Too trustful, man.
> (Exits)

> (LARRY sits down, FLORA passes by,
> has grocery bags.)

FLORA
> (Sits down)
Nothing better than a bench to rest on a
sunny spring morning ... I can already see
the daisies all around.

LARRY
> (Looks at the bags)
So you're planning to cook a big meal, huh?

FLORA
Would you like to come up for dinner?

LARRY
With great pleasure, Flora.
> (FLORA, LARRY exit, JENNY arrives,
> sits down, PHIL arrives.)

PHIL
Mind if I sit down, Miss?

JENNY
No, not at all ...

PHIL
Phil Bakers, fifth floor.

JENNY
Jenny Smith, fourth.

PHIL
Thanks to this bench I had the chance to
meet you ... and perhaps, to ask you out this
evening ...

JENNY
Why not?

PHIL
No need to come and pick you up, I'll just
get out of the elevator and ring your bell.

JENNY
> (Laughs)
We're neighbors, aren't we?
> (PHIL and JENNY exit happily. JOE
> arrives, sits on the bench. HELEN arrives.)

HELEN
Where on earth did that bench come from?
> (Sits down)

JOE
Basking in the sun warms up the heart,
Helen. Say, couldn't we try and be good
neighbors instead of fighting all the time?

HELEN

No more TV so loud and stinking butts on my
balcony?

JOE

Promise.

HELEN

(Gets up)

Hum ... Never thought an old bench could
make life easier.

(Exits)

(LARRY passes by with a bunch of
daisies.)

JOE

Hey, Larry, who are those daisies for?

LARRY

For Flora, sixth floor.

JOE

Seems this bench does wonders.

LARRY

You bet. Good benches, good neighbors!

END

Category: U
Cast: 6 plus Ensemble
Gi60 UK 2012

HOLIDAY SEASON
By Bill Grabowski
Huntington Station, NY, USA

Setting
(Five to nine people stand in a separated line implying a crowded subway train. A few stand as
if holding onto the above strap/bar, with briefcases, etc. – one man (Newspaper) sits reading a
paper – all the others stand holding above straps, checking watches, etc.)

(Someone silently counts off so all simultaneously start together to bounce and hum as
if train is moving.)

(After about 10 seconds, all movement stops – implying a subway stop. Off stage
someone yells "Jamaica Station. Two more stops till the end." A NEW man then gets on
and moves between people. As train starts to move again, NEW begins to sing.)

NEW
Jingle Bells. Jingle Bells. Jingle all the way …. Oh what fun it is to ride … (He's interrupted.)

PERSON 1
Yo pal. Whaddya doin'? It's April dude.

NEW
(happily) Yep.

PERSON 2
You OK buddy? Everything OK?

NEW
(Still happily) Yep. Just love Holiday songs. (Sings again) … on a one horse open sleigh – ay!!!
(Quiet for a few seconds, then back to it.) Jingle Bells – Jingle Bells Jingle all the way … Oh
what fun it is to ride Christmas in a one horse open sleigh …
(At this point one of the other passengers looks forward and starts to sing in with him.
"Jingle Bells – Jingle Bells Jingle all the way …" (big finish, slowly).) Quickly then all
the others sing in too, except the guy reading the newspaper. They all sing together
finishing the song, smiling approvingly. The passengers then jostle to show the train has
stopped. "Oh … what … fun … it … is to ride Christmas in a one … horse … open …
sleigh …")
(Matter-of-factly, NEW walks out and away – as it's his train stop. The others look
surprised and sad – as they then start to bounce again, implying the train moving. In a
few seconds, one of them starts to sing:)

PERSON 3
Frosty the snowman is a jolly happy soul …, (now all the others sing – except NEWSPAPER)
with a corn cob pipe and a button nose … (they all get closer together) and two eyes made
out of coal …

(Now NEWSPAPER bolts up, shocking the others, arms outstretched with newspaper, to beautifully sing the final line as a solo – with much feeling.)

NEWSPAPER

"Frosty the snow man
Had to hurry on his way,
But he waved goodbye saying,
'Don't you cry,
I'll be back again some day.' "
        (All others join in.)
"Thumpetty thump thump,
Thumpety thump thump,
Look at Frosty go.
Thumpetty thump thump,
Thumpety thump thump,
Over the hills of snow ..."
        (All the others then freeze for a couple of seconds, then quickly do a group hug.)

("Last stop" is announced off stage.)

(All quickly hug once more and then separate to walk off the train in different directions and back to their lives.)

END

Category: U
Cast: 1 M, 6–10 Gender Neutral
Gi60 US 2009

KAPTAIN KAMOO'S TV FUN HOUSE
By M. Rigney Ryan
Queens, NY, USA

KAPTAIN KAMOO

So instead of the frog being transformed into a handsome, virile prince, the princess was instantly changed into a wizened, toothless hag. Can any of you tell Kaptain Kamoo what the moral of the story is?

CHILD 1

Careful what you wish for?

CHILD 2

Don't judge a book by its cover?

CHILD 3

Never try to rise above your station?

CHILD 4

Amphibians of all kinds are mysteriously disappearing?

CHILD 5

Always wear safety glasses?

KAPTAIN KAMOO

No! No! No! Is it possible that all of you can be that dense? Have all my words been wasted?
    (CHILD 6 timidly raises hand.)

KAPTAIN KAMOO

(irritably) Yes?

CHILD 6

There is no God?

KAPTAIN KAMOO

Ah!

END

Category: U
Cast: 3 F, 3 M, Ensemble
Gi60 US 2012

KING KWIK
By Alex Bernstein
Cranford, NJ, USA

Characters

ISAAC, middle-aged – speaks to the audience, off to the side of the stage.
MARGARET, 60, thin, white-haired, chipper, behind a counter. She speaks to an unseen child.

ISAAC

King Kwik was the greatest store on Earth. It had everything you could possibly need: comics, candy, pizza, 25 cent airplanes, a big spy mirror, and, of course, Icees. But more than anything, King Kwik had Margaret.

(ISAAC speaks to the audience, off to the side of the stage. Lights come up on MARGARET, behind a counter. She speaks to an unseen child.)

MARGARET

Is that candy? Oh, that's a lot of candy.

ISAAC

Margaret was dependable and not at all complicated. At exactly 3:05 pm, hundreds of kids would race the two blocks from school to see who could be first to victimize Margaret.

(A horde of kids, including IZZY and TIM (both 11), come onstage and huddle around the counter, shoving food and items at MARGARET and yelling orders at MARGARET.)

KIDS

Heat my pizza, Margaret! Icee! Icee! I want change! Stop pushing! Take out my pizza! Icee! I dropped a quarter! Where's the bathroom? He hit me, Margaret. I want change! Heat my pizza!

MARGARET

Okay! Settle down! Settle down, honey!

ISAAC

She liked the girls best. Called them "honey."

(She spots a boy in the corner.)

MARGARET

You! Over there! I saw that! Out for a month! I know you, now! Out for a month!

ISAAC

That was her punishment for delinquents. No King Kwik for a month.

(TIM, a tough kid in a white t-shirt, grabs something, sticks it under his shirt, and bumps Izzy. He starts to exit.)

MARGARET

You! Alright! I saw that! Empty your pockets!

(Tim turns, angry and defensive.)

TIM

I din't do nothin'!

MARGARET

Oh yes you did. I saw you in the spy mirror.

TIM

DID NOT! DIN'T DO NOTHIN'!

MARGARET

… Oh! Out! And don't come back for a month!

TIM

Aw, bite me, ya' witch! I"ll come back tomorrow!

(The kids are stunned. TIM storms out.
MARGARET is shocked, hurt. Tears well up
in her eyes and she turns and covers her
face with her apron. All the kids leave but
IZZY. He watches her, compassionately,
and approaches the counter.)

IZZY

C'n I have an Icee?
(MARGARET, shaking, makes the Icee.)

IZZY

Are you okay?
(MARGARET nods. She hands him the
Icee. He pays, starts to leave.)

MARGARET

Those Pop-tarts are 85 cents.
(IZZY stops, frozen. He backs up,
sheepishly, puts the pop-tarts and
change on the counter.)

MARGARET

And I'm sorry, but you can't come in for a
month.
(IZZY runs off, head hung low.)

MARGARET

(Calling after him)
Don't forget your Pop-tarts!

ISAAC

But they'd only have a bitter taste.
(A girl comes in, puts a piece of candy
on the counter. IZZY, off to the side,
presses his face to the glass, watching –
a sad criminal.)

MARGARET

Thirty cents, honey.

END

Category: U
Cast: 7 or more F
Gi60 US 2014

MR & MRS?
By Rachel Avison
York, UK

(A hen party EM (bride to be) and FI (chief hen) are chatting excitedly with female friends in a bar or at a hen party.)

FI
Okay girlies, time for the first game of the night!

FRIENDS
(Share excitement and anticipation)

EM
What have you been up to?

FI
We might have asked Dave a series of questions about his favorite subject – you!
(Pulls out a piece of paper)

EM
Aww bless him.

FI
All you have to do is try to guess his answers, see how well you two know each other.

EM
Ha! You'd think so after three years.

FI
Let's see. First question, nice and easy. We asked Dave, what's your shoe size?

EM
4. I've got tiny feet.

FI
(Looking confused at the answers) He said 6 or 7, never mind, my Gary wouldn't know. Next question.

GIRL 1
We asked, what's your favorite film?

EM
He should've got this one because it's the film we saw together on our first date. "500 Days of Summer."

GIRL 1
His actual words, "Dirty Dancing" or something cheesy.

EM
Oh.

FI
Moving on.

GIRL 2
We asked, what's your favorite place?

EM
Aww. This'll be under the weeping willow in Field Park. We sit there for hours on sunny days.

GIRL 2
(Shakes head, looks uncomfortable)
He said, Oceana nightclub, five shots, five quid?

EM
(Frowns)

GIRL 3
Annoying habit?

EM
(sighs) Worrying? I've made the wrong decision.

GIRL 3
He's made a list (everyone laughs). Interferes in the kitchen. Perfectionist about cleaning. Generally a control freak.

EM
Thanks Dave.

GIRL 4
Your most embarrassing moment?

EM
Probably right here, right now.

FI
Shall we play a different game girls. Pin the tail on the "donkey," truth or dare, I have never?

EM
No, no. Carry on.

GIRL 5
One thing he would save in a fire – after his ego.

EM
It should be me, but I'm going to go for car keys, iPad, or signed ManU t-shirt?

GIRL 5
(Looks at the piece of paper, looks at EM awkwardly and folds the paper away in her pocket.)

END

Category: U
Cast: 3 F, 2 M, 1 Gender Neutral
Gi60 US 2012

WHY BABIES ARE BORN CRYING
By Catherine Clyne
Babylon, NY, USA

Setting
MAN greets WOMAN as she enters. There is a
desk and chair on the set. There is a bell on
the desk and a huge book and there are two
small paperbacks in a drawer.

MAN
(Looking on clipboard) Angelica? (she nods)
Welcome to the new life chosen especially for
you! Are you ready?

WOMAN
(Sits in chair cautiously, he looks
puzzled. She is very nervous.)
Can you go over some of the highlights for
me?

MAN
You know I can't do that. We've been through
this before. The only thing I can go over with
you are the lessons you yourself have chosen
to learn: Patience, Forgiveness, Compassion.
Good for you!

WOMAN
I feel I will be much better prepared if I know
a little more.

MAN
(Thinks a moment) Alright. I'm not supposed
to, though. (Sits at desk and takes out large
book, looks something up. Is obviously
disturbed by what he has read and tries to
gloss over it.) It's the usual, you know.
Dysfunctional family – who doesn't have one,
right? (small uncomfortable laugh), alcoholic
father, two children – take my advice and stop
after the first one – divorce – should have

listened to your mother – then there's the
unfortunate scuba diving incident –
remember: always follow the bubbles – don't
worry, you make it, (then almost inaudibly)
terminal illness.

WOMAN
What was that?

MAN
(Softly, caught) Terminal illness.

WOMAN
(Gets up, panicked) I've changed my mind.

MAN
You can't do that, you signed a contract.
(Produces contract)

WOMAN
Then I demand to speak with my lawyer.

MAN
You've evolved too much. We don't have
lawyers here. You have to go to a much lower
level for that.
(Thinks a moment and takes out a
book and hands it to her)
Here, take this with you.

WOMAN
"Why Bad Things Happen to Good People"?

MAN
(Looks back at large book, thinks a
moment and then takes out another
copy)
Here, better take two.

WOMAN

Okay, I'm getting out of here.
> (She begins to leave, he rings a bell and two women dressed in white enter.)

MAN

(To the women in white) Angelica is a little resistant.
> (The two WOMEN grab her and start to drag her out.)

WOMAN

(Pleading) No, please ….

MAN

Just think, you won't ever have to do this again after you're done.

WOMAN

That's what you said the last time!

A VOICE FROM OFF STAGE

The contractions are getting closer together, make it snappy.
> (Women in white drag her off.)

MAN

(After her) Hey, you forgot your books!
> (Angelica is heard crying "no" as she trails off.)

> (In another part of the stage a doctor enters and speaks to a MAN who is waiting.)

DOCTOR

Well, Steve, it looks like you have yourself a beautiful, healthy baby girl. Want to hold her?
> (STEVE nods and follows doctor off.)
(annoyed) Maybe you can get her to stop crying.

END

Category: U
Cast: Ensemble
Gi60 UK 2012

SIX CHARACTERS + PLAYS

BREATHE
By Steve Ansell
Holmfirth, UK

Setting
The ensemble walk on stage. One cast member has a stop watch.

ACTOR
Okay, I want everybody to take a breath and hold it when I say. Ready, steady, go.
  (The rest of the ensemble also hold their breath. Actor checks the stop watch throughout
  the scene.)
We breathe all the time, day and night, asleep or awake without a single thought. 10 seconds.
We go for long walks to get some country air, we tell children to go outside and get some air
in your lungs. 20 seconds. Just how often do we stop and consider the air we breathe?
  (Two of the ensemble have stopped holding their breath and sit down.)
30 seconds. Carbon emissions, deforestation, pollution, climate change
  (More cast members have now sat down having run out of breath.)
all seemingly distant and disconnected from our daily lives ... until you hold your breath. 50
seconds.
  (Only one cast member remains standing and holding their breath.)
Breathe ...
  (The cast member holding their breath breathes with a great deal of relief.)

END

Category: U
Cast: Ensemble
Gi60 UK 2009

THE COLLECTIVE MEMORY OF HUMANS, BEING
By Helen Elliott
Strood, UK

Setting
Two or three POLITICIANS standing slightly elevated giving a press conference addressing a crowd. Below them, the people, broken down, in various positions showing their submission, e.g. on their knees, prone, prostrated on the ground. Some looking as though their hands are handcuffed behind their backs.

POLITICIAN
(As if we are coming in part way through his speech)
... but we are all working together, striving towards the same goals. And that, (Beat) that is why you must believe me when I say to you, We will solve the problems. Global warming, unemployment, the threat of global terrorism ...
(During this speech, MEMORY appears at the back of the broken-down people; she is standing up tall, completely confident and unbowed.)

MEMORY
Stop.

POLITICIAN
What? Who are you?

MEMORY
I'm MEMORY.

POLITICIAN
MEMORY?

MEMORY
I am MEMORY, your MEMORY, his, hers, and I remember. I remember famine and war, I remember the War to End All Wars,

I remember Passchendaele, Gallipoli, Ypres, the Somme.
(As she speaks she starts walking through the broken people, touches a head or a hand as she passes, "waking them up.")

MAN
I remember 1929, The Wall Street Crash. Hooverville ...

MAN
I remember Hitler Youth ...

MAN
I remember Oswald Mosley, Fascism, The Nazis, The Final Solution ...
(As each MAN is woken he begins speaking and stands and touches the next MAN so that as they wake up a ripple or wave effect happens until at the end, they are all standing facing the POLITICIANS. MEMORY is standing at the back, having started the wave and watched it grow. The lines of speech need to overlap one another but still be distinguishable.)

MAN
I remember Auschwitz ...

MAN
I remember The Blitz ...

MAN
Kristallnacht ...

MAN
Pearl Harbor ...

MAN

Hiroshima and Nagasaki …

MAN

I remember Partition …

MAN

I remember Slavery, Segregation, Jim Crow, Ku Klux Klan …

MAN

Ethnic Cleansing …

MAN

Apartheid …

MAN

Rwanda …

MAN

Cambodian Genocide, Pol Pot, Khmer Rouge …

MAN

I remember Tibet, Human Rights …

MAN

Tiananmen Square, The Dying Rooms …

MAN

The Falklands War, the *Sir Galahad*, the *Belgrano* …

MAN

Vietnam, Korea, The Gulf War, Iraq …

MAN

Guantanamo Bay …

MAN

(This can be more than one voice at a time as they advance on the POLITICIANS.)

Deforestation, Global Warming, Poverty, Drought, Sweat Shops, Pollution, Capitalism, Globalization, Famine, Torture, Refugees, Cash for Questions, Global Recession, Nuclear Proliferation, The Iron Curtain, The Cold War, Shareholders, Multinational Corporations, The Credit Crunch, MPs' Expenses …

ALL

We remember.

MAN

There are more of us than there are of you …

ALL

And We Remember.

MEMORY

Now, tell us we can trust you. Tell us that you're right.

END

Category: U
Cast: Ensemble
Gi60 UK 2009

CONFRONTATION
By Amy Ignatow
Philadelphia, PA, USA

(A VICIOUS ARMY of several thousand enters stage right. They are well armed with knives, swords, scimitars, machine guns, sawn-off shotguns, armored vehicles, and several war elephants. They are full of war-like bluster.)

(ANOTHER VICIOUS ARMY of several thousand enters stage left. They are equally well armed with bows, cannons, AK47s, grenades, rocket launchers, daggers, throwing stars, and lassos, and they are carrying a Stealth Bomber above their heads. They, too, are full of the vim and vigor that precedes total carnage.)

VICIOUS ARMY
(in unison) We see that you have arrived, and now we are going to kill you a lot!

OTHER VICIOUS ARMY
(also in unison) Oh, were only that true, for in fact, today shall be the day of your most certain demise, for it is we who will annihilate you!

VICIOUS ARMY
We will take your sorry lives from this earth with ruthless efficiency!

OTHER VICIOUS ARMY
We will both kill you and disrespect you!!!

VICIOUS ARMY
We can see that we have already caused you to quake in mortal fear!

OTHER VICIOUS ARMY
We laugh at your assertions, as we've just made that one guy pee himself in terror!

THAT ONE GUY
It's not pee, I spilled coffee on myself! And not out of fear! The lid was difficult to close properly.

VICIOUS ARMY
Did you put club soda on it?

OTHER VICIOUS ARMY
The bubbles lift out the stain if you put it on while the coffee is still wet.
(That One Guy shakes his head.)

VICIOUS ARMY
Can we meet you back here in 15 minutes? We have to go to a convenience store.

OTHER VICIOUS ARMY
We'll give you 10.

VICIOUS ARMY
We only need five.

OTHER VICIOUS ARMY
You might as well take 10, there may be a line.

INDIVIDUAL VICIOUS ARMY GUY
And I have to get money from the ATM.
(Both VICIOUS ARMIES exit their respective sides of the stage.)

END

Category: U
Cast: Ensemble
Gi60 UK 2012

DEAL WITH IT
By Ivy Vale
New York, NY, USA

Setting
An adult birthday party. FRIENDS toast BOB, the guest of honor.

GUESTS
Speech, speech!

BOB
Can I just say that I'm touched? I am damn lucky to have such thoughtful, caring friends in my life. I have to be honest with you guys. I was a little depressed about turning 50 – actually, I was dreading it – but it's all good now. So thanks, everyone, for the best birthday a guy could ask for.

FRIEND #1
40 is the new 50, Bob!

FRIEND #2
We love you, Bob!

FRIEND #3
Open the gifts!
      (BOB is handed a gift, which he opens. He holds up a sweater. Guests "ooo" and "ahhh.")

BOB
Looks like a perfect fit, Jane. I love it!
      (FRIEND #4 hands BOB an envelope.)

BOB
I hope it's a check. That would be a perfect fit, too!
      (Laughter. BOB's expression turns to shock.)

BOB
(Reading) *Deal With It – How to Face the Inevitable. We are all going to die, including you …* What is this, some kind of sick joke?

FRIEND #4
You said you wanted to be buried near Mount Rushmore, remember? This cemetery is only 12 miles away.

FRIEND #1
Your plot faces Jefferson, your favorite founding father.

FRIEND #5
It's perfect for you!

FRIEND #2
And we all signed the card.

BOB
You mean this is a group gift? You got together to plan my death? I also said I wanted a leather jacket. You could have all gone in on that. I still have all of my own teeth. I play racquetball.

FRIEND #3
(whispers to FRIEND #2) I'm not telling him about the free coffin.

END

Category: U
Cast: 2 Gender Neutral, Ensemble
Gi60 US 2015

DRILL
By Stephen Kaplan
Bogota, NJ, USA

(A high school classroom. The TEACHER stands before three STUDENTS sitting at their desks taking notes.)

TEACHER

And what's the main theme of Wordsworth's poem? (Beat.) "The things which I have seen I now can see no more"? (Beat.) Anyone? (Beat.) Think what his title –
(A loud beep from the loudspeaker. The VICE-PRINCIPAL's voice is heard.)

VOICE OF VICE-PRINCIPAL

(Matter-of-factly and almost bored)
Ladies and Gentlemen, this is an Active Shooter in Building Drill. Again, this is an Active Shooter in Building Drill. Please lock your doors and turn out your lights.
(The TEACHER, matter-of-factly and almost bored, goes to lock a door and the lights dim as they turn out the lights. The STUDENTS sit up from their desks and move to a corner of the room, where they sit on the floor. They are not scared. They do not goof off. They just follow the instructions, matter-of-factly, almost bored. The TEACHER stands near them. They remain there. They do not make eye contact. They sit. They are thinking of their homework, their after school practice, their prom date, the groceries to pick up after work. They sit and stand.)

VOICE OF VICE-PRINCIPAL

Thank you, ladies and gentlemen. Code Green. Again, this is a Code Green.
(TEACHER turns the lights back on and STUDENTS and TEACHER return to their spots and to their lesson.)

TEACHER

Think about the title of his poem. What are the "things" from childhood "which [you] have seen [but] now can see no more"?

END

Category: U
Cast: 7 Gender Neutral plus Ensemble
Gi60 UK 2012

ENJOY EVERY SANDWICH
(For Warren Zevon)
By Steve Ansell
Holmfirth, UK

Setting
(A group of actors are sat casually on
stage, looking out at the audience.)

THE VISITOR
Excuse me … is this heaven?

PERSON A
It's just through there.

THE VISITOR
Thank you.
(Pause)
Are you all …

PERSON A
Dead? Yes.

THE VISITOR
What's it like?

PERSON A
Calm. Serene … peaceful.

THE VISITOR
Why are you out here?

PERSON A
It's the only place you can see "them."
(PERSON A motions towards the
audience.)
The "living."

THE VISITOR
Do you miss it?

PERSON A
Being alive? Sometimes.

THE VISITOR
What do you miss?

PERSON A
Oh, I don't know … Brunch.

PERSON B
With really great Canadian bacon.

PERSON A
And a cup of hot coffee

PERSON B
… and that first sip of an ice cold beer as it
hits the back of your throat on a hot day.

PERSON C
rain... I miss rain.

PERSON D
And the wind biting your face.

PERSON E
Crying.

PERSON D
The knot in your stomach on a first date.

PERSON F
Kissing.

PERSON A
Fear … joy …

THE VISITOR
I'm not ready for this … I want to go back.
Do you think I can?

PERSON A
Nobody has come to collect you yet?

THE VISITOR
Thank you.
        (THE VISITOR begins to leave.)

PERSON A
Hey!
        (THE VISITOR stops.)

PERSON A
Enjoy every sandwich.

END

Category: U
Cast: 2 Gender Neutral, Ensemble
Gi60 UK 2012

FLYING INTO THE JAWS OF DOOM
By Julian Kaufman
Woodford Green, UK

Setting
A spaceship. Some distant part of the galaxy.
Exploratory mission. In the future, probably.

HARDING
This is it, boys. Hold her steady. Tilt starboard
booster 9 degrees. Enhance pulse laser by
seven microns.

GONDO
Sir.

HARDING
Okay. Take us into the jaws of doom!

GONDO
What?

HARDING
You heard me. Take us into the jaws of doom.

GONDO
That's ridiculous.

HARDING
Is it?

GONDO
It sounds so clichéd – "take us into the jaws
of doom."

HARDING
Well, I'm the captain. It's my job to say things
like that.

GONDO
Well, you could try to be more original.

HARDING
Could I?

GONDO
You could try. It might inspire us. After all,
we're all putting our lives on the line. Risking
all, for the mission. This blasted mission to go
beyond the realm of civilization, to forward
mankind's hungry thirst for knowledge, to
discover new planets, explore the unexplored,
shift paradigms like they have never been
shifted before, to …

HARDING
… fly into the jaws of doom.

GONDO
No, no, no! It just sounds bad.

HARDING
Well, do you think you could do better?

GONDO
I thought I just did!

HARDING
Yes, but that didn't make sense – "forward
mankind's hungry thirst for knowledge"?
I mean, what does that mean?

GONDO
I thought it was quite bold.

HARDING
It's illogical. "Hungry thirst"? Uh?

GONDO
It's oxymoronic.

HARDING
It's moronic.

GONDO
Alright, alright. I'll keep my mouth shut then.

HARDING
Fine. No complaining.

GONDO
None.

HARDING
Then we shall continue. In silence. Happy.

(GONDO nods.)

HARDING
The jaws of doom will simply have to be flown into, without comment. Fine.
(They sulkily fly into the jaws of doom.)

END

Category: U
Cast: 2 Gender Neutral, Ensemble
Gi60 UK 2006

GOLDFISH QUEST FOR DOMINATION
By Zachary Elliott-Hatton
Harrogate, UK

Setting
A Goldfish Bowl. A group of fish listen intently to their leader.

LEADER
Right, men, the time has come to reclaim the land, we will take back what is rightfully ours.

SHOAL OF FISH
Sir! Yes, Sir!

SINGLE FISH
(Breaking away from the main shoal and staring out into the audience)
Ooh! This is new.
(The single fish returns to the shoal.)

LEADER
This is the moment we have been waiting for, the moment every fish knew would come.

SINGLE FISH
(Breaking away again from the main shoal and staring out into the same part of the audience)
Ooh! I've not seen this before.
(The single fish returns to the shoal.)

LEADER
We will fight them on the river beds, we will fight them on the pond weed, we will fight them in the fishmongers.

SHOAL OF FISH
Sir! Yes, Sir!

LEADER
Now! ... How do we get out of this tank?

END

Category: U
Cast: 2 Gender Neutral, Ensemble
Gi60 UK 2009

INVERSE NINJA LAW
By Russ Thorne
York, UK

Setting
Enter grasshopper, SR, on tiptoes, carrying
three dummy boards in the style of that
Subterranean Homesick Blues video. The first
dummy board reads: "HELP." The second
dummy board: "SOME NINJAS ARE AFTER
ME." The third dummy board reads: "I NEED
TO KEEP REALLY, REALLY QUIET OR THEY
WILL CATCH ME AND DO UNSPEAKABLE
THINGS TO MY NETHER PARTS."
        (Enter JACKIE, SL, cheerfully. He sees
        GRASSHOPPER and greets him loudly.)

JACKIE
GRASSHOPPER! Hey, GRASSHOPPER!
        (GRASSHOPPER jumps and rushes to
        him making "shhhh!" noises.)

GRASSHOPPER
No, no, no, no, no!

JACKIE
What?

GRASSHOPPER
Ninjas!

JACKIE
How many?

GRASSHOPPER
What? They are ninjas. NINJAS! There's loads
of them. Loads of Ninjas!

JACKIE
Then we're fine. Inverse ninja law. Stand back
to back.

(They stand back to back. Loads of
ninjas rush on, yelling lustily, and there
is a burst of sort-of kung fu fighting.
The ninjas are a bit rubbish and are
beaten up in seconds by GRASSHOPPER
and JACKIE.)

GRASSHOPPER
What just happened?

JACKIE
Inverse ninja law. The more ninjas there are,
the more rubbish they become. One ninja?
Unstoppable wraith of doom. Ten ninjas?
About as hard as candyfloss. That's why James
Bond can always beat up loads of them just
by swinging his arms a bit.
        (Enter one very small ninja, SR. It
        should be as ridiculously small as
        possible compared with the other
        ninjas. GRASSHOPPER and JACKIE look
        at it with horror. The ninja adopts a
        fighting stance.)

GRASSHOPPER
That's just one tiny ninja.

JACKIE
Yup, we're finished. Run!
        (Exit, pursued by a ninja. The fallen
        ninjas get up and limp off. If there's
        time, one can mutter: "Right, next
        time, I'm being the lone warrior. This
        sucks.")

END

Category: U
Cast: 1 Gender Neutral, Ensemble
Gi60 UK 2011

THE ONE MINUTE, NON-MUSICAL, LA BOHEME FOR ONE OR MORE ACTORS
By Meron Langsner
New York, NY, USA

The one (wo)man, one minute, non-musical La Boheme. Ahem.
> (Modify this line if performed by multiple actors.)

We are bohemian. (Pause) La.

We are the poets! We are the painters! We are the unemployed and very broke.

But still, we are bohemian. (Pause) La.

Who is that? It is the landlord. Is he bohemian? La? No.

Then let us cheat him.

Yes, that would be rather bohemian. La.

I am the landlord. It is time for you bohemians to pay.

Join us in our bohemian celebrations. Landlord, tell us of your womanizing. We are bohemians and valorize such behavior.

I am a great womanizer.

How impressive. But are you not married?

Ah but I am.

We are shocked. We are outraged.

We are bohemian. (Pause) La.

Get out of here you filthy, filthy man. Be gone.

What about rent?

What about your wife? Now be gone.

Is he gone? He is gone. We are so clever.

Yes. Because we are bohemian. (Pause) La.

And now, we come to a café. With bohemians everywhere. (Pause) La.

Who is she? She is beautiful. Is she bohemian? (Pause) La?

She is.

I love you.

I love you.

You are bohemian?

I am. (Pause) La.

La.

Let us have a mad, passionate, ill-fated affair.

Yes, let's. It is very bohemian. (Pause) La.

And now our affair is over. Because you are sick and I am abandoning you.

And I am dating a very rich man instead.

He is not bohemian.

No, but he is Very rich.

And you are still very sick.

I am.

And I still love you.

And I you.

We should get back together. But only until you die.

It would be … bohemian. (Pause) La.

We must now get her medicine.

I am dying.

She is dead.

But I loved her.

And she died, a bohemian. (Pause) La.

And we gather.

As artists. As poets. As thinkers.

As bohemians. La.

With time to mourn.

Because we have no jobs.

We are bohemian. (Pause) La.

END

Category: U
Cast: 7–9 Gender Neutral, Ensemble
Gi60 US 2012

THE PLAY
By Aurora Stewart de Peña
Toronto, ON, Canada

Setting
A row of actors sitting in chairs across the stage. They have programmes in their laps.
>   (The lights dim to BLACKOUT. The audience gasps. The lights fade back up. The audience have shocked, awed expressions on their faces. They begin to clap. JAY turns to JOAN.)

JAY
I thought that was really incredible.

LORI
>   (Sitting on the other side of JOAN)
I'm crying a little bit. Is my make-up running?

JOAN
No, no. It's fine.
>   (LORI begins to smile. She claps very enthusiastically. So do the rest of the audience. She leaps to her feet. So does MACK.)

LORI AND MACK
Whoo-hoo!

JAY
I'm going to stand, too.
>   (JAY stands, so do CHRISTIAN and SABRINA. The audience claps harder.)

CHRISTIAN
That woman with the blonde hair –

SABRINA
She did the choreography, too!

MACK
Oh, my God, I want to marry her!

CRISTINA
>   (Leaping to her feet)
Whoooo!

ADAM
>   (Jumping to his feet to join CRISTINA)
You really loved it, didn't you?

CRISTINA
How could you not?
>   (The whole audience is standing now. They are standing and cheering, smiling and laughing. One person whistles. Everyone except for JOAN. She sits and claps thoughtfully. Holding her programme in her lap. The clapping dies down. The audience files out. LORI and JOAN stay. LORI sits down next to JOAN.)

LORI
You didn't like it?

JOAN
No, I did.
>   (Pause)
I did. Sometimes I just feel so full, and I –

LORI
You want to take it all in.

JOAN
I don't want to let any of it out.

END

Category: U
Cast: Ensemble
Gi60 UK 2015

A LIFE
By Gary Wadley
Louisville, KY, USA

ALL – LINES SPLIT BETWEEN CAST
I am
Born.
I grow.
I cry.
I poop.
I pee.
I eat.
I grow.
I am.
Son.
Daughter.
I learn.
To speak.
To burp.
To fart.
To sing.
To draw.
To dance.
To smile.
To laugh.
To scream.
To tell.
A lie.
To tell.
The truth.

To be.
Silent. (Pause)
To compete.
To trick.
To tease.
To please.
To work.
To hurt.
To love.
To be.
Loved.
I become.
Mother.
Father.
I grow.
Old.
I forget.
I am.
Forgotten.
I am.

ALL TOGETHER

No more.

END

Category: U
Cast: Ensemble
Gi60 UK 2006

BAGGAGE
By Mark Harvey Levine
Pasadena, CA, USA

Setting

A group of suitcases slowly ride around the carousel at baggage claim. Some flop over. Some get claimed and taken off the carousel during the following ...

VARIOUS BAGS

Spare a moment for us. As we slowly ride the carousel. We are the checked luggage. Not important enough to be carried on. Too big to fit in the overhead compartment. Or underneath the seat in front of you.

BLACK BAG

I'm a black bag.

BLACK BAG

I'm a black bag, too.

DUFFEL BAG

I'm a big ol' duffel bag.

VARIOUS BAGS

Waiting to be chosen.
It's like being at a dance.
And we are the blushing ingenues.
Waiting for someone to ask us out on the floor.

BLACK BAG

Black bag.

BLACK BAG

Black bag.

VARIOUS BAGS

We're mostly black bags.

GUITAR

I'm a guitar case, covered with stickers. Aren't I cool? Don't you wish you were the person picking me up? You should have practised more when you were little ...

BOX

I'm a badly taped up box. Did my owner just not care? Have they no pride?

SUITCASE

I'm an unclaimed bag. I've been here for hours. Maybe I'm a bomb! Ha ha, no. I'm just some shirts and socks and stuff. I'm supposed to be in Atlanta. Could somebody please come get me ...? Somebody?

BLACK BAG

Black bag.

BLACK BAG

Black bag.

BLACK BAG

Careful! Many of us look alike.
        (The bags continue to go slowly
        around the carousel.)

FADE OUT

END

Category: U
Cast: Ensemble
Gi60 UK 2011

RU A GHOST?
By Ramona Floyd
New York, NY, USA

Setting
Whole group of people are walking through
a haunted house with a tour guide.

GUIDE
(Holding up a paddle, leading the
group across, then off stage)
Now, through this hallway is the Great Room
where many "strange" things were recorded.
Stay close to the group, now.
(As the group exits, one CHILD slowly
brings up the rear. He/She is a bit
bored and a lot precocious. CHILD
notices a MAN standing off to the
side – he has been standing there all
along, but the others did not see him.
CHILD stops and stares at the MAN. The
MAN stares at the child. Each silently
judges the other and neither speaks for
a full moment.)

CHILD
Are you a ghost?

MAN
Yep.

CHILD
I don't believe in ghosts.

MAN
Fine. I don't believe in children.

CHILD
You're not very scary.

MAN
Boo.

CHILD
Very disappointing.

MAN
Maybe your standards are too high.

CHILD
Is this your house?

MAN
Dunno.

CHILD
Did you die here?

MAN
Dunno.

CHILD
Can you fly?

MAN
Dunno – never tried it.

CHILD
You're not much of a ghost.

MAN
I wasn't much of a man, either.

CHILD
Why don't you try and scare somebody.

MAN
I much prefer disappointing snotty little
children.

CHILD
If I kick you, will you feel it? Would it hurt?

MAN

Dunno. Why don't you give it a try.
(Considering this option. With a satisfied grin, the CHILD gets into position to give a good kick in the shins.)

MAN

You're not afraid?

CHILD

I'm not afraid of you. (Winds up for good stiff kick … BUT maybe it's not such a good idea after all … tries to play it off cool.) Awww, stupid old ghost … you're no fun.

(Child blows off the man and heads toward the same exit as the group … as the child is walking away he/she feels a swift kick in the seat of the pants. Child stops, shocked and stunned … and slowly turns and glares at the man, who hasn't moved.)

CHILD

(Angry and embarrassed) Did you kick me!?

MAN

(Grinning) Dunno.

END

Category: U
Cast: Ensemble
Gi60 UK 2009

SCHOOL OF THOUGHT
By Mark Harvey Levine
Pasadena, CA, USA

Setting
A school of fish is swimming in the ocean.
The fish in front is the LEADER. It speaks:

ONE FISH
I am the leader of this school of fish. The
weight of responsibility lies heavily upon me.
But I bear it, because it is my duty as ...
> (The school of fish changes direction
> en masse, like fish do, and now there is
> a new "front fish," who speaks.)

TWO FISH
A change of leadership was called for. A new
era has dawned. We now move forward,
confident that ...
> (The school changes direction again,
> creating a new leader ...)

RED FISH
I am correcting the mistakes of the previous
administration. We have a tough road ahead,
but our school will ...
> (They change direction again ...)

BLUE FISH
It is time to move back to our traditional,
core values. We are now moving in the right
direction ...
> (They change direction again. It should
> start becoming obvious that they are
> not actually going anywhere.)

BLACK FISH
I have corrected our course! Our badly
misguided leaders have ...
> (They change direction. BLUE FISH is
> in lead again.)

BLUE FISH
I would like to thank the people for their
renewed faith in me, and I promise that ...
> (Change direction.)

OLD FISH
Change is what is needed! Change is ...
> (Change direction.)

NEW FISH
NOW we are finally headed in the right
direction. Now we know where we are going!
> (Change direction. They begin to swim
> off in the same direction they entered.
> As they exit ...)

SAD FISH
I have no idea where we're going. I didn't ask
for this job ...

END

Category: U
Cast: 5 to 17, Gender Neutral
Gi60 US 2007, 2014

SHOEBOX
By Stacey Lane
Miamisburg, OH, USA

Setting

The stage is bare except for an open shoebox center in a pool of light. The actors, there may be as few as two or as many as ten, stand in a line behind the box. Each steps forward into the light, "reads" a greeting card, and then drops it into the box and returns to the back of the procession.

ACTOR #1

There is no gift more precious than the gift of new life. Welcome to the world, baby girl!

ACTOR #2

Ice cream and lollipops and candy kisses too. And a special birthday wish for a girl as sweet as you.

ACTOR #3

May you dream big and then make those dreams come true. Happy Graduation.

ACTOR #4

Make this birthday alcohol free … Get your friends to pay!

ACTOR #5

Congratulations on your new job!

ACTOR #6

You're engaged!? Many cheers to many years!

ACTOR #7

On your wedding day, remember to always cherish each other and not let a single moment pass you by.

ACTOR #8

You never knew there could be such joy. Congratulations on your baby boy!

ACTOR #9

What do you mean you didn't get a birthday card from me? At your age, I'm surprised you even remember who I am. Happy belated.

ACTOR #10

With a mom as great as you, everyday should be Mother's Day!

ACTOR #11

And the World's Greatest Grandma Award goes to … You! Happy Grandparents Day!

ACTOR #12

Now it's your job to sit back, relax, and enjoy this new chapter in your life. Congratulations on your retirement.

ACTOR #13

Your love has stood the test of time and is an inspiration to us all. May it blossom for many more years to come. Happy Anniversary.

ACTOR #14

Get well soon.

ACTOR #15

With deepest sympathy and heartfelt prayers. May your treasured memories comfort you in this time of loss.

> (The next ACTOR closes the lid to the box and all exit, leaving just the shoebox, as the pool of light gets smaller and smaller and then darkness sets in.)

END

Category: U
Cast: 1 Gender Neutral, Ensemble
Gi60 US 2011, 2014

TECH NO LANGUAGE
By Mack Exilus
Brooklyn, NY, USA
(for Rosie)

Note: there should be no dialogue throughout this piece. The main ACTOR should only use non-verbal actions to communicate with the TECH NO LANGUAGE ZOMBIES.

(An ACTOR walks on stage with a map in hand looking about trying to get his/her bearings. The ACTOR sees a group of kids walking sluggishly with portable video games in their hands. The ACTOR then tries to communicate with the kids, but they are so wrapped up in their video games they ignore him/her and continue to move around the space.)

(The ACTOR then sees a couple. They are both on their respective cell phones walking around, zombie like. The ACTOR tries to communicate with them and they too give him/her the cold shoulder. As this is happening, TECH NO LANGUAGE ZOMBIES begin to trickle onto the stage. The stage becomes cluttered with people on cell phones, texting, swiping their fingers on a tablet or iPad, listening to music on their huge headphones.)

(The ACTOR tries to get someone to help with directions. He is moving around the space much faster and with more intensity then the TECH NO LANGUAGE ZOMBIES. The ACTOR then gives up, becoming so frustrated that he/she stomps their foot. The TECH NO LANGUAGE ZOMBIES all turn and look at the ACTOR.)

(One of the TECH NO LANGUAGE ZOMBIES takes the map from the ACTOR and hands him/her a GPS. The ACTOR then goes into a zombie-like state.)

END

Category: U
Cast: 7–20 Gender Neutral
Gi60 US 2010

TREE
By Ramona Floyd
New York, NY, USA

Setting

Two actors center stage (trunk actors) with their arms lifted are joined at each hand with four other actors with their arms lifted. If possible, some of these four actors are joined at the ankle by additional actors. This can be accomplished with all actors lying on the floor to create this pattern or possibly in various seated, standing, or lying combinations. The idea is to create an image of a tree trunk and branches with all actors available. Downstage center of the two "trunk" actors, a single actor sits with legs apart.

BRANCH ACTOR 1
I was a hunter. I dreamed of flying like a leaf on the wind.

BRANCH ACTOR 2
I loved a short man with a wicked smile and a lust for the sea.

BRANCH ACTOR 3
I built the rails that changed many lives. And I loved to dance.

BRANCH ACTOR 4
I was a scoundrel.

BRANCH ACTOR 5
I was a dandy.

BRANCH ACTOR 6
I was a scoundrel and a dandy.

BRANCH ACTOR 7
Never saw the child I gave birth to.

BRANCH ACTOR 8
I could sing – with a voice that made evil men weep.

BRANCH ACTOR 9
I had a simple, uneventful life.

BRANCH ACTOR 10
I took the lives of many and lied to the rest.

BRANCH ACTOR 11

I had 14 children.

BRANCH ACTOR 12

I had a whole town named after me. But it's no longer called that.

BRANCH ACTOR 13

I was a traveling healer.

BRANCH ACTOR 14

I broke my children's hearts.

BRANCH ACTOR 15

I broke my parents' hearts.

BRANCH ACTOR 16

I stood up and faced a mob to help a stranger.

BRANCH ACTOR 17

I collected thimbles.

BRANCH ACTOR 18

I ran a tight ship.

BRANCH ACTOR 19

One day I just disappeared.

BRANCH ACTOR 20

I drank more than I should have.

TRUNK ACTOR 1

I taught.

TRUNK ACTOR 2

I learned.

SINGLE ACTOR

I work my way up
    (Glances back at the others)
Until I am just another leaf flying on the wind.

END

Category: U
Cast: Ensemble
Gi60 UK 2010

TWEET SORROW
By Jim MacNerland
Los Angeles, CA, USA

(This should be performed as Performance Art, like in the early sixties. Broad and mime like. Very theatrical, very "Symbolic," and have performers who are able to bend their bodies in ways that would make a Cirque du Soleil performer jealous. The readers should see this as sort of a Beat Poem.)

SINGLE PERFORMER
The

WHOLE GROUP
Tweet

SINGLE PERFORMER
Came

THREE OR FOUR PERFORMERS
Silent

WHOLE GROUP
As a hawk.
(All the performers grab their hearts. All but one performer do an exaggerated baseball pitch: arm way back, one leg up in the air, they pitch and stomp their foot on the ground on the word "Smashed." All moves by the group are big and exaggerated.)

SINGLE PERFORMER
Pink iPhone

WHOLE GROUP
Smashed

SINGLE PERFORMER
On the wall.
(The next four words are said by four groups of three or four people.)

GROUP 1
Pieces

GROUP 2
Drop

GROUP 3
Like

GROUP 4
Tears.

GROUP 1
I am anger!

GROUP 2
I am hate!

GROUP 3
I am vengeful!

SINGLE PERFORMER
One hundred

SINGLE PERFORMER
Forty

WHOLE GROUP
Characters

SINGLE PERFORMER
Is not

WHOLE GROUP

Enough
> (The group mimes picking up the
> shattered cell phone as if it were a
> baby bird.)

SINGLE PERFORMER

But now

WHOLE GROUP

Is too much.
> (They slowly walk away sadly.
> Lights dim.)

END

ADULT THEMES
GENRE "A"

Category: A
Cast: 1 M
Gi60 US 2008

A BULLET FOR EVERY BRAIN
By John Weagly
Chicago, IL, USA

(LIGHTS UP. STERLING addresses the audience.)

STERLING

My mind is a gun.
I walk down the street in the city. I look at people and shoot them with my mind.
> (He points his finger in a random direction.)

The guy in the hybrid car parked in the middle of the crosswalk.
Bang!
> (He points his finger in another random direction.)

The woman talking on her cell phone so loud that I can hear her a block away.
Bang!
> (He points his finger in another random direction.)

The homeless man that won't stop following me, asking me for the money I've earned.
Bang!
I shoot them all. In my head they all fall down.
Once I get home, I sit on the couch and stop thinking.
My mind reloads.
It's the same street every day.

END

Category: A
Cast: 1 F, 1 M
Gi60 US 2009, 2014

CONVERSATION
By Jay Nickerson
New York, NY, USA

Setting

A middle-aged couple, HE and SHE, sits reading. Think Geoffrey Palmer and Judi Dench.

HE

Observation.

SHE

Question?

HE

Observation again.

SHE

Acknowledgment.
    (Pause)

HE

Related observation.

SHE

Sarcastic reply.

HE

Injured self-justification.

SHE

Placating concession.
    (Pause)

HE

Immature, defensive self-justification.

SHE

Typical wise feminine rejoinder.
    (Pause)

HE

Request for affirmation of undamaged virility.

SHE

Tender, though somewhat disingenuous, affirmation.

HE

Somewhat pathetic attempt to claim limited victory.

SHE

Polite threat of continuing contention.
    (Pause)

HE

Grumbling acceptance of lower status.
    (Pause)

SHE

Unexpected proposition of sexual activity.

HE

Feigned lukewarm interest, followed by request for clarification.

SHE

Reminder that proposition has an early expiration.

HE

Expression of genuine interest, masked by George Clooney joke.

SHE

Reminder of history of disinterest in George Clooney.

HE

Same joke without George Clooney. Substituting Benedict Cumberbatch.
    (SHE stands.)

SHE

Direct offer of sex.
    (SHE exits. He rises to follow.)

HE

Mediocre mandatory exit punchline! Throw-away reference to Benedict Cumberbatch.
    (HE exits.)

END

Category: A
Cast: 2 M
Gi60 US 2013

DIAMONDS ARE FOREVER
By Patrick Gabridge
Brookline, MA, USA

(MARK sits in some seats at Fenway Park, looking very cold. SAM, a cop, walks over to MARK.)

SAM
Hey, buddy. Game's over. Time to go home.

MARK
I'm trying to make the moment last.

SAM
It's January. Ballpark's closed. The players are all home and clean shaven.

MARK
I can still hear the crowd. I can still see Uehara thrusting his glove into the air.

SAM
Yeah. Still gives me chills.

MARK
Makes me feel all warm inside.

SAM
Well, it ain't warm out here. Look, you can't stay.

MARK
It's the one place where things make sense. Balls are fair or foul, the runner is safe or out.

SAM
Unless a jack-off ump calls interference.

MARK
It was in the rules. Bad call, but it was right. Out there, people blow up crowds at the Marathon, bosses lay off people by the hundreds. Maybe a guy's wife says she's leaving him. His kids say they hate him. I don't know what the rules are anymore. Maybe nothing makes sense.

SAM
Except right here.

MARK
I can still hear the crack of the ball off Victorino's bat.

SAM
Yeah.
(SAM sits next to MARK and looks out over the field.)

END

Category: A
Cast: 2 M
Gi60 US 2013

FISHING FOR MEN
By Dwayne Yancey
Fincastle, VA, USA

(A brooding man sits by a stream, staring into the water. A sunny angler approaches him.)

SUNNY
Catching anything today?

BROODER
Not fishing.

SUNNY
(Confused)
Oh. What you doing then?

BROODER
Looking in the water.

SUNNY
Oh. Whatcha see? Minnows? Crawdads? You know, I hear there's a great spot down around the bend a ways —

BROODER
The devil's in that water.

SUNNY
The devil? He goes fishing?

BROODER
They're having a baptism upstream.

SUNNY
Oh. So it ought to be Jesus in the water then.

BROODER
Upstream maybe. But down here, it's the devil.

SUNNY
I don't follow.

BROODER
They say baptism washes away your sins, right?

SUNNY
Yeah —

BROODER
So ever wonder where they go?

SUNNY
I don't know. Away.

BROODER
Downstream.

SUNNY
Downstream?

BROODER
Look down there. What do you see?

SUNNY
Umm. Water. Rocks. Why?

BROODER
You know what I see?

SUNNY
What?

BROODER
I see all the sins of mankind flowing right past us.

SUNNY

Really? You see that?

BROODER

Don't believe me? Lean down a little closer.
Get a better look.

SUNNY
(Bending down to the water)
Like this?

BROODER

Exactly.
(BROODER pushes SUNNY'S head
under the water.)

SUNNY
(Trying to resist being drowned)
Hey!

BROODER
(Holding SUNNY under water)
Get a good look, boy. A good long look.
(SUNNY goes limp from drowning.)
I told you I saw the devil in that water.

END

Category: A
Cast: 1 F, 1 M
Gi60 US 2007

GOD AND MY MOTHER
By Michael Burdick
Linden, NJ, USA

BELLA
You know why we've managed to stay together all these years?

VINCENZO
Booze and the absolute certainty that things could be worse.

BELLA
It's because of God and my mother.

VINCENZO
One reigns in heaven and the other ...

BELLA
Watch it ...

VINCENZO
In Jersey.

BELLA
My mamma used to say, "Bella, you marry a man, you marry the whole man. You have to deal with a lot."

VINCENZO
My mother used to say, "Women destroy a man's balls deep down." She said, "You wanna keep your balls, Vinnie, never let a woman catch 'em once."

BELLA
I hate your mother.

VINCENZO
I hate all women.

BELLA
Including me?

VINCENZO
Most the time.

BELLA
Then, why stay?

VINCENZO
Cause you're the best I could get.

BELLA
I could have done better.

END

Category: A
Cast: 1 F, 1 M
Gi60 UK 2011

HERE THEN GONE
By Amy L. Bernstein
Baltimore, MD, USA

Setting
A bare stage. MAN and WOMAN, dressed all in black, stand shoulder to shoulder, facing the audience.
    (MAN and WOMAN emit primal birth screams simultaneously.)

MAN AND WOMAN
Waaahhheeeeeaaawwwwooooowww!!!

MAN
Mmmm, sucking, sucking –

WOMAN
Sucking, so good, whoops, too fast –
    (MAN and WOMAN belch loudly.)

MAN AND WOMAN
Ahh, better.
    (Speaking together)

MAN	WOMAN
Ma-ma!	Da-da!

MAN
The round circle goes in the square hole.

WOMAN
Red, yellow, blue, green.

MAN
Look, I'm Superman! I'm going to save the world! Ta-da!

WOMAN
I'm going to be a doctor. Or maybe a TV news lady.

MAN
Pass it to me! I'm open! Pass the ball!

WOMAN
Don't be mean!

MAN
Play fair!

WOMAN
I look terrible in this!

MAN
Hey, cut me some slack!

WOMAN
You don't know everything and I don't have to listen to you!

MAN
I'm outta here, and I'm never coming back!

WOMAN
Oh, God, I'm so shit-faced.

MAN
Give me the keys. I'll drive. I'm sober enough.

MAN AND WOMAN
I don't want to go to this stupid party.
    (MAN and WOMAN turn to face one another.)

MAN
Hello. Pretty lame party, huh?

WOMAN
Yeah, I didn't want to come.

MAN
Me, neither. Wanna get outta here?

WOMAN
Let's go.

MAN
I love –

WOMAN
– you.

MAN
Well, I'm under pressure, too!

WOMAN
Think about somebody else, for a change!

MAN
Thirty years with the same damn company
and nothing to show for it!

WOMAN
I want to go to Paris.

MAN
I'm going to the pub.

WOMAN
I'm going to Paris.

MAN
My legs hurt.

WOMAN
What? I can't hear you.
    (MAN and WOMAN turn back toward
    audience, shoulder to shoulder.)

MAN
I can't remember –

WOMAN
Who?

MAN
It doesn't matter.

WOMAN
I need to lie down.

MAN
Now it makes sense.

WOMAN
Too late.
    (MAN and WOMAN emit primal death
    sighs.)

MAN AND WOMAN
Ahhhhhh.

END

Category: A
Cast: 1 F, 1 M
Gi60 US 2011, 2014

ILLNESS
By Jim MacNerland
Los Angeles, CA, USA

Setting
A man is sitting near a table with a bottle of pills on it. The woman is standing as if about to leave.

MAN
I don't want you to leave. I'm sorry, okay? I'll take my medication.
(Beat)
I'll always take my medication.
(She picks up the bottle and moves it toward him.)

MAN
No. Not until you say you'll stay.

WOMAN
I don't want to be alone … in this, anymore.

MAN
What are you talking about? I'm here. I'm here every day.

WOMAN
So am I.

MAN
I know that.

WOMAN
But, I don't know that. You don't do things for us.

MAN
Do what? Take the medicine? It's my medicine. I take the medicine. That doesn't make any sense.

(She turns and walks away.)

MAN
Where the hell you going? I need you.
(She continues to the door.)

WOMAN
I wanted you to need us.

MAN
I don't know what the hell that means.

WOMAN
(Resigned)
I know.
(She moves further away.)

MAN
Fine. I'll take your stupid medicine. There. You got what you wanted.

WOMAN
No. I didn't.

MAN
I did that for you.
(She exits. As the lights fade, the man yells angrily, and throws the bottle across the stage. He stops, looks at the door, spits the pill he had taken into his hand and puts it on the table. He looks at the door and exits.)

END

Category: A
Cast: 1 F, 1 M
Gi60 US 2016

IT'S NOT WHAT YOU THINK
By Jay Nickerson
New York, NY, USA

(A man and a woman sit across from one another at a table in a restaurant.)

HE
I'm sorry to cut you off, but I need to say something to you so, can I just say it?

SHE
Um, sure.

HE
I love you.

SHE
(Surprised) Oh.

HE
I know it's only been a few weeks and, I mean, we haven't even slept together, but I really … I've fallen for you. I'm completely in love with you.

SHE
(She takes his hands.) I don't know what to say. The weeks we've spent together have been the most wonderful I can remember. But …

HE
What, you have a shady past, we all have indiscretions, mistakes …

SHE
(A pause) I have a penis.

HE
What?

SHE
I'm a pre-op transgender woman who used to be a man.

HE
Oh. (He stands up. He sits down in his chair. He stands up again. He sits down.)

SHE
Look, I know this is difficult for you …

HE
No, it's just … I'm crazy about you. Everything is so much better when we're together. It's just that … are you going to get rid of it?

SHE
What?

HE
The … penis.

SHE
Well …

HE
I mean, I wouldn't know what to do with it.

SHE
With what?

HE
A penis.

SHE
Well, what do you do with yours?

HE
Good point.

SHE
Look, if this is too much for you …

HE
No. I meant it when I said I love you.

SHE
You're a lovely man. But let's take this slow.
(Pause) So, what don't I know about you?

HE
(A real confession) I have a Back to the Future
tattoo on my inner thigh.

SHE
The DeLorean?

HE
Marty's mom.

SHE
(She takes his hands.)
We're even.

END

Category: A
Cast: 1 F, 1 M
Gi60 UK 2006

MISTAH
By Sean Burn
Newcastle-Upon-Tyne, UK

(A MAN, nervous, approaches a young
WOMAN on the street.)

MAN
What do you want?

WOMAN
Thirty.
        (Pause)
Mister .... I said thirty.

MAN
Fifteen.

WOMAN
Fuck off.

MAN
Twenty then.

WOMAN
Twenty-five.

MAN
You better be good.

WOMAN
Best you'll ever have.

MAN
You're my first.

WOMAN
You'll love me ... I swear.

MAN
How old are you?

WOMAN
How young do you want?
        (Pause)

MAN
What choices do I have?

WOMAN
Anything you want for thirty.
        (They exit together.)

END

Category: A
Cast: 1 F, 1 M
Gi60 US 2009, 2014

MOMENT BEFORE IMPACT
By Ruben Carbajal
Los Angeles, CA, USA

(The horrible screeching of tires. SHE (early forties), frozen in an expression of terror. HE (mid-forties), seated next to her, pantomimes a steering wheel, carefree expression. Lighting change. HE loses the steering wheel. They address the audience directly: their delivery should be impassive, pleasant but clinical.)

SHE

Moment before impact: I'm helpless to react.

HE

(Almost jolly)
I never know what hit me.

SHE

He was my best friend's husband. The one rash act of my life.

HE

(Almost proud)
Ruining one marriage while consummating the next: tricky.

SHE

Terrorism. Poverty. Shark Attacks. Outliving our son. Balding.

HE

Things She Worried About.
    (Beat)
Impotence. The new VP of Sales. Being Bad Father. Balding.

SHE

Things He Worried About.

HE

My whole life I'm told I'm capable of great things. I bask in my potential and accomplish nothing.

SHE

I work hard. Nose to grindstone. T's crossed, I's dotted. I'm rarely, and mildly, acknowledged.

HE
>(Gingerly)
I slept with interns.

SHE
Things He Thinks I Don't Know.
>(Beat)
I'd trade him in to have my best friend back.

HE
Things She Thinks I Don't Know. Final score: 2 Marriages, 2 Children, 3 Continents, 17 Lovers.

SHE
Two Children?

HE
Things He or She Didn't Know.

SHE
Oh.

HE
>(Musing)
What a mess.

SHE
>(Correcting)
What a lovely mess. I'll miss it. If it's possible to miss anything now.

HE
>(Cheerfully)
Probably not.
>(THEY hold hands. Stare into each other's eyes.)

SHE
>(To the audience)
This is a dramatic conceit. When it happens, we don't actually hold hands.

HE
>(To the audience)
There is no time for that.
>(Lighting change. Sound of screeching tires. SHE, frozen in an expression of terror. HE, holds the steering wheel, joyfully oblivious.)

END

Category: A
Cast Size: 1 F, 1 M
Gi60 US 2005, 2014

MONDAY IN C MINOR
By Lauren Feldman
Miami, FL, USA

Setting
HE is sitting, finishing his coffee before
work. SHE enters in a frenzy. We can hear
Beethoven's *Symphony No. 5 in C Minor,* "allegro
con brio," underscoring and driving the
dialogue, which is spoken in time with
the music.

SHE
Can't find my keys.
Can't find my keys.
I tried the desk, I tried my coat, I checked
the car.

HE
How 'bout the floor, how 'bout the bath,
how 'bout the bar?

SHE
I checked the bar.

HE
Oh yeah?

SHE
I checked the tub.

HE
Okay ...

SHE
My meeting starts. At. EIGHT.

HE
It's quarter of.

SHE
I hate my job, I hate my boss, I hate my life –

HE
It's not that bad.

SHE
I hate my hair –

HE
I like your hair –

SHE
I hate my shoes.

HE
You're like your Dad.

SHE
Can I take your car?

HE
You think I'm crazy?

SHE
But I'll be late.

HE
And so will I.

SHE
Your boss won't care.

HE
My boss would die.

SHE
Please Honey please.

HE
Oh Love don't cry.

We'll find your keys, let's look around, they must be here, I'll check the ground.

SHE

I'll call a cab, I'll be dead meat, I just looked there, please lift your feet.

HE

I'm sure they're here, retrace your steps, were you upstairs?

SHE

I am a mess.
All Mondays suck.
Oh Shit Oh Fuck.

HE

I think I found … Your …

SHE

Keys!

(She kisses him. The music fades out.)

END

Category: A
Cast: 2 M
Gi60 US 2010, 2014

NOT EXPECTING THAT
By Arthur M. Jolly
Marina del Rey, CA, USA

(STEVE staggers on and collapses on a
seat next to BOB.)

STEVE
They don't tell you about the shit. They didn't
tell me. Anyone tell you?

BOB
No. No one told me.

STEVE
Can't face it either, huh? … Her water breaking, sure. Hey – I can handle water. Mucus
plug? Okay. Disgusting, but okay. I've seen her
snot into a hanky a coupla times. She gets the
flu – I'm right there. Makin' her soup, pickin'
up the used Kleenex off the floor. You handle,
right? That's part of being a – that's part of – I
mean, right? Part of it.

BOB
Yeah.

STEVE
Blood, sweat and tears? Breathe: whoo whoo
whoo, give her an ice chip. No one told me
about the shit! He says push – she pushes,
boom! Like the Hindenberg was filled with
sewage. They could warn a guy! Give him –
you know – a heads up would be nice. …
Know what the worst part is?

BOB
I can't imagine.

STEVE
I'm not in there. This is meant to be like –
you know. I'm out here. We're out here.
Sitting out here, we can't face them. Can't go
in there and deal with our own wives. Can't,
can ya?

BOB
Can't what?

STEVE
Go in there. Deal with her.

BOB
No. No, I can't.

STEVE
Exactly! Does that make us cowards? Does
that make us bad husbands?
    (Beat)
Still … It's all worth it in the end, right? You
go through all the shit, but at the end, it's all
worth it. Cause you have a – you know … a
new life. Right?

BOB
    (Agonized)
No. Not always.
    (STEVE looks at BOB. BOB looks back at
    the door, but can't make himself get up.
    A long moment.)

END

Category: A
Cast: 1 F, 1 M
Gi60 US 2016

SO WHAT'S HARD ABOUT CONSENT?
By Jo Muswell
London, UK

(Couple are in bed, cuddled up close, watching the news.)

MALE
It's lucky that he got off. God, something like that could ruin his career and his life.

FEMALE
What are you on about? What about her life and career? If he did it, he should pay.

MALE
Yeah, no I know. That's not what I meant. Of course if he did it he should pay, but what if it was a publicity stunt on her part? We don't know what happened.
    (FEMALE pulls away a little but remains holding him.)

FEMALE
Exactly. We don't know what happened. The only people who know are the two of them, regardless of how the judge ruled.

MALE
I only meant that she should have to prove it before she ruins his life. Innocent until proven guilty, right?

FEMALE
    (While pulling away to lie next to him, facing him but no physical contact)
I'm not saying false accusations don't exist but you have no idea how hard it is to prove. I know so many people who have been sexually assaulted, and how many of us make it to a guilty verdict? None.

MALE
Well obviously it would be difficult to come forward –

FEMALE
Yes, it would be. And let's say you did come forward, you have police telling you maybe it's too hard for you to recount the worst day of your life to strangers and not even get a conviction. We all know how low the conviction rate is. Innocent until proven guilty … right?

MALE
But consent is hard, right? Maybe it wasn't clear to him that she didn't want it.

FEMALE

If I, at any point, said no and told you to stop, would you continue?

MALE

No!

FEMALE

(Sits up.) And if you were kissing me and I was stone cold and wouldn't kiss you back, or touch you, or look at you. Would you continue?

MALE

Of course not, no one would.

FEMALE

So what's hard about consent?
      (As MALE talks, FEMALE rolls feet away to sit on the side of the bed, facing away
      from him.)

MALE

I see what you're saying. I just meant that it could have been a stunt, playing the victim and all
.... Are you OK, babe?

FEMALE

(Massages face with hands and stands and walks away, never turning back to MALE.)
Yeah, fine. Do you want tea? I'll go put the kettle on.

END

Category: A
Cast: 2 M
Gi60 US 2007

STATING THE OBVIOUS
By Meron Langsner
New York, NY, USA

(DARREN stands in front of a hospital bed. ARTHUR lies in the bed. DARREN alternates between addressing ARTHUR and addressing the audience.)

DARREN
A lot of people are asking if I am OK. The answer is no. I am not OK, and I haven't really been OK since this all started years ago. But certain things help me get by. Yesterday a business partner of my father's says, "Arthur, this is a very difficult question I know, but what would you like me to do if you die?"

ARTHUR
Come to the funeral.

DARREN
And you say you wonder about my sense of humor.
     (Turns to ARTHUR)
Listen, we fought for a long time over my choice of career. I know this was because you worried about me. I want you to know that I am in sight of major success; you don't have to worry about me anymore. We don't have to fight anymore.

ARTHUR
This makes me very happy. You don't know how happy this makes me. I want you to know, I enjoyed most of your plays.

DARREN
Some very wise people stated the obvious to me recently. They said to say the things I need to say now. That I have time. That I should say them while he can hear them. He implied once about a year ago that he did not expect to live to see me finish my doctorate. Of course he also said outright that he was surprised to have lasted as long as he has. I insist on believing that he can beat it.

ARTHUR
Darren. I am a miracle.

DARREN
Tell me sir. Why are you a miracle?

ARTHUR
The doctors, they told me a month ago that I had a week to live. I am still here. Look at me being a miracle.

DARREN

This is very impressive. And for your next trick?

ARTHUR

You think this is a time for jokes? I am very sick.
 (Pause)
You know, it has been a long time since anyone did that trick with the Red Sea. Maybe they will make another movie. Maybe you will write it.

DARREN

 (With humor)
You think this is a time for jokes?

ARTHUR

I would not joke about your writing. I know you take it very seriously. When you make a movie of this, make sure that I am played by someone good looking. Audiences like good looking people. And put in jokes. It's can't be serious the whole time. People like jokes too.

DARREN

I am not OK. I am getting by. My strength is his and his is mine. And if there isn't another miracle, I will go to the funeral too. Maybe I will tell them about this. Maybe I will write about it too. Maybe I will remember to put in a joke or two.

END

Category: A
Cast: 2 Gender Neutral
Gi60 UK 2010

THE TIME MACHINE
By Michael Maiella
Brooklyn, NY, USA

(PANCHO and LEFTY are sitting at their cubicles at the end of the work day. PANCHO has a box. It is his "time machine.")

PANCHO

So I'm retiring tomorrow.

LEFTY

Right.

PANCHO

No. Really. I am.

LEFTY

You've only been working here for two weeks.

PANCHO

I have a secret.

LEFTY

Did you murder someone?

PANCHO

What? Don't be crude.

LEFTY

Well?

PANCHO

Now don't laugh, but I built a time machine. I'm going back in time. (Pause) Did you hear what I said? I'm going back in time. Time travel. I did it. Well, I'm going to do it. I mean, I've built the machine. It works though. I swear, it works. All I need now is to actually do it.

LEFTY

What are you talking about?

PANCHO

Listen, don't you remember all those times we'd come in here wishing we could escape? Be anywhere but here?

LEFTY

I've known you for two weeks.

PANCHO

(Not paying attention to LEFTY) Now, in order to prove that it works, I'm going to shoot you … well, kill you actually.

(Pulls a gun from out of his box. LEFTY does not see the gun.)

But don't worry. I'll simply go back in time and stop myself from shooting you. It's basically fool-proof.

LEFTY

(Noticing the gun) OK. I get it. You're upset because I didn't switch vacation days with you. And I understand. I'm sorry. But if this is your idea of some kind of joke, you're messed up. OK? This isn't funny.

(While LEFTY is still talking, PANCHO calmly shoots him. As LEFTY is dying, PANCHO immediately begins fidgeting with whatever is in the box.)

PANCHO

(Realizing his "time machine" does not work) Damn it!

END

Category: A
Cast: 1 F, 1 M
Gi60 US 2010

YES
By Bill Grabowski
Huntington Station, NY, USA

Setting
A MAN and a WOMAN are looking at artwork in a local gallery. Each is looking at different pieces. She comes up to him.

	I have something I need to tell you. Let's go over there.
(they move)	Uh.mmm
	Michael and I are separating.
— — — – – (no response)	
	Are you surprised?
No. I guess not …… No – I'm not.	
	… a lot of things I need to do …
Yes.	
	A lot of things. I don't know. It's just.
Are you OK?	Yeah. Sure. My idea. But. Don't tell anybody – No one knows. Only one of my kids knows.
No one. Yes. Zero. You'll be fine. You –	
You jump off cliffs. That's what you do. But you – fly. Always. I …… I can't – I'm not going anywhere –	
	Yes. Yes. I know. Yes OK. Of course. Well. Uh. Gotta go. We'll talk. I have some things to tell you.

—— —— —— —— —— —— ——

Next …
Next lifetime ….
You get the first call.

                                                      —— —— —— —— —— —— ——
                                                      —— —— —— —— Promise ???

YES !

                                        END

Category: A
Cast: 3 F
Gi60 US 2013, 2014

THREE CHARACTER PLAYS

THE LONGEST MINUTES
By Rosanne Manfredi
Bay Shore, NY, USA

Setting
MS JONES and MS SMITH sit in separate chairs "not really reading" magazines. They are in hospital gowns. A couple seconds of silence.

MS JONES
I really like this waiting room. The fountain. The lighting. The music. Very Zen.

MS SMITH
Very relaxing.

MS JONES
Well, as relaxing as it can be.
(A couple seconds of silence)

MS JONES
You know, I had a friend who went for his first prostate exam. He was gay and afterwards he told me that he felt like he'd been molested. "Really," I said. "And what, you think women just sit and play with puppies and kittens for their exams?"
(They laugh. A second of silence)

MS SMITH
And then there's this.

MS JONES
Yeah, there's this.

MS SMITH
(Confiding)
They had to take a couple extra views. I'm gonna be really bruised tomorrow, but I said, "Whatever you need to do."

MS JONES
I hear that – you do what you have to be safe.
(Nurse comes in.)

NURSE
Ms Smith, you're done. We'll see you next year.

MS SMITH
(Huge relieved smile as she heads past the nurse)
Thank you.

NURSE
Ms Jones, will you follow me to the doctor's office?
(MS SMITH turns back and both women exchange stricken looks.)

END

Category: A
Cast: 2 F, 1 M
Gi60 US 2010, 2014

PARENT TEACHER
By Arthur M. Jolly
Marina del Rey, CA, USA

CLARICE
I know that most parents have aspirations for
their children – they push them to achieve,
sometimes it can be hard to accept that …

BRENDA
We only want what's best for Tobias.

ALEX
He's a bright kid.

CLARICE
He's dead.

ALEX
What are you saying?

CLARICE
I'm saying … well, he's dead.

ALEX
Is he disruptive?

CLARICE
Well – it's not so much that he's disruptive
per se –

BRENDA
We know he maybe can't participate as much
as some of the other children –

ALEX
Or at all.

BRENDA
But we feel, if he's in a positive learning
environment –

CLARICE
Yes – but he's dead.

ALEX
You're fixating on the negatives. He's a good
kid. Smells a bit.

CLARICE
He's decomposing. There's an insect issue.

ALEX
Well, some of his classmates have nits. Head
lice. I don't see the school doing much
about –

CLARICE
I'm just trying to –

BRENDA
We just want what's best for our son.

CLARICE
There are funeral services –

ALEX
I'm not paying for goddamn funeral
services – I already pay taxes. I pay your salary.
You sit here, you tell us our son is – some
kind of defective – he can't learn –

CLARICE
'cause he's dead.

ALEX
That's not his fault! It's your job to overcome
these little – you're meant to be a teacher,
dammit! So teach!
(A beat)

BRENDA
I'll do my best. Thanks for coming in.

ALEX
(To BRENDA)
I want to know how many other kids in his class are dead – she doesn't even know it.
(As they leave, BRENDA turns back)

BRENDA
Oh one thing – the other day, Toby came home without one of his arms – so if you see it anywhere –

CLARICE
I'll keep an eye out.

BRENDA
Thank you.
(They leave.)

END

Category: A
Cast: 1 F, 2 M, Ensemble
Gi60 UK 2013

PERSISTENCE PAYS
By Alan Jozwiak
Cincinnati, OH, USA

(Scene opens with TINA and RICK, drinks in hand, standing around a crowded bar. They are together, but are looking around the room for someone, anyone to connect with. JOHN comes confidently onstage and approaches TINA.)

JOHN
Hi. I'm John. Have sex with me.
(TINA slaps JOHN and throws her drink into JOHN's face. TINA exits.)

RICK
(To JOHN)
Hey buddy, your pickup line's not working.

JOHN
It'll work – on the right woman. I've been shot down 500 times so far. It's all a matter of persistence.

RICK
Good luck with that.

JOHN
Luck has nothing to do with it. Excuse me.
(JOHN approaches REBECCA, who has just come onstage.)

JOHN
Hi. I'm John. Have sex with me.

REBECCA
And then?

JOHN
We'll lie side by side learning the intimate contours of our lives.

REBECCA
And then ... commitment? Cohabitation?

JOHN
Make it marriage.

REBECCA
In that case, our first girl will be named Rebecca – after me.

JOHN
And our first boy will be named John – after me.

REBECCA
My place's just around the corner. Good thing I came in here for some change.

JOHN
Lots of things will change now that I've found you.
(JOHN and REBECCA exit, arm in arm. JOHN gives RICK a knowing look before leaving. TINA returns onstage, this time with a noticeably larger drink. RICK primps himself and approaches TINA.)

RICK
Hi, I'm Rick. Have sex with me.
(TINA contemplates her drink.)

END

Category: A
Cast: 3 F
Gi60 US 2007

SUBWAY
By Aurora Stewart de Peña
Toronto, ON, Canada

The slide changes to show morning rush hour on the subway. ANGRINA, AGRESSA, and INTERVENA are businesswomen.

ANGRINA
Excuse Me!

AGRESSA
Ouch!

ANGRINA
You are in my way!

AGRESSA
Who said this way was yours?

ANGRINA
I wouldn't start with me if I were you.

AGRESSA
This is the subway. It belongs to no one.

ANGRINA
I wouldn't start with me if I were you.
(AGRESSA shoves ANGRINA. INTERVENA stands up.)

INTERVENA
Whoa!
(AGRESSA and ANGRINA stare at INTERVENA.)

INTERVENA
Whoa!
(ANGRINA sinks to her knees and covers her head with her hands.)

ANGRINA
(Quietly and tearfully) I wouldn't start with me if I were you.

INTERVENA
Whoa.

ANGRINA
(Quietly and tearfully) I'm going to kill the next person who bumps me, or shoves me, or touches me on the subway. I'm going to kill them.

END

Category: A
Cast: 5 F, 1 M
Gi60 US 2015

THE DELICATE GRACE OF A SEVERED LIMB
By Stephen Gracia
Brooklyn, NY, USA

Setting

Six muses have sat down at a café for a session of drinking and gossip. The pace is quick and the liquor flows, and the poses are ever changing and elegant. In fact, if at all possible, the muses should change poses after every line.

KIKI
Did you hear about Picasso?

GALA
That man was a trick of the light.

CAMILLE
He did have a problem with dusk.

HELGA
His heart followed the sun!

GEORGE
I heard he hung the moon.
(Pause)

KIKI
The moon hung herself.

PEGGY
What was it that Burton said of melancholy?

GALA
That melancholy can only be overcome by melancholy.

GEORGE
As drunkenness can only be overcome by more liquor.

PEGGY
Would anyone care for another drink?
(They all raise their glasses. PEGGY refills them.)

GALA
Why is it our hearts that must guide another's hand? Why is our despair only real if it is expressed through the brushstrokes of he who watched us flare and die? We always speak of what happened to the artist, when nothing happened to him, in point of fact, it was he who happened to a muse.

HELGA
To be fair, Picasso is dead.

GALA
Yes, but death is such a small part of an artist's life, it barely warrants notice.

HELGA
There's a sadness. A soft one. But still. It doesn't go unnoticed.

GALA
It should, though, Helga, dear. Art endures. The hand is immaterial.

HELGA
To be so cold!

GALA
I adore the hand while it works. Don't misunderstand me. I praise it; I pamper it; sometimes I even guide it. But it is ethereal and intangible, and I get no tingle from a ghost limb.

PEGGY
As a world, we cannot function without art.
(Takes a long sip)
We function quite well without artists.

KIKI
In fact, we may yet regain the feeling in our hands.

END

YOUTH APPROPRIATE GENRE "Y"

Category: Y
Cast: 1 M
Gi60 #NextGen 2014

ONE CHARACTER PLAYS

MS JOHNSON
By Jim MacNerland
Los Angeles, CA, USA

(An eighth- or ninth-grade boy, JOHN, rolls in on a wheelchair. Actor can have crutches and leg braces, too, or other physical disability.)

JOHN

Today was supposed to be a happy, happy day. Last day of school, summer vacation and I would have D. Johnson for honors English, again. I loved Ms Johnson. She understood what it was like for me to be trapped in this ... body.

And she taught me to "Write my stories." About the way people treated me. And how trapped I felt. And when they got put in the paper, she smiled and hugged me so close ... She wears the greatest perfume.
     (Beat)
But, today, she said that "Ms Johnson won't be back next year." But not to worry, because Mr Johnson will be here. "Your husband?" I said. "No." She smiled at me. That same smile she had when she hugged me.

I ... (angry, confused, at a loss for words) cried.

Mr Kretz said that I was a bigot for saying the things I said, and that I will learn to love Mr Johnson just as much as Ms Johnson, because they are the same person.

But they are not the same person. I loved Ms Johnson for who she was. And now, I ... just don't know.

END

Category: Y
Cast: 1 Gender Neutral
Gi60 UK 2013

NO. 56
By Jessica Hilton
Blackburn, UK

I love getting the bus. I always get the 56 into town. I just love watching people, you know?
I sit there and just look at people. I see all the students and their hairstyles get on and off, I see
the mums and their pushchairs. I just like to watch them.

I used to have this friend you see, who I used to ride the bus with. We used to get on the bus
on a Tuesday morning and have a brew together in M&S. She doesn't get the bus with me
anymore though. Things happen like that.

So now I just sort of sit on my own and watch people. There's always someone on their mobile
phone – sometimes speaking in English – and that's sort of like a conversation, I guess. I always
want to chat with people, but I get the impression they don't always want to chat to me.

It's a nice route anyway. Not quite scenic but there's a lot to look at. All sorts of people really,
all walks of life. I like going past the university. The bus half empties once all the clattering
students get off. They're all so loud, so full of life. I was like that when I was 21.

But I do my shopping anyway, nip to the market. For a while I went for a brew in M&S on my
own but it just wasn't quite the same. So I just do my bits and get back on the bus.

I think one of these days I'll just sit on the bus, and watch as it drives right past my stop. I'll
pay the right fare mind – but I'll just stay on the bus, and see what happens. See where I'll end
up. I'll just sit there and watch the world go by, and no one will notice. No one will know I'm
not supposed to be there. I'll just watch.

END

Category: Y
Cast: 1 F
Gi60 UK 2013

PROS AND CONS
By Amy Gijsbers van Wijk
New York, NY, USA

Note: DIANA may or may not read the numbers, but she is listing her reasons mentally to herself.

DIANA

To keep it ... or not to keep it ... That is the question.
(This is crazy; she laughs at herself, really in an unhealthy way.)

1. Didn't I always want to have children? 2. But I – this is fucking crazy. Diana, you're being nutso! 3. What if – what if everything happens for a reason and 4. This could be good for me? What if somehow this could be good for me? 5. Do I believe in God? 6. Maybe I am supposed to believe in God? 7. ... what if this is my only chance to be a mom? 8. What if this kid is, like, a demonic crazy sonufabitch? 9. I. I like kids! 10. ... maybe this kid ... maybe this kid needs me. 11. This is its only chance. 12. This could be a huge mistake! 13. This could be a huge mistake! 14. I don't have to get married, now. No one can give me shit about not getting married. 15. I kind of want this kid. 16. Maybe it's a girl. 17. What if this kid is really fucked up? 18. What if I do this and I hate myself? 19. What if I don't do this and I hate myself? 20. What if I don't and I always wonder who it could have become? Is it – what if the world misses something because I don't let it?

END

Category: Y
Cast: 1 M
Gi60 UK 2007

RUN!
By James Harvey
York, UK

A YOUNG MAN

(A YOUNG MAN stands centre stage with his right hand hidden behind his back. He is a picture of barely restrained violence.)

I'm standing 20 paces away from you and I can see the whites of your eyes, man. I see your scrambled thoughts. You wish you were anywhere else but facing me. You wish you could run. But you ain't going nowhere, mate. I've got 10 of my boys in a ring around you. You're surrounded. I smell your sweat from here, man. I hear your fast breath. I see you desperately running through your options. Should you try and attack? It's 11 against 1; I don't like your chances. Are you gonna take the hits? Soak up the punishment? Show us how hard you are? What would that prove, man? You'd better try and run! But you can't run can you? You can't get away.

Your eyes slowly stray to my right hand and it dawns on you that I'm hiding something behind my back. What am I holding in my right hand? It feels sleek and smooth and very, very dangerous. How you gonna like this thing shooting towards you at 90 miles an hour?

I shrug my sleeve on to my shoulder, turn, and walk away.
    (Pause)
Do you feel relief? Ill advised, man. I'm just finalizing my plans.
    (Pause)
I turn back. I lock my eyes on to yours and I steam forward. I'm tearing towards you.
My boys are slowly closing in around you. There's nothing you can do but take it, son. All eyes are on you. I thunder towards you. My fast feet thudding on the ground below. I raise my arm high, high to the sky. My boys are ready like a pack of wild dogs. I'm ready, I'm ready and I let it go. Hurl it through the sky like a missile, man. Your eyes open wide. Panic sets in. All you can do is duck out the way like a frightened baby. But it's useless. The whole gang's almost on top of you and we're screaming and there's sticks flying in all directions, and I'm howling, I'm howling ...
    (In slow motion he crouches down in a position of entreaty and yells ...)
OWWZZAAATTTT?????
    (Calmly and smugly)
"That's out" smiles the umpire. And you trudge back to the pavilion for a consolation cup of tea and a slice of scrumptious chocolate cake.

END

Category: Y
Cast: 1 and an audience member
Gi60 #NextGen 2016

TWO CHARACTER PLAYS

SCENE #6
By Derick Edgren
Bronxville, NY, USA

(ANY ONE PERSON stands onstage for an uncomfortable amount of time. This person approaches an audience member and whispers the following so that no one else can hear it.)

ANY ONE PERSON

I am very afraid that I am not living the right life and that this is all illusory. So please tell me it will be okay, but don't say it above a whisper. Go ahead, say it. … Thank you. Now you have to swear to me, on your own life and maybe mine too, that you'll never tell anyone what I've just said to you. It's a secret. It's our secret. Do you promise? Please promise. … Okay. I'm going to leave now.

(Exits)

END

Category: Y
Cast: 2 Gender Neutral
Gi60 UK 2011

CUSTOMER FOCUS
By Hedley Brown
Leeds, UK

(A CUSTOMER walks up to a customer services desk.)

CUSTOMER
You turn up. They say ...

CUSTOMER SERVICES
It's next week.

CUSTOMER
You come back next week. They say ...

CUSTOMER SERVICES
It was last week.

CUSTOMER
You try to reschedule. They say ...

CUSTOMER SERVICES
We can't fit you in for another month.

CUSTOMER
You come back in a month. They say ...

CUSTOMER SERVICES
You've missed the deadline.

CUSTOMER
You say "That's not fair!" They say ...

CUSTOMER SERVICES
Not my Problem.

CUSTOMER
You say "I want to see your manager." They say ...

CUSTOMER SERVICES
I am the manager.

CUSTOMER

You shout "Now look here ..." They say ...

CUSTOMER SERVICES

Please don't raise your voice sir.

CUSTOMER

You say "I'll raise my bloody voice if I want to!" They say ...

CUSTOMER SERVICES

If you don't calm down sir, I'll have to call security.

CUSTOMER

You say "Oooo I'm soooo scared." They call security!
    (Two burly SECURITY GUARDS enter and grab the customer.)

CUSTOMER

You say "Leave me alone! Get your hands off me!" They say ...

SECURITY GUARD

Don't struggle sir or I'll have to use the taser!

CUSTOMER

You struggle. They use the taser.
    (CUSTOMER is tasered by the SECURITY GUARD and instantly falls to the floor. Security
    guards exit. Pause. CUSTOMER comes to and raises his head. As he says the next line a
    POLICE OFFICER enters.)

CUSTOMER

You come to in a police van. They say ...
    (POLICE OFFICER puts handcuffs on the CUSTOMER, securing his arms behind his
    back.)

POLICE OFFICER

You're nicked!
    (POLICE OFFICER gets the CUSTOMER to his feet and marches the CUSTOMER to exit.
    Just before they exit they stop and the CUSTOMER has a final word with the audience.)

CUSTOMER

... And they say this time it's going to be custodial.

END

Category: Y
Cast: 1 F, 1 M
Gi60 UK 2006

DATE IN A DUMPSTER
By Bruce Shearer
Melbourne, Australia

WAL
I'm really glad that after all this time, you've finally agreed to …

ZENDA
Did you feel that? They touched us.

WAL
Did they?

ZENDA
I felt the touch. Can you get out and check?

WAL
(Long pause)
Is that the car that touched us?

ZENDA
You know it is.

WAL
Can you see those people in it? I do not want to speak with them, because if I do it might be one of my last conversations.

ZENDA
They've probably scratched my car. Get out and check, then speak to them.

WAL
Are you trying to get me killed?

ZENDA
We are in the right here. They've committed the crime.

WAL
Can you keep your voice down?

ZENDA
If they cause the accident, they need to own up to it.

WAL
They're coming over.
(Pause)
All of them are coming over!

ZENDA
To apologize.

WAL
They don't look apologetic.

ZENDA
Get out and give them a good piece of your mind.

WAL
If I do they'll cut out a good piece of my heart. I'm not getting out. They've surrounded the car.

ZENDA
Just checking the damage. I hope they take note of every scratch.

WAL
They're rocking the car.

ZENDA
Making sure they haven't affected the suspension in the collision.

WAL
They're going to tip us over.

ZENDA
That would be very unwise.

WAL
It might not seem possible, but it's happening.

ZENDA
Oh no, I don't think so.
(Pause)
Could it be part of an elaborate apology?

WAL
If only it was.
(Pause)
Did you feel that?
(Pause)
They're carrying us.

ZENDA
Do they know whom they're dealing with?

WAL
Do you think they care? We're heading for
that dumpster.

ZENDA
They are going to regret this!

WAL
Someone certainly is.

ZENDA
Open the window and tell them …

WAL
(Enormous crashing noise)
We're in the dumpster!

ZENDA
I'm aware of that.

WAL
You did say you wanted to go somewhere
different!

END

Category: Y
Cast: 1 F, 1 M
Gi60 UK 2011

DISCOUNTS
By Olivia Arieti
Torre del Lago, Puccini, Italy

(MR CLARK is behind his desk. MRS PARKER enters. Has a handkerchief.)

MR CLARK
(Gets up.) Bill Clark, at your service, Mrs …

MRS PARKER
Parker … (Sits down. Sobs.) George, my husband, is about to pass away …

MR CLARK
Great!

MRS PARKER
I beg your pardon?

MR CLARK
I mean I'm delighted to have such a becoming widow-to-be as our customer.

MRS PARKER
Why, thank you, Mr Clark.

MR CLARK
So when is this fortunate … err, sad event going to take place?

MRS PARKER
I'm afraid in a month's time …

MR CLARK
That means May! Wonderful choice! There's up to a 50% discount on all types of roses.

MRS PARKER
I love roses.

MR CLARK
Was sure you did. Should he unfortunately leave in June …

MRS PARKER
Yes?

MR CLARK
Prices will rise steeply, (Smiles) brides' month.

MRS PARKER
Oh, I see …

MR CLARK
May is perfect. We also provide a special gift for the bereaved.

MRS PARKER
How thoughtful.

MR CLARK
Our company's pride, (Takes her hand) Mrs Parker.

MRS PARKER
I'll make all the arrangements for May. When you have to go, a few days earlier make no difference.

MR CLARK
A very practical woman.

MRS PARKER
Nothing quicker than an overdose to simplify everything.

MR CLARK
I perfectly agree. Say, what about discussing the details over a drink?

MRS PARKER
Will seven be fine, Mr Clark?

END

Category: Y
Cast: 2 M
Gi60 UK 2013

DRAMA (A COMEDY)
By Vincent Krasauskas
Yorkshire, UK

(Two men wearing suits with ties
loosened are relaxing with a pint.)

MAN 1
So there we are. The end of the working week.

MAN 2
Aye.

MAN 1
It's a great feeling isn't it? The satisfaction of a
hard day's work.

MAN 2
Aye.

MAN 1
A pint in your hand, a cheeky cigarette or
two, and the knowledge that it's all over for a
couple of days.

MAN 2
Aye.

MAN 1
You know what I like the most?

MAN 2
What's that?

MAN 1
Getting away from all that fakery and drama.
People acting like they're too good to be seen
with you. All that drama.

MAN 2
Drama?

MAN 1
Yeah, y'know, like, they're all bustling around
talking about just how bloody busy they are
these days. Moaning about how they'll be
stuck there all night instead of just, y'know,
getting on with it and clocking off at five like
they're supposed to.

MAN 2
I know what you mean. Everything's such a
performance with them isn't it? They're just
flapping about and creating so much …

MAN 1 AND MAN 2
… DRAMA.

MAN 1
Aye, exactly.
          (Pause. They sip from their pints.)

MAN 1
I've been sleeping with my secretary.

MAN 2
I've been sleeping with your secretary as well.
          (They both gasp, then point at each
          other knowingly.)

MAN 1 AND 2

DRAMA!
(They clink glasses.)

END

Category: Y
Cast: 2 F
Gi60 UK 2008

FATHER
By Aurora Stewart de Peña
Toronto, ON, Canada

(PRUNELDA is sitting in one of two chairs facing each other. Enter EFFERVESCENCE.)

VOICE
Father ...

EFFERVESCENCE
Hello Prunelda.

PRUNELDA
Effervescence, sit down.
(EFFERVESCENCE sits down.)

PRUNELDA
I have some fantastic news for you.
(Pause)

PRUNELDA
Are you ready?

EFFERVESCENCE
Yes, I think so.

PRUNELDA
You have a father!

EFFERVESCENCE
I do? You told me I was an Immaculate Conception!

PRUNELDA
Well, that's what we all thought. He was in and out so quickly I really had no time to process what had happened. It turns out that that man who has been visiting sporadically all of these years is the man whose genetics make up half of your own!

EFFERVESCENCE
You mean Hezekiah the gardener?

PRUNELDA
Yes!

EFFERVESCENCE
Oh my God.

PRUNELDA
And he wants to have a relationship with you starting now! He's coming by momentarily to take you out for ice cream! He'll be referring to you as "Princess" from now on.

EFFERVESCENCE
I'm 29 years old!

PRUNELDA
Are you saying you don't want a Father?

EFFERVESCENCE
I really have no idea.
(We hear a knock at the door. PRUNELDA gets up to answer. She comes back.)

PRUNELDA
That was a Greenpeace canvasser, but he should be here any moment. Sit tight.

EFFERVESCENCE
Oh my God.

END

Category: Y
Cast: 1 F
Gi60 UK 2011

GIFTWRAP
By Emily Lawrenson
Barcelona, Spain

(A young woman steps forward to the front of the stage, and begins to speak.)

I remember one Christmas, how immaculately my present was wrapped. Every gift-wrapped corner was perfectly smoothed, beautifully folded, a work of art.

I can't remember what I got that day. I just remember how much love went into the presentation.

We don't talk about what our parents do for us.

We rarely acknowledge what the past has stamped on our minds and how much we are grateful for everything you've done.

My memory throws out leaning against your leg, wrapped in my dad's jumper, 10 sizes too big for my body, biscuit crumbs across my face and my thumb in my mouth, eyes lulling as I tried to keep walking. The sun set over the sand as we walked back to the car, where you bundled me in.

Now I'm the one wrapping you up.

Your skin is like paper, so thin, so veined, I'm afraid to touch you. I want to keep you as pristine as that gift, fold your delicate corners away, keep you safe and treat you with the love and care you once bestowed on me.
    (Long pause)

You don't remember me anymore, mum, but I've got enough memories for the pair of us.

END

Category: Y
Cast: 2 M
Gi60 US 2005, 2014

GOING TO KEVIN'S
By Tom Gerhard
Winter Park, FL, USA

Setting
One boy (BOY 1) squatting center stage,
looking intensely at something on the
ground. Another boy (BOY 2) comes in
from stage left, walking slowly, wheeling a
bicycle.

BOY 2
Whatcha looking at?

BOY 1
Bug. A shiny little black one. I followed it all
the way down the sidewalk to here.

BOY 2
What's it doing now?

BOY 1
I think it's resting. That was a long walk for a
bug.

BOY 2
(Three second pause)
It hasn't moved in a while.

BOY 1
It's a really pretty bug. See? It's black and
shiny and purple and has many busy legs.

BOY 2
They're not very busy now.

BOY 1
He was looking for food for his family – like
going to work. He had to go a long way for
them. Like going to work like my Daddy.

BOY 2
He's not moving.

BOY 1
My Daddy comes home every night.

BOY 2
I think he's dead.

BOY 1
(Startled)
What?

BOY 2
The bug, I think it's dead.

BOY 1
(Pokes lightly / gently at the bug)
I think he's gone to Kevin's.

BOY 2
Where?

BOY 1
Kevin's. I heard my Mom and Dad talking
about it when my sister died before I was
born and they said she'd gone to Kevin's. They
said it's a happy place.

BOY 2
You want to bury the bug?

BOY 1
(Standing)
No. A bird can eat him.

BOY 2
(Walking off stage with BOY 1)
Wanna ride bikes?

BOY 1
Sure. Let's go to my house and get mine.

END

Category: Y
Cast: 2 M
Gi60 #NextGen 2015

THE GOLD DOUBLOON
By Barry M. Putt, Jr
Somerset, NJ, USA

(LIGHTS UP as TOM, virile, slinks in.)

(He scans the ground, then tiptoes over to a toppled chair. He lifts it up and finds nothing. He spots another toppled chair in the distance. He walks over and reaches under it, pulling out a GOLD DOUBLOON. He grins from ear to ear.)

(BRAD, a cocky brute, charges out and tries to grab the doubloon. It falls.)

(TOM reaches for it. Brad knocks him down.)

(TOM gets up and charges at BRAD. A vigorous fight ensues as they block each other's punches like they were dueling with swords.)

(Suddenly, TOM twists BRAD's arms behind his back.)

(BRAD winces, then kicks TOM, releasing himself from TOM's hold.)

(TOM lunges at BRAD. BRAD darts off. TOM grins, then scans the ground and spots the doubloon. He picks it up and carefully peels its gold edges away to reveal chocolate underneath.)

(He pops the chocolate in his mouth, savoring every chew with utmost delight. TOM tosses the wrapper down and strolls off.)

END

Category: Y
Cast: 2 Gender Neutral
Gi60 #NextGen 2015

HOTLINE
By David Storck
Savannah, GA, USA

Two characters, 1 and 2, sit by phones. They
are in different locations.

1
(Picks up telephone and dials)

2
(Phone rings)
Hello, OCD Hotline.

1
(Hangs up, then redials)

2
(Phone rings)
Hello, OCD Hotline.

1
(Hangs up, then redials)

2
(Phone rings)
Hello, OCD Hotline.

1
(Hangs up, then redials)

2
(Phone rings)
Hola, el teléfono caliente.

1
(Hangs up, then redials)

2
(Phone rings, 2 picks up, then just
listens. 1 says nothing. They both just
listen. Finally …)
Hello, OCD Hotline.

1
(Hangs up, then redials)

2
(Phone rings, 2 picks up, then just
listens. 1 says nothing. They both just
listen. Silence lasts longer than previous
time. Finally …)
Hello … (waits) OCD … (waits) Hotline.

1
(Hangs up, then redials)

2
(Phone rings, 2 picks up, then just
listens. 1 says nothing. They both just
listen. Silence lasts longer than previous
time. Finally …)
Hello … (waits) OCD … (waits) Hot …
(waits) LLLLLLLLLLLLLLLLLLLLLLLLLLLLL –
IIIIIIIIIIIIIIIIIIIIIIIIIIIIII – ne.

1
(Hangs up, then redials)

2
(Phone rings. 2 stares at the phone.
It continues to ring. And ring. 1 grows
anxious. Finally, 2 answers and mimics
a recording …)
Hello. You have reached the OCD Hotline.
Our offices are now closed. If this is an OCD
emergency, please press 1.

1
(Presses 1, but that doesn't satisfy his/
her compulsion, so he/she presses 1
again. Then again. And again. Repeated
pressing grows in speed and urgency.)

2
(Trying to help, 2 blurts out ...)
Just once!
(Then immediately freezes, having
realized the error.)

1
(Upon hearing 2 speak, 1 also freezes.
After a moment, 1 hangs up.)

2
(Throws up hands in exasperation)

END

Category: Y
Cast: 1 M, 1 Gender Neutral
Gi60 UK 2010

THE INTERVIEW
By Matt Allen
Leeds, UK

Setting

There is a table with a chair next to it and another chair far across the room. LISA is sat at the chair next to the table. MATTHEW enters and hands LISA a sheet of paper.

LISA

Hello Mr Jones, please take a seat.
    (LISA waits for MATTHEW to sit across the room.)

LISA

Ah Mr Jones. Can I call you Jeff?

MATT

Erm, well. My name's not Jeff.

LISA

Oh yes, sorry I should have stated that, I do know your name, I have it written down here, it's just a little game we play here. I like to pretend I don't know your name.

MATT

Oh. Okay.

LISA

Now it says here that you are interested in the supervisor position. Now Jeff, let me ask you one question. Have you got it?

MATT

Well …

LISA
(cutting MATT off)

That's rhetorical Jeff. We operate a no seniority policy here. That answers can you be senior? No. There is no seniority. There are partners. A workforce of partners not supervisors. That means that you have the fortunate circumstance of having the potential and requirement to fulfil the "supervisor" duties whilst being an equal. As such you will of course receive minimum wage.

MATT

So I'll be doing a supervisor position but on the same wage as everyone else?

LISA

Well that's if you get the job Jeff. Don't go assuming yet, we still have other candidates to see.

MATT

OK. (Pause) Sorry.

LISA

Now it says here on your curriculum vitae that you studied GCSE Spanish, how wonderful. Tell me, can you still hablah en Espanola?

MATT

Well, I know basic Spanish.

LISA

That's fantastic. I'm just going to make a note on your account that you're Spanish.

MATT

But I'm not Spanish. I have a GCSE in Spanish …

LISA

Woah, woah, woah. This is just for statistical purposes, it will in no way affect the outcome of your application.

MATT

Okay, but I'm not Spanish.

LISA

Look, I'll be frank Jeff. It's all about multiculturalism. We are a family here and are proud of diversity. I'll just put down that you are (writing) Jew (Pause) Ish, Span (Pause) Ish. And Homosexual.

MATT

I'm sorry, I'm not Spanish or Jewish or what was the last one.

LISA

Hey. Hey Hey! What you do in your own time is 100% up to you. I don't let that affect our relationship, I'm not prejudiced, I have attended four seminars. Now as a new starter you will be on a trial period. You will be on what we call the three levels of commitment – have you heard of this before?

MATT

I think so.
(LISA waves for him to continue.)

MATT

Is it like … when … every time you are sick or late you get a strike. And you get three strikes.

LISA

Yikes. Wow. What kind of horrific company have you been dealing with? That won't promote a good atmosphere if you are afraid to be ill! Haha. (forced laugh)

MATT

No, sorry.

LISA

The three levels are a tried and tested monitoring scheme. If for any circumstances you are absent or are delayed in clocking in you will ascend a level. You will then be assessed and asked to explain why and how this happened. If you pass by the third level your contract will … erm … be evaluated.

MATT

Isn't that just the same?

LISA

No, no. It gives you a chance to tell us why the action happened so we can strive to avoid it in the future. For example, if you have flu we can and will require a list of all you have been in contact with in the days leading up to your first day off so we can discipline those responsible for passing the flu onto you.

MATT

Oh.

LISA

Now. Everything seems to be in order with your paperwork. If you could just sign this non-disclosure here. Initials here, mother's maiden name here, sign and date here. And here, and here, and here. If you could please leave three copies of passport photos, sign the 816a form and we will be in touch.

END

Category: Y
Cast: 2 F
Gi60 UK 2015

KNEADING
By Theeda Phe Kali Winter
Leeds, UK

Setting

The text is a monologue spoken by the mother to her child. The child, who pretends to make gingerbread people, has no dialogue. The mother stands opposite her daughter with a table in between them, as if it were a mirror image, while they busily make gingerbread people.

MOTHER

Her little face was mine as a child. Especially some facial expressions when her hair was pulled up from her face. Looking at my little reflection was like rewriting my past. "No pressure then to get it right the next generation on." The fear in my furrow told of the intense need to get it right. Failure was not an option.

She followed my instructions carefully. One cup of flour, one egg, five tablespoons of sugar, half a teaspoon of ginger, and two dashes of cinnamon. I watched her kneading the dough together and lovingly rolling it out. I kneaded her to get it right, to produce well put together gingerbread men that she could feel proud of. I kneaded her to feel confident and able.

Using the cutter she stamped out several gingerbread men and lots of friends. She added two raisins for breasts and declared that it was a gingerbread woman. I placed them on a baking tray as if my life depended on it. Not waiting to dismember or break any of her gingerbread people or break her spirit with the taste of failure and disappointment.

In the oven went the small community of people that came out brown and sweet and whole and near perfect, except the buttons and breasts that were a little more cooked than desired. They sat in the tray in perfection as she admired them, soaking up the feeling of self-satisfaction.

I left them to cool, prolonging the moment when I was to do my part in the process and spatula them off the tray with a steady, at ease, adult confidence that I wasn't sure I had. Her eyes transfixed on me as the drum roll of my mind played on. My hand struggling to scrape one off the tray.

"Shit! I had forgotten to butter the tray!" A fragile leg broke off and I crumbled. I took a deep breath and attempted another, this time decapitating a head. I tried again this time with no expectation of success and I won! A whole person popped off the surface, then another and another. I was developing a technique for it now. She smiled at the plate of perfect people and munched away at the injured, until all of evidence of my failure had been devoured and only our achievements were on display.

END

Category: Y
Cast: 1 F, 1 M
Gi60 US 2007

THE LAKE
By Aren Haun
San Francisco, CA, USA

A bench by a lake.

Characters
BOY: About 17 years old.
GIRL: Slightly older. A year ahead.
>   (A BOY and a GIRL, seated. Pause)

GIRL
When I was a little girl, I used to go
swimming in this lake. I remember, one
time, I was swimming, and, for some reason,
I decided to find out how deep it was. So I
swam straight down, straight down as far as I
could go, but I couldn't ... I couldn't reach it.
I couldn't reach the bottom. But I kept going
... My eyes were open but I couldn't see
anything. I couldn't see. Everything was black.
The water was black. I got all turned around
and ... I wasn't sure which way was up or
down. I was scared. I thought ... I wondered
if I was going to drown. And I remember
thinking if ... if I don't turn back now ... I
might ... I might not ...
>   (Pause)

BOY
You might not make it back.

GIRL
I might not reach the bottom.
>   (Long pause)

BOY
I've been thinking, you know, a lot, lately.
And I don't think you should go. I think you
should put it off another year. And then we
can, you know, go together.

GIRL
I've already been accepted. The arrangements
have all been made.

BOY
But what'll happen to us if you go?

GIRL
What'll happen to me if I stay?
>   (Pause)

BOY
So how deep is it?
>   (Pause)

GIRL
I have no idea.

END

Category: Y
Cast: 1 F, 1 M
Gi60 US 2013

LOVE FINDS A WAY
By Mark Harvey Levine
Pasadena, CA, USA

Setting
Two T-Rexes on a date at a nice little Italian restaurant. The actors hold their arms against their chests to indicate their tiny forearms.

SUSIE
It's really hard to eat spaghetti with our little tiny forearms.

DANNY
I'm sorry, Susie. I shouldn't have taken you to an Italian restaurant.

SUSIE
No, no, I didn't mean that! It's really nice. The Microraptor Meatballs are so fresh.

DANNY
I know, right! Some of mine are still moving!
(He attacks one in a dinosaur-like manner.)

SUSIE
No, I just mean ... it's hard. Here we are, the best the Cretaceous has to offer, and I'm struggling to eat a simple plate of pasta.

DANNY
Seriously. I'm surprised we haven't gone extinct yet. (They laugh.) Still, I'm glad you came out with me, Susie.

SUSIE
I am too. Could you pass the grated cheese?
(During the following he struggles to reach it.)

DANNY
I liked you from the first moment I saw you. It was like I was ... struck by a meteor, or something.

SUSIE
Me too. Oh Danny ...
(She reaches out to hold his hand. He tries to take her hand. But they don't reach across the table.)

DANNY
Oh this is ridiculous. I don't think this is going to work. How can we have a romance? I can't even hold your hand!

SUSIE
There's got to be a way! Try!
(They lean further in, trying to get their hands to touch. They lean in so far that their heads meet and they kiss before they realize it.)

DANNY
Oh!

DANNY AND SUSIE
(Gesturing with their tiny arms) Check!

END

Category: Y
Cast: 1 F, 1 M
Gi60 UK 2007

LOVE STORY
By Joel Dean
Harrogate, UK

Setting

A high school Form Common Room. DENNIS sits a few seats away from LYNDA. LYNDA cannot hear what DENNIS is saying.

LYNDA

Wait a minute. There was something I was going to say.

DENNIS

You were going to say that you have fallen in love with me, deeply and passionately. That you want to spend the rest of your life with me. That secretly, everything might as well disappear if my hand is not there for you to hold and my lips not there to kiss.

LYNDA

Oh that's right. I've got to buy some crisps at the Co-op.

DENNIS

Crisps, my sweetheart! You are above crisps. You should be showered with flowers, jewels, and chocolates. We should all bow down and worship your supreme beauty. Your desirable countenance would make even the cruellest men melt at your feet.

LYNDA

I wonder if Dennis would like anything.

DENNIS

Only your heart, soul, and promise that you will be mine forever!

LYNDA

Should I ask him?

DENNIS

My darling, you know the answer would be yes every time.

LYNDA

Was there anything you wanted Dennis? Were you going to say something?

DENNIS

(LYNDA hears this.) No.

END

Category: Y
Cast: 1 F, 1 M
Gi60 UK 2015

NERVOUS
By Jessica Hilton
Blackburn, UK

A couple on a date.

BOY
I like your dress. It's the one on your profile
picture isn't it?

GIRL
Yes it is. You liked that picture didn't you? You
like a lot of my pictures. And my statuses. And
my check-ins sometimes too. You liked that I
went to ASDA with my mum. And you poked
me. (Giggles)

BOY
Oh yeah, I do. (Giggle) Sorry – is that weird?

GIRL
No, no, it's … nice.

BOY
Well, you know, you're pretty and that. I'll
tell you a secret. I used to always look at you
when you were waiting for the bus.

GIRL
Really? I never saw you.

BOY
Sorry – is that weird? I don't want to sound
like some sort of stalker. I'm not. I mean it's

not like I love you. I mean, I'm … Well I mean
I'm not saying I don't. I just. Oh you know.
You're pretty. That's what I'm trying to say.

GIRL
Well, thanks. That's … nice.

BOY
I mean maybe we could go for another drink
sometime. Maybe. Or, maybe you could come
home and meet my parents? And um, maybe
you could meet my friends. And my cat. Or
maybe you can come out with me and a
few work colleagues, or come to my works'
do next week. Or maybe we could go away
together, or maybe. (Sort of joking) I mean
maybe we could just get married now and get
it all done with. Maybe. And maybe, (sort of
serious) maybe we could grow old together in
arm chairs next to each other and cups of tea.

GIRL
Maybe. Let's go for that drink.

END

Category: Y
Cast: 1 F, 1 M
Gi60 UK 2011

NOTHING
By Alex Bernstein
Cranford, NJ, USA

(PAM and JEFF, both mid-twenties, are standing in a corner at a crowded party.)

JEFF

I had this dream: I'm at the camp of book people at the end of *Fahrenheit 451*. The one where all the books in the world have been burned? So everyone has to memorize a book and then they become that book completely? And I'm *Crime and Punishment*. And I can't remember anything. Russian names. Text. Nothing. Everyone's staring at me. And then you show up and you're *Green Eggs and Ham*. And everyone loves you. And I'm just so pissed —

(She smiles. She pulls him close and kisses him deeply, but unexpectedly.)

JEFF

What was that?

PAM

Nothing.

JEFF

Nothing?

PAM

I just felt like trying it.

JEFF

Do — do you want to try it again?

PAM

No.

JEFF

No?

PAM

Not right now. Maybe later.

JEFF

Okay. So — so — so — this was just a — does this —

does this mean anything? I mean —

PAM

You're thinking too much.

JEFF

Okay. I —

PAM

Don't worry about it. I just wanted to see what it was like.

JEFF

Okay. What was it like?

PAM

It was pretty good.

END

Category: Y
Cast: 1 F, 1 M
Gi60 UK 2007

PINTER PAUSE
By Henry Raby
York, UK

Setting
The stage has a chair. Enter Harry and Viv.

HARRY
Please sit down.

VIV
(She sits.)
I hear you like Pinter.

VIV
I like Pinter.

HARRY
But do you love Pinter?

VIV
I like Pinter. (Pause)

HARRY
I need to get a new chair. I really need to. This
one's getting rather knarled.

VIV
Knarled?

HARRY
Knarled. (Pause) Don't you hate knarled
things?

VIV
Like you?

HARRY
Yes, like me.

VIV
Yes. I do hate knarled things. (Pause) Do
you think this little chat will ever get to a
conclusion, Harry?

HARRY
(Genuinely uncertain) Are you implying
something subtly or are you asking me
outright?

VIV
What do you think, Harry?

HARRY
I ... think ... I think ... (Pause) I don't think.

VIV
No, you don't. Would you like a seat? (Pause)

HARRY
Does that mean I've got the power or you?

VIV
Oh, you've definitely got the power, Harry.

HARRY
Oh. Thanks Viv. Ta.
(He sits and she stands.)

END

Category: Y
Cast: 1 F, 1 M
Gi60 UK 2012

THE QUIZZER WHO CAME TO TEA
By Terry Collins
Harrogate, UK

Setting

(Sophie and her mummy are having tea with a Quizzer. The Storyteller addresses the Audience.)

STORYTELLER

Sophie and her Mummy were having tea with a very hungry quizzer.

MUMMY

Tea, Quizzer?

QUIZZER

Ah yes. A tisane of the flushes of *Camelia sineniensis* first infused in tenth-century China.

MUMMY

Milk?

QUIZZER

One enjoys milk. A negatively charged colloidal suspension of butterfat micelles secreted by female mammals, pigeons, flamingos, and Emperor Penguins. And a source of casein adhesive.

MUMMY

Sugar?

QUIZZER

From Medieval Latin *succarum*. A refined disaccharide first crystallized in ancient India, from whose language our word candy is derived.

(The QUIZZER drinks up his tea and they all wave goodbye.)

STORYTELLER

The quizzer told Sophie and her Mummy all about the orange juice in the fridge, the hops that go into beer, the water in the taps, the world's first biscuit, the plaster on the walls – oh yes – until Sophie's Mummy thought she might open a vein. But Quizzer did at last leave and Sophie and her Mummy went to the shop and bought the biggest tin of weed killer they could find and they wrote on the tin in the biggest blackest letters "Quizzer Food" and they kept it in the cupboard in case he should come to tea again one day, but he never did.

END

Category: Y
Cast: 1 F, 1 M
Gi60 US 2008, 2014

SEE YOU ON THE OTHER SIDE
By Kirsty Sedgman
Shropshire, UK

Setting
Two cliff-edges separated by a narrow, deep
chasm. BOY is sitting on the right-hand cliff,
silently plucking petals from daisies.
(Enter GIRL, from left)

BOY
I wasn't sure you'd come.

GIRL
I'm sorry. My sister –

BOY
How is she? (Pause) I'm sorry. (Pause) I'm
glad you came.

GIRL
It wasn't easy. They're getting more alert.

BOY
If they catch you –

GIRL
It's worth it.

BOY
I wish –

GIRL
What?

BOY
I wish I could help you.

GIRL
You can't.

BOY
This damn drop –

GIRL
It's what's keeping you safe.

BOY
Still –

GIRL
I dream about it sometimes. I'm running
along and the ground opens up underneath
me. I wake up screaming. They don't like that.

BOY
I wish you could be with me.

GIRL
If I could jump I would.
(Pause)

BOY
Then do it.

GIRL
What?

BOY
What's stopping you?

GIRL
It's too far.

BOY
I'll catch you.

GIRL
I'll fall.

BOY
You won't.

GIRL

I'm scared –

BOY

I know.

GIRL

I'm *scared* –

BOY

It's just one minute. Isn't that better? One
minute and it'll be over. Isn't it better? I think
it is.
(Pause)

GIRL

OK.

BOY

OK?

GIRL

I'll do it. Step back.

BOY

Get a good run-up.

GIRL

Here?

BOY

There.

GIRL

You promise you'll catch me?

BOY

I'll catch you. I'll try.
(Pause)

GIRL

Here we go.
(She closes her eyes and prepares
to run.)

BOY

Hey?
(She opens her eyes. He smiles.)

BOY

See you on the other side.
(She starts running. As she begins to
jump –)

END

Category: Y
Cast: 2 M
G(hosts) in 60 2010

SLEEP TIGHT
By Alex and Charlie Bernstein
Cranford, NJ, USA

Setting
A little boy's bedroom.

DAD
Good night, sport.

NICK
G'night, Dad.

DAD
I love you.

NICK
Love you, too.

DAD
I'm gonna turn off the light now, okay?

NICK
Kay.

DAD
That's a big boy. Nothing to be afraid of.

NICK
Nope.
        (Yawns)

DAD
Great. Y'know these shadows on the wall are just shadows. Not monsters.

NICK
I know.

DAD
And no monsters in your closet either, right? Nothing to worry about.

NICK
Okay.

DAD
No giant bugs will drop on you at night while you sleep –

NICK
What?

DAD
And crawl in your ears – and eat your brains or anything –

NICK
Wait – what –?

DAD
What?

NICK
What did you say?

DAD
No giant bugs are going to –

NICK
Why would they do that?

DAD
They wouldn't.

NICK
Do we have giant bugs?

DAD
No, no – I'm saying we don't.

NICK

Oh. Okay.

DAD

And no monsters in the closet. No evil clowns hiding in the dresser –

NICK

What?

DAD

– with broken, glow-in-the-dark teeth.

NICK

What?!

DAD

Fangs –

NICK

What are you –

DAD

Honey! Nothing's going to happen. It's all shadows! Relax. It's just the mind playing tricks.

NICK

Oh, oh, okay –

DAD

You okay?

NICK

Mm-hmm.

DAD

Alright. I love you.
(He gets up.)
Sleep tight. Turning off the lights now.

NICK

Kay.

DAD

And no Dracula in the basement.
(He turns off the lights.)
BLACKOUT

NICK

AHHHHHHH!

END

Category: Y
Cast: 2 F
Gi60 US 2014

SPIRALING
By Buffy Aakaash
Seattle, WA, USA

Setting
AT RISE: A hospital psychiatric ward. Two
women and a baby. RACHEL and BEETA.
    (RACHEL holds a baby. BEETA holds a
    piece of paper.)

RACHEL
What's he staring at?

BEETA
He loves that fan.

RACHEL
Spiraling. Like he was doing ... How many
hours ago? Coming down. From wherever
babies come from. Before they become
babies. (Pause) What did you say before about
the cord?

BEETA
It was wrapped around his neck.

RACHEL
Oh god!

BEETA
He's okay, Rachel. Look at him. See? Have you
thought about ...?

RACHEL
His name?

BEETA
What's his name?

RACHEL
It just doesn't seem real.

BEETA
What?

RACHEL
That this happened.

BEETA
It happened. I was there. I held your hand.

RACHEL
You did? That was you?

BEETA
But you're here now. You've gotta ... Get
yourself together. So you can be his momma.

RACHEL
I am his momma.

BEETA
What about me? I could watch him. In the
meantime.

RACHEL
No.

BEETA
I could do that for you.

RACHEL
I dunno.

BEETA
I adore him. And ... Rachel ... It's either me
or them.

RACHEL
But ...

BEETA
I have something for you to sign.

RACHEL
So that you can take him away?

BEETA
It's just temporary. They won't let you take
him home.

RACHEL
But he's mine, Beeta. He came from me.
(Pause) For how long?

BEETA
Just until they say. (Pause)
    (RACHEL is gazing into the fan.)
Rachel ... What are you doing?

BEETA
Whenever I look at this fan here, I'll think
of him ... And you. You and him together.
Spiraling.
    (BEETA puts the paper down in front of
    her.)
Spiral. That's his name. Spiral.
    (RACHEL hands over her baby.)

END

Category: Y
Cast: 2 F
Gi60 US 2015

WE CAN BE HEROES
By Allie Costa
Studio City, CA, USA

Lights come up on two teenage girls, ZAYAH and KEELY, leaning against a wall of lockers, sipping Slurpees.

ZAYAH
Did you see Danny's shirt today?

KEELY
No. I'm not as hyperaware of him as you.

ZAYAH
It said, "Always be yourself. Unless you can be Batman. Then always be Batman." What if I don't want to be Batman?

KEELY
Then be Superman. (sips Slurpee)

ZAYAH
No, Batman's cooler. He doesn't need superpowers to fight crime. (sip) As cool as he is, if I were given the opportunity to be Batman, I would politely decline. I would rather be myself.

KEELY
(approvingly) Good for you.

ZAYAH
Of course, I wouldn't mind having the Batmobile. Or the butler.

KEELY
Just don't make me your sidekick.

ZAYAH
Why not?

KEELY
I wanna be a hero, too. I like that poster in Miss Martin's classroom: "You are the protagonist of your own story."

ZAYAH
True. But other people still kinda help you write it.

KEELY
True. And if our life was a movie, we'd have equal billing. (holds out her pinky) Yeah?

ZAYAH
Definitely.
(They pinky swear, then take long slurps from their cups.)

END

Category: Y
Cast: 2 M
Gi60 UK 2013

WINGMAN
By Ted Wenskus
Rochester, NY, USA

Setting
A local pub at lunch time. GEOFF is sitting at a table when TREV bursts in.

GEOFF
Trev, you won't believe what happened to me last night! I'm in love.

TREV
You met a bird on the way home? Way to go!

GEOFF
Well, I didn't meet a bird exactly … more like a frog.

TREV
Uh, what?

GEOFF
A gorgeous, magical frog.

TREV
(Beat) You've gone off your meds, haven't you …

GEOFF
I'm serious! I was cutting through the woods last night, stopped to tie my boot … and that's when she spoke to me.

TREV
And what did your frog say?

GEOFF
She told me she was really a beautiful princess that some evil wizard had cursed and the only way to break the spell was for a handsome bloke to kiss her.

TREV
You did not kiss a frog.

GEOFF
Well. I was a bit drunk, so it seemed reasonable at the time. I leaned in, gave her a peck, and suddenly there she was – the most beautiful woman I've ever seen. Look here!
       (GEOFF shows TREV a picture on his phone.)

TREV
Well, you may be nuts, but she is stunning.

GEOFF
There's just one problem before we can be together forever.

TREV
What?

GEOFF
The evil wizard also cursed her sister … are you busy tonight?

END

Category: Y
Cast: 1 F, 1 M, Ensemble
Gi60 UK 2006

SOUNDTRACK
By Jasmine Bown
Harrogate, UK

Setting

A young couple are in love.

HIM

Amazing … you're amazing. I've been wanting to do this for a while now.
    (They kiss and as soon as they do the ensemble appear and start to sing an overly sweet
    love song, e.g. "Puppy Love.")
Guys … guys!
    (The ensemble stop singing.)
We're having a bit of a moment here and I'm not going to lie, I'm being slightly distracted.

ENSEMBLE

(Variously)
Sorry, apologies, sorry, etc.

HIM

Anyway, where were we …
    (The ensemble return singing an upbeat love song, e.g. "Love Is in the Air," with gusto,
    some are dancing.)
I said …
    (The ensemble stop.)
Do you mind!

HER

You know what, maybe I should just go?

ENSEMBLE and HIM

No, no … etc.

HIM

Don't go, stay. Ignore them, it isn't about them. It isn't about anyone else. It's about me and you
… together.
    (The ensemble begin to sing an empowering love song, e.g. "All you Need Is Love.")

HER

No, I'm sorry, I can't do this … I … I … I'll see you around.
    (She leaves the stage. The ensemble immediately sing a break up song, e.g. "All by
    Myself." Frustrated, he exits in the opposite direction.)

END

Category: Y
Cast: 1 F, 2 M
Gi60 UK 2010

THREE CHARACTER PLAYS

ENDS
By Anton Krasauskas
Pontefract, UK

(Two men sit staring upwards.)

ALAN
I can't see anything.

BILL
She says it's "very bleedin' obvious."

ALAN
Well, I don't know where she's looking,
because I can't see anything.

BILL
Maybe it was just one of them trick of the
light things.

ALAN
Must be. I have absolutely no idea what we're
looking for.

BILL
Well, she's not going to have brought us in to
look at nothing for a joke, is she?

ALAN
Maybe we're over-thinking it. What would
she want us to have a look at, that is very
bleedin' obvious, that she's not at all happy
about.

BILL
I don't know. It could be like ... a crack, or a
bit where someone hasn't painted it right ...
or ... something.

ALAN
I bet it's not even that big a deal. You know
how women get when you're redecorating.
Everything has to be just so.

BILL
(Chuckles) Yep. You got it right there my son.

ALAN
Don't call me that. How many times ...?

BILL
I'm trying to bring it back as a popular
phrase.

ALAN
Well, all you're actually doing is bringing it
back as a creepy weirdo.

BILL
Nah ...

ALAN
That cardigan doesn't help much ...

BILL
What's wrong with the cardigan? This is the
height of fashion. This screams fashionable ...

ALAN
It's screaming something ...
    (From off stage)

CARLY
Have you sorted it yet?
    (BILL and ALAN look at each other and
    shrug. They both shout "Yeah.")

CARLY
Good. It's going to take some doing ... but
I think we'll be able to sort it out before the
end of the week, yeah?
    (ALAN and BILL look at each other and
    shrug. They both shout "Yeah.")

(CARLY walks in looking pleased, looking up at the ceiling. She stops dead in her tracks, her expression changing to frustration.)

CARLY

Oh for god's sake. Can you not see it?
(ALAN and BILL shrug.)

BILL

I'll be honest. Whatever it is, I think it's just you wanting everything perfect. It's nothing anyone else would notice.
(ALAN nods in agreement.)

CARLY

Oh is that what it is?
(The boys both nod.)

CARLY

OK. Fair enough. (She exits, clearly giving up on them both.)
(The boys look at each other, pleased with the day's work. Then they look up again.)

ALAN

Hey hold on ... didn't this room used to have a ceiling?

BILL

(We see realization spread across his face.)
That's what it is ... I knew it was something.

END

(handwritten) To our great friend, George, with love. Altenir 05/11/17 NYC. 341

Category: Y
Cast: 3 M
Gi60 US 2015

FRIENDSHIP
By Altenir Silva
Rio de Janeiro, Brazil

AT RISE: BOY is looking for a PIRATE and a MAGICIAN. We know that because the magician uses a magician's hat and the pirate uses a pirate's hat.

PIRATE
So, which one of us will you choose?

BOY
I have not decided.

MAGICIAN
If you choose me, I'll always do amazing magic, like how to get the rabbit out of the hat, disappear and appear in another place … and much more.

PIRATE
I'll tell incredible stories of lost treasures, ghost ships, caves with wizards … every day I'll tell you a new story.

BOY
And me? What do I do?

PIRATE
You listen to the story.

MAGICIAN
And applaud the magic.

BOY
I prefer a true friend.

PIRATE
What makes a true friend?

BOY
Play with me.

PIRATE
A friend doesn't know how to tell stories of pirates.

MAGICIAN
Much less do magic.

BOY
A true friend doesn't need to do any of this because he loves me.
(PIRATE takes off his hat; the MAGICIAN takes off his hat as well.)

PIRATE
Let's play ball?

MAGICIAN
I'm the pitcher.

BOY
I'm at bat.

PIRATE
I'm the catcher.
(They begin to play baseball.)

END

Category: Y
Cast: 1 F, 1 M, 1 bus driver
Gi60 US 2013

LAST CHANCE SALOON
By John Hawkhead
Yeovil, UK

Setting
A bus. The YOUNG WOMAN is seated.
The YOUNG MAN walks past the YOUNG
WOMAN and takes a seat behind her.

YOUNG WOMAN
Here he is again, every night the same.

YOUNG MAN
There she is. Always the same seat – like
clockwork.

YOUNG WOMAN
I can feel him looking at me; or is he?

YOUNG MAN
Her hair looks different, I could almost touch it.

YOUNG WOMAN
I wonder if he's noticed my hair?
Probably not.

YOUNG MAN
Should I speak? All these weeks and not a
word. I should speak.

YOUNG WOMAN
He never speaks. Why? Weeks and not even
"Hi, my name's …?"

YOUNG MAN
I don't even know her name. Why the hell
don't I just ask?

YOUNG WOMAN
Perhaps I should speak. Why not?

YOUNG WOMAN
I must speak this time, before he gets off. This
is my last night on the bus, but he can't know
that! So just turn round and say hello.

YOUNG MAN
OK, here goes, but what do I say? I must say
something.

BUS DRIVER
Langton Grove!

YOUNG WOMAN
    (Leaves seat)
Too late now. He didn't want to speak. I won't
look back. Don't look back.
    (She walks forward – she looks back –
    she exits quickly.)

YOUNG MAN
Why didn't I speak? What's stopping me?
That's it! Tomorrow I'll ask her. Tomorrow …
I will tell her.

BUS DRIVER
Overton Park! Final Destination!
    (Lights fade with YOUNG MAN still
    in seat.)

END

Category: U
Cast: 3 M plus Ensemble
Gi60 UK 2015

LEVI IS DEAD
By Rebekka Pattison
Dortmund, Germany

Setting

JOSEF is a soldier. LEVI is a prisoner. JOSEF kisses LEVI. Another soldier, THOMAS, joins JOSEF and LEVI.

THOMAS

To the wall! To the wall!
  (Six men, women, and children run on and line up at the wall, with their backs to
  JOSEF, LEVI, and THOMAS. JOSEF and LEVI stare at THOMAS.)

THOMAS

What?
  (LEVI smiles at JOSEF and walks to the wall. LEVI faces the two soldiers. JOSEF gets out
  his gun. Six shots are fired, six bodies fall to the ground, dead. LEVI waves. A seventh
  shot is fired. LEVI is dead.)

END

Category: Y
Cast: 2 F, 1 M
Gi60 US 2009

SHOULD I STAY OR SHOULD I GO?
By Natasha Geffen (grade 7 at time of writing)
New York, NY, USA

Setting and Time
Living room. Evening on the weekend.
Characters: ALI, age 13, MOM, DAD
(The sound of TV and noise around the house is heard. DAD and MOM are watching TV. ALI stands in the middle of them. She is all dressed up to go to a party: wearing a black dress, too much make-up, her hair elaborately done, and she is wearing over-sized fuzzy, teddy-bear slippers. She fidgets with her dress and hair.)

MOM
(Soft voice, barely taking her eyes off the TV)
Ali ... darling ... aren't you going to finish getting ready ...? They'll be here in a minute to pick you up ....

ALI
Well, I'm just not so sure if I really want to go tonight.

MOM
ALI, you can't be serious?

ALI
Should I stay or should I go ...?

MOM
You should go!

ALI
Who knows what could happen? It's the first actual party that I've been to! I could get a headache, other people might think I'm a bad dancer, they might not like what I'm wearing, or the food might be gross and I'll ...

MOM
Ali, stop worrying so much – you're gonna have a great time! Just think about it, Kendra will be there ...

ALI
That's true ...

MOM
(continuing) ... and Robby ...

ALI
Ew, that boy that threw up in math class?

MOM
Well, what about Mason?

ALI
Fine, I'll go ... I guess it will be OK (She turns to go finish getting dressed.)

MOM
... and your friend Julia will be –

ALI
(She stops in her tracks and turns back around.) – there is no way I'm going if that selfish brat does!

MOM
Well, if she isn't nice, just walk away ...

DAD
Maybe there'll be someone nice to dance with ... (DAD laughs in a goofy way and MOM joins him.)

ALI
Stop ...

MOM

It took me an hour to do your hair!

DAD

(without taking his eyes off the TV) You really do look great, honey ...

MOM

Yes, look at you! All you ever do is sit in front of ...

DAD

Listen, she's a big girl! If she doesn't want to go she can make up her own mind. The last thing she needs is someone on her back ...

MOM

I'm just doing what's best for her — all teenagers need some fun in their lives ...

DAD

You worry too much — she'll have fun ... look at us.

MOM

(over the TV) mmmmm ...that's true ...
(By now, ALI has sat in the empty seat and has dismantled her hair. She grabs the remote from her father to raise the volume. We quickly hear something recognizable from the TV — like Simon Cowell bashing an American Idol contestant ...

The three of them stare blankly at the TV as the lights start to fade to black ...)

END

Category: Y
Cast: 1 F, 1 M, 1 Gender Neutral
Gi60 UK 2010

STRANGERS ON A TRAIN
By Dee Grijack
Otley, UK

(MAN enters imaginary train. WOMAN
sitting in middle of carriage.)

MAN
Is this the Chatham train?

WOMAN
Yes.
(MAN looks around, up and down.)

MAN
Is that seat taken? (points to seat opposite THE
WOMAN)

WOMAN
No.
(MAN sits down: shuffling, sitting,
getting comfortable.)

MAN
I thought I'd missed the train.
(The WOMAN is silent.)

MAN
Thought I'd missed it. Didn't expect it to be
still here.

WOMAN
No.

MAN
Didn't expect it to be empty either (looks
up and down the carriage). S'pose you're
wondering why I chose to sit here, with all
those empty seats?

WOMAN
You don't like being on your own?

MAN
On my own! That's a laugh. I've never been
on my own in my life.

WOMAN
That's what I mean: you don't like being
alone.

MAN
Well, I like meeting people. New faces – new
places. You're quite safe, though – I'm a
married man … you married?

WOMAN
Yes.

MAN
Good to have a break, though. Any kids?

WOMAN
No.

MAN
Take my advice – wait.

WOMAN
I did.

MAN
Sorry.

WOMAN
I waited. For a long time. Then I found myself
alone. I don't like travelling alone.
(The MAN is silent …)
(WOMAN is silent too, at first.)

WOMAN
Where did you say this train was going?

MAN
Chatham. Look … are you OK?

WOMAN
I just thought I might have missed my station … does the train terminate here? I've been sitting here a long time.
(MAN starts to say something, then suddenly gets up.)

MAN
… Is this train moving or what? I'm going to check on the train – OK?
(Gets up and walks along the carriage and seems to lean out of the door, while the WOMAN looks around, confused: she leaves in the other direction.)

MAN
Oy, mate, what's the problem with the train?

STATION STAFF
You deaf or something? We cleared you lot off half an hour ago. There's one under.

(MAN looks confused.) Fatality. Jumped when the train pulled out.

MAN
Oh … Do us a favour, can you tell the other one?

STATION STAFF
Other what?

MAN
Passenger. In this carriage.

STATION STAFF
(Gets on train): Where'd you all come from? Haven't you got a home to go to? … No, there's no one here. Not unless you've got an imaginary friend. Lonely are we?

END

Category: Y
Cast: 3 Gender Neutral
Gi60 UK 2015

YOU DON'T SAY
By Dan Morra
Middletown, PA, USA

Setting
A man is seated at a desk feverishly typing on a laptop, occasionally glancing at a piece of paper and swearing under his breath. A woman rushes in.

WOMAN
(urgently) Well?

WRITER
(without looking up as he continues typing)
Well what!

WOMAN
The press conference is starting. The governor needs his speech.

WRITER
Excuse me for not doing a better job of anticipating the flood and our inadequate preparations.

WOMAN
Don't say that.

WRITER
You mean they weren't inadequate? Tell that to the 12 people who drowned when their homes were washed away.

WOMAN
You know what I mean. You can't use words like that; they're on the banned list. We'll get fired.
(The man finishes typing triumphantly.)

WRITER
There; it's on his pad. Another literary masterpiece.
(The WOMAN exits quickly; the lights come up on a podium where the GOVERNOR is set to speak.)

GOVERNOR
(obviously reading from his pad) Let me begin by saying how tragic this hydro anomaly has been. Recognizing the possibility of widespread structural disintegrity, we ordered the temporary reallocation of human resources late last night; unfortunately, 12 individuals were subjected to a challenging non-viable water situation and did not remain sentient.
(Begin fade out.)
Despite our concerted and limitless efforts ....

END

Category: Y   **FOUR CHARACTER PLAYS**
Cast: 2 F, 2 M
Gi60 UK 2015

THE LACK
By Alex Dremann
Philadelphia, PA, USA

Setting

Sitting side by side, a MAN and a WOMAN share a soft pretzel off a paper plate that has a glop
of mustard on it they are using as dip. WINNIFRED and DONOVAN approach them as if they
were an art installation and slowly circle them, inspecting every detail during the following.
WINNIFRED wears uber-trendy black-framed glasses.

DONOVAN

Now, this, this is fascinating. Notice the use of color – see how the yellow of the mustard is
repeated here on his shirt.
        (pointing to a stain on the MAN's shirt)
Genius ... and the use of gritty urban texture throughout. The bags under her eyes speak of a
world-weariness. And look at the bottom-heavy composition as a whole. Simply stunning!

WINNIFRED

Or simply simple.
        (Beat)

DONOVAN

Expound.

WINNIFRED

I think the artist is making a statement on the averageness of the Average. Capital A. And that's
just so ... Average.

DONOVAN

        (not agreeing or disagreeing)
Capital A.

WINNIFRED

They are literally everybody. Every man, every woman. Every soft pretzel for that matter. There
is nothing unique or interesting about them. Watch as she chews.
        (WOMAN chews, eyeing WINNIFRED without emotion.)

DONOVAN

I disagree. Their lack of distinction is exactly what's so interesting about them. What you are
looking at is a void. The artist has captured an emptiness, a vacuum. A cultural, emotional, and
spiritual lack. Do you not see the brilliance of that?
        (MAN dips his soft pretzel chunk into the mustard and eats it.)

WINNIFRED

It's like painting with the brush an inch off the canvas – the effort immense, the result, nothingness.

DONOVAN

Perhaps you're projecting your own lack. Perhaps this piece is exactly that; an empty canvas upon which you project your inner self. Perhaps you are seeing your own nothingness.
(WINNIFRED has leaned in close to inspect WOMAN.)

WINNIFRED

If there's one thing I lack, Donovan, it's lack.

DONOVAN

(skeptically)
Uh-huh.

WINNIFRED

Let's just go. You know I only come to First Friday for the free wine and do you see any wine? If I lack anything besides "lack," it's a Pinot Grigio and the last thing I need is to look at "lack" by some hack, sober.
(WOMAN dips her pretzel stub in the mustard and smudges mustard onto WINNIFRED's glasses. WINNIFRED just takes it unfazed.)

WINNIFRED

OK, now I love it.

DONOVAN

Meh.

END

Category: Y
Cast: 4 Gender Neutral
Gi60 UK 2014

MONSTER FACE
By Oscar Allen
Leeds, UK

Setting
GODZILLA, RODAN, KING GHIDORAH
the three-headed monster, and GIGAN the
Cyborg Chicken are sat at a table playing a
card game. It's GIGAN's turn. He goes to
make a move. GODZILLA stops him.

GODZILLA
I wouldn't do that if I were you.

RODAN
You're looking at his cards and helping, you
can't do that!

GODZILLA
I'm the king of the monsters, I can do what
I like!

GIGAN
Gigan think it *good* idea!

GODZILLA
See!

RODAN
That proves nothing, Gigan agrees to anything
if you offer him oil for his chain-saw tummy-
button.

GIGAN
Gigan see no problem with this.

GODZILLA
Besides, look at that! King Ghidorah's got
the worst poker faces around. You're hiding
something ...

KING GHIDORAH
Oh, come on, you're ganging up on me again
... It's just not fair!

GIGAN
Gigan think it fair!

KING GHIDORAH
Why is it always me, Godzilla? Sometimes
I think you just have a grudge. Look me in
the eye, and tell me this isn't because I'm the
only girl at this table.

GODZILLA
... You're a GIRL? But your name is KING
Ghidorah!

KING GHIDORAH
I can't help it if my parents had avant-garde
naming traditions.

GODZILLA
No, look, the only girl at this table is Rodan!

RODAN
Hey! I'm a guy!

GODZILLA
That's not possible, you LAY EGGS!

RODAN
SO DO YOU!

GODZILLA
Yeah, well, I'm a girl! Well, sort of both,
sometimes ... When I want to be, LOOK IT'S
COMPLICATED!

GIGAN
Gigan is a chicken!
    (Everyone stares at GIGAN before
    GODZILLA lets out an awkward
    cough.)

GODZILLA
Well, at least now that I know ... I mean, umm, if you're free, maybe you'd like to umm ...

KING GHIDORAH
Grab a bite to eat?

GODZILLA
Yeah! Well, if you want ...

KING GHIDORAH
How about Tokyo?

GODZILLA
My favourite!

(The two smile and walk off stage together. GIGAN and RODAN are also smiling and watch them walk away. As they watch, GIGAN slowly moves to put his arm around RODAN's back.)

RODAN
(Without looking) No.

GIGAN
Awww.

END

Category: Y
Cast: 6–8 Gender Neutral
Gi60 US 2009, 2014

SIX CHARACTERS+ PLAYS

GHOSTS
By Aurora Stewart de Peña
Toronto, ON, Canada

Setting
(ELENA comes home from a long day
at work to find six or seven ghosts in
her living room, relaxing casually
around her apartment.)

ELENA
Ahhh!

GHOSTS
Ahhhhh!

ELENA
Who are you?

GHOST 1
We're ghosts.

ELENA
Why?

GHOST 2
Your house is haunted.

ELENA
It is?

GHOST 1
Well, it's full of ghosts, isn't it?

GHOST 4
Yeah, if we're here it means your house is
haunted.

GHOST 3
Yeah, we're haunting it.

ELENA
Have you always been here?

GHOST 3
I can't remember.

GHOST 5
I have.

GHOST 6
I used to live here.

GHOST 1
I died a sudden and violent death not far
from here.

ELENA
Are you benevolent spirits that are watching
over me?

GHOST 2
I don't think so.

ELENA
Are you evil spirits that want to harm me?

GHOST 5
Probably not.

ELENA
Well, what are you?

GHOST 6
We're just ghosts.

ELENA
How come I couldn't see you before?

GHOST 3
I don't know.

GHOST 2
Has something changed recently?

ELENA
Like what?

GHOST 4
Like, I don't know, a shift of some kind?

ELENA
Like how?

GHOST 6
Like something significant?

ELENA
Like, what kind of significant?

GHOST 1
Like, did you die?

END

Category: Y
Cast: 2 M, Ensemble
Gi60 US 2008, 2014

I.D. PLEASE
By Jose A. Rivera
Buffalo, NY, USA

(A security guard stands at the entrance to a college campus. Two students walk by the guard. One flashes their I.D. card to the guard. The other does not.)

SECURITY GUARD
I.D. please.

STUDENT
Yea sure.
(Searches through things)
Uh … wait I know I have it … it's just … damn come on … ugh … I'm … I'm sorry I can't find it now …
(A student passes with no I.D., the guard doesn't notice.)

SECURITY GUARD
Then you can't go through.

STUDENT
(Another student passes with no I.D.)
But I –

SECURITY GUARD
You can pick up a guest pass at the main gate.

STUDENT
But then I have to go all the way around … C'mon I'm already late for class.
(Another student passes with no I.D.)

SECURITY GUARD
Not my problem.
(A very mysterious and seedy-looking person walks by the guard and student.)

STUDENT
Hey look –

SECURITY GUARD
You can pick up a guest pass at the main gate.

STUDENT
Just give me a break.

SECURITY GUARD
No. I need your I.D.

STUDENT
I'm a student; why would I lie –

SECURITY GUARD
I don't know that until you show me some I.D.
(A larger group of people pass by: some students, some bizarre characters. Maybe zombies or pickpockets.)

STUDENT
Look I just can't find – OH COME ON!!! Like 20 freaking people just went by!!! You didn't ask any of them for – You got to be kidding me!!

SECURITY GUARD
I'm going to have to ask you to calm down.
(A girl runs past the guard and student, frantic and screaming. A masked murderer holding a bloody knife is stalking her.)

STUDENT
Oh, for crying out loud!

(Optional: As masked murderer passes
SECURITY GUARD, he wordlessly holds
up an I.D. card, never breaking stride in
his pursuit of screaming girl.)

SECURITY GUARD
I don't see an I.D. card.

STUDENT
YOU CAN'T BE SERIOUS!

SECURITY GUARD
I.D.

STUDENT
But –

SECURITY GUARD
I.D.

STUDENT
This is –

SECURITY GUARD
I.D. Card. Please.

END

Category: Y
Cast: Ensemble
Gi60 #NextGen 2015

THE REHEARSAL
By Julia Coyle (age 11 at time of writing)
Leeds, UK

(Small group of children sit round in a
semicircle with TEACHER standing.
They are in a small village library.)

TEACHER
(Claps hands) Gather round everyone,
rehearsals are starting.

ELLIE
(ELLIE stands up.)
Uuumm, Miss, I can't get any black shoes and
my mum ...

TEACHER
Sit down ELLIE. (ELLIE sits down with a
frown on her face.) Now let's get started.

JAMES
Miss, (JAMES stands) my dad says he doesn't
want me to have any dairy products on the ...
(James trails off as he is interrupted)

TEACHER
(Points to floor) SIT!
(James sits back down with his head
down.)

LIBRARIAN
Could you ask your kids to settle down
please? I know the school hall is shut so mind
your manners.

LUCY
Should I sing that extra part Miss? I'm sooo
good at singing.

TEACHER
Yes, Um, No, LUCY! SIT DOWN.

ELLIE
Can't YOU get me some black shoes?

GRAHAM
I feel sick Miss?

CHILD 1
My head is hurting.

CHILD 2
I have a tummy ache.

ELLIE
I can't come any more miss if I can't get
black shoes.

JAMES
I can't eat nuts and ...
(TEACHER glares at Kids.)

JAMES
I have to quit 'cos I can't have dairy.
(TEACHER's phone rings.)

TEACHER
(Pause) ... that's okay, we'll get someone else
to do his part.

LUCY
My dad says if I don't sing then I have to
leave.

TEACHER
KIDS, there is no more production. Please go
Home!!

END

Category: Y
Cast: 1 F, 6–12 Ensemble
Gi60 US 2007

SOME ZOO STORY
By Joan Lunoe
Bronx, NY, USA

Setting
The Bronx Zoo. On stage a female GORILLA is seen relaxing in her enclosure. She should be exhibiting standard GORILLA behavior, i.e. sitting on her haunches eating berries found on the ground, walking calmly on all fours, scratching arm/face, etc. It should not be the frenzied behavior of a chimpanzee – no chest beating, jumping around, "monkey" cries. GORILLAS are calm and quiet, very distinct from chimps.

(An enthusiastic Zoo volunteer GUIDE enters leading a school group of hyper 10 year olds.)

GUIDE
If you'll all follow me this way we're now entering the Congo Gorilla Forest – which is my favorite place at the zoo.
Here there are two families of gorillas living in a six and a half acre enclosure …

(The following should be said in quick succession but each line needs to be heard completely, no cutoffs.)

KID 1
Where are the monkeys?

KID 2
Can we go in there?

KID 3
I bet he could bust through that window.

KID 4
Does he like Pop Tarts?

KID 5
My dad says we don't come from apes, we come from God.

(The GUIDE begins to stutter some response but quickly looks imploringly to the GORILLA in bewilderment.)

GORILLA
(to the GUIDE w/gentle but firm reassurance)
I think I can field these.
(to the KIDS, spoken very quickly in quiet tones of complete disgust)

First of all, Sonny, I am not a monkey, I'm an APE, a primate of the subfamily Hominoidea. We are distinguished from the monkey by our large brains, a small appendix and NO TAIL.

Secondly, you don't want to come in here because even though we look nice and calm we're still wild animals and you don't know what we might do, yadda, yadda, yadda.

And yes, *she* (I may not be your definition of delicate but I am a *lady*) could bust through this window but I make a conscious choice not to.

Pop Tarts … well, my diet consists largely of raw fruits, leaves, and seeds, so I don't see where Pop Tarts would fit into the picture, and certainly not those wretched cinnamon crème with raspberry sprinkles.

And as for the Ape–God, Evolution–Intelligent Design debate, don't get me started! But hey, what do I know. **I'm just a big GORILLA!**

(Throws a quick little "boo!" to the KIDS and goes back to peacefully scratching and picking gnats.)

END

Category: Y
Cast: 1 M, 2 Gender Neutral, 3–7 Ensemble
Gi60 US 2009

SUPER FLAVOR
By Jose A. Rivera
Buffalo, NY, USA

Setting
Cold Stone Creamery. Two employees stand
behind the counter. EMPLOYEE #1 is serving
a customer. More customers stand in line
waiting to be served.

EMPLOYEE #2
Hi! Welcome to Cold Stone, home of the Cold
Stone, can I take your order?
(Just as the customer is about to order
we hear a large gush of wind. All the
customers quickly look to the
entrance.)

CUSTOMER #1
What was that?!? A bird?

CUSTOMER #2
A plane?

CUSTOMER #3
No it's –

EMPLOYEE #1
Here we go again …
(Enter SUPERMAN.)

ALL CUSTOMERS
SUPERMAN!!!
(EMPLOYEE #1 and #2 share a glance;
they are not happy.)

EMPLOYEE #2
Fuckin' Superman …

SUPERMAN
Greetings citizens! Yes, it's me. I'm excited to
see you too.

(SUPERMAN works his way through
the beaming customers to the front of
the line.)

SUPERMAN
(Rhetorically) May I?

CUSTOMER #1
Not at –
(SUPERMAN moves immediately to the
counter.)

SUPERMAN
Thank you. (To the employees) Greetings
Cold Stonians!

EMPLOYEE #1
(sighs) What can we get you Super –

SUPERMAN
(Note: When Superman orders the ice
cream he's always playing to the
customers' attention and relishing in it.
You can add in him signing autographs
or posing for pictures.)
I *overheard* about a new flavor: Peppermint
Chocolate. May I have a sample?

EMPLOYEE #1
Of course … (Hands him a little pink sample
spoon)

SUPERMAN
Mmm. That's just super! (The crowd swoons.)
What about some Orange Dreamscicle.
(EMPLOYEE hands him another little
spoon.)

SUPERMAN
Mmm, mmm, MMM! Lemme try the uh, the
Raspberry Sorbet, and the Macadamia Nut.
    (Takes the samples. SUPERMAN savors
    the ice cream slowly for the crowd,
    who are in awe.)
The flavors are just … overwhelming!

EMPLOYEE #1
Fucking Superman. Comes in here once a
week and never buys a damn thing.

EMPLOYEE #2
He'll learn his lesson today.

EMPLOYEE #1
Whaddya mean?

SUPERMAN
That Mint Green Chocolate Magic looks
delicious. Lemme –

EMPLOYEE #2
Here ya go!
    (SUPERMAN takes, eats.)

EMPLOYEE #1
What are you up to?

SUPERMAN
Oh! (Suddenly he's in tremendous pain.)
What's happening?!?

EMPLOYEE #2
Yes! I got him!
    (Jumps on the counter)

SUPERMAN
This isn't Mint!

EMPLOYEE #2
That's right Superman! It's Kryptonite!

SUPERMAN
No!

EMPLOYEE #2
That'll teach you to only sample and never
buy ice cream at Cold Stone!
    (Evil maniacal laughter)

END

Category: Y
Cast Size: 5–12 Actors
Gi60 US 2010

WHY DEATH SHOULDN'T GO TO THE MOVIES
By Jennifer Russo (age 13 at time of writing)
New York, NY, USA

Setting
A movie theatre.
(Enter cloaked person, DEATH. He has popcorn in his hand (but no soda) and a scythe. DEATH is followed by an USHER.)

USHER
'Scuse me sir, I'm going to have to take that.
(Gestures at scythe)

DEATH
Are you sure?

USHER
Yes.
(The USHER grabs the scythe and screams in agony, falling on the floor.)

DEATH
(Shrug)
(DEATH begins to climb over people after spotting an empty seat.)

DEATH
Excuse me.

PERSON 1
Oh sur– AHHH!
(Dies)

DEATH
(Scooching over more people to get to an empty seat a few seats down)
I'm sorry, ooh 'scuse me. My bad.

PEOPLE IN SEATS
(Screams of pain)
AHH!! Ooooh!!
(All dying as he passes them.)

DEATH
(Bumps into a big hefty guy)

HEFTY GUY
(Turns around)
HEY WATCH IT.

DEATH
(Touches his shoulders apologetically)
I'm so sorry.

HEFTY GUY
(Screams in agony like a little girl)
(As DEATH is going along, his phone rings. "It's a Small World" or something happy and peppy as his ringtone)

DEATH
(Answers phone)
OH HEY MARTY! Yeah I've had quite a week. Next Tuesday? Sure, that works!

MOVIE GOER
SHUSH! There's a movie going on here!

DEATH
(Touches him apologetically)
I'm sorry, man.

MOVIE GOER
(Dies screaming)

DEATH
(Finally sits down in an empty seat. A second ticks by.)
OH MAN! I forgot my soda!
(As DEATH stands up, the entire aisle in front of him scramble for dear life.)

END

Appendices

Appendix A

Please/No

An exercise about being completely present with your partner; objectives, committing to specific actions, listening, and having a willingness to let go of a tactic that isn't working and committing to a new action. Two partners, A and B; group observes.

- Guider sets up an open area to include a few pieces of random furniture; perhaps four to six chairs, a cube or two. These should be placed at distances from one another; they are there to offer participants options for random movement during the exercise, they should not indicate any specific environment.

- "Please" has the goal of getting "No" to change their mind to say "Yes." "No" is under no obligation to do so; they must be honestly persuaded to change their mind.

- "Please" and "No" should have good, clear reasons; "Please" needs to be clear on why they need "No" to say "Yes," and "No" needs to be clear as to why they feel strongly about their position and disinclined to change to a "Yes." However, they should not devise complicated back stories. Guider should encourage them to find simple, human reasons for wanting what they want, i.e. "Please" should not create a deep back story about a betrayal that they need forgiveness for; "No" should not create unreasonable circumstances that must exist before they change their minds ("I will only say "Yes" if "Please" hops up and down on one foot"). Imaginations will create circumstances as the exchanges evolve, but starting with "story" instead of objectives and tactics has the potential to take the participants out of the immediacy of the moment.

- Guider designates who will be "Please" and who will be "No"; e.g. Participant A will be "Please" and Participant B will be "No." These are the only lines of text they can say out loud.

  - "No" will be asked to ground themselves somewhere in the playing area. (They are instructed not to move during the actual exchange with "Please.")

  - Once they have done so, "Please" must approach "No" – make physical contact in some way – and then ask/say "Please" in an effort to get "No" to change to "Yes." "No" will very likely say "No" – and then after the exchange is complete, "No" must move to a different place in the playing area, ground themselves again.

  - Once "No" has grounded themselves in the space again, "Please" makes a new attempt to get "No" to change to "Yes." Each time, "Please" must make – and maintain – physical contact with "No" while trying to persuade them to change to "Yes." This can be foot touching foot, a hand on the shoulder, etc. Again, physical contact cannot be broken during the exchange once it's been made.

  - If/when "No" says "No," they must then move again. It is their choice how far or where to move to.

  - The round will end either when "No" changes to "Yes" or the Guider decides to end the round after a period of time/exploration. Make certain that "Please" and "No" maintain the structure throughout; once "No" finds a new place in the playing area, they remain grounded for the next attempt of "Please."

- Be mindful if the participants start to add words, or want to say their single piece of text multiple times. By compelling them to stay with the structure of those single words in each exchange, it helps them put the rest of what they *want* to do in their bodies and in their choices. Adding extra words can defuse the strength of purpose.

Tips

This exercise is more challenging than it appears. As you side coach, be mindful of whether "Please" is truly taking in "No"'s response to their choice. Is "No" offended? Annoyed? Exasperated? Encourage "Please" to really take in their partner; listen to their responses, observe the body language as "No" responds and moves away after saying "No." What information can be gleaned from close listening and observation? What effect are the choices of "Please" having on the partner? And how can "Please" use that information to adjust their next choice of action? Is "Please" getting closer to getting a "Yes," or are they driving "No" more firmly into their position of "No"? Also, is "No" being open to "Please"? Are they listening and allowing, or are they digging in no matter what, simply to give their partner a hard time?

Observe if "Please" immediately casts their eyes to the ground when/if they get a "No." They may be spending time focusing on beating themselves up for not getting a "Yes," or they may be completely in their heads, thinking "Huh. Why didn't that work?" Or "What else *could* work?" In the meantime, the very thing that can help them get a "Yes" – their partner's honest response – is being missed, and is now walking away from them. Also observe whether "Please" struggles to make or maintain the physical contact. Do they "tap" their partner on the arm and then let their arm flop? Gently remind them of this element.

Notes

Please/No focuses on being present, listening, committing fully to objectives and actions, observation, taking care of your partner, and being open and willing to be affected by your partner and to let go of an action that isn't working for the success of your objective. This exercise helps actors become aware of when they are disengaged from the listening process, when they are disengaged from their partner and the circumstances, and when they are clinging to an action that isn't working because they're too busy thinking "hey, it *should* have worked ..." Perhaps most importantly, it explores the idea that to get what you want, you need to find what your partner wants or needs and be willing to give that.

The physical structure of this exercise can also reveal when actors are anticipating failure. Physical contact is intimate, and "Please" can see how "No" feels about that threshold being crossed. It's a risk to try a new tactic while touching your partner; "Please" will sometimes ask "do I *have* to touch them?" And that's the point; the touch is intimate, it makes it personal, and it creates a visceral response. The physical component helps keep actors out of their heads, and helps make the scene active, connected, personal, and immediate.

The physical component of "No" moving also provides a strong visual clue as to what "No" needs or wants from "Please" before they can consider giving a "Yes." Are they only moving a few feet away? "Please" may be getting closer to discovering what action may be affecting "No" that can help them get a "Yes." How can they pursue that choice more deeply, more fully? Or, did "No" go straight across the room, creating as much distance as possible? That distance communicates how close/far "Please" may have been off the mark.

Appendix B

Scheme of work 'Writing plays'. Note: Get your students to hand in their scripts at the end of each class so you can make photocopies. This Scheme of work uses the exercises listed in Chapter 1 of this book.

Week	Length of activity	Activity	Assessment	Resources
1	5 mins	Introduction to project: what is a 1 min play	Reading aloud – literacy	Teacher explanation
	5 mins	Hand out example scripts to group and get them to read in groups or pairs		Gi60 example scripts
	15 mins	Work out your 1 min play – small group work to stage script given		
	15 mins	Share 1 min play given with group		
	10 mins	Group discussion: What facets of playwriting do these plays share? What is good or bad? Group teacher leads discussion with notes	Peer evaluation Verbal – three positives Evaluation of writing techniques used	Pens and paper/ could be done as a flipchart sheet in groups
2	5 mins	Introduction – ? Reminder of the structure required, explored at the end of last class If you are writing for 1 min script how long is a minute?	Group discussion with aide memoire	Flipchart sheets from previous class
	10 mins	Pen Head Exercise – Generating basic ideas for a script	Tutor lead observations of scripts	Pen and paper
	10 mins	"What's in a Name" Exercise		
	15 mins	Write a script. Work with a partner – use the character/s created in the What's in a Name Exercise and the ideas generated in Pen Heads to write a short dialogue between characters	Group identify positives	
	5 mins	Share some scripts – gather in ideas generated		
3	5 mins	Introduction – how do I get an idea on how to write a play – reminder of lessons learnt last class and the structure required for a play	Tutor observation of information retained	PowerPoint or notes on board
	15 mins	"The Ballad of X & Y" – can be played more than once, with students to decide if their final sheet is worth keeping or not		Pen and paper

(Continued)

Week	Length of activity	Activity	Assessment	Resources
	5 mins	With their ideas sheets, students are to find a partner and to discuss these concepts and how they may form together to form a short script	Literacy	Paper and pens
	15 mins	Students to write a play either individually or in pairs observing the structure previously discussed with a story between the two characters		
	10 mins	Students to share writing with group	Peer observation Three positives and one area to expand on	
4	5 mins	Introduction – getting script ideas from other sources, reminder again of how to apply structure	Literacy Teamwork peer observation	
	15 mins	Exercise What's in the Box – students to pick an item from the box and to spend time examining it and noting down any thoughts they have about their object in a spider graph (for younger groups) or five minutes of continuous writing		Pen and paper Box containing random objects/ newspaper stories/poems/ items of costume
	15 mins	Writing scripts – can you make these ideas into a one minute play for a cast of two?		
	15 mins	Share your idea with a partner – can you get both scripts on to their feet?		
5	10 mins	Introduction and warm up game, using improvisation to generate script ideas – best suit a focus game such as Bobby's Balls		Balls
	5 mins	Game Alfred's Cat – Students to sit in a circle and to tell the story of Alfred's cat in turns. Starting their sentence with a consecutive letter of the alphabet, i.e. Alfred's cat: "Ate apples on a Monday" "Belched in the face of his owner" "Cooked hamsters for tea"		
	5 mins	Status – randomly give out status cards ranked in power 1–10, ask the student to consider what a person of that status level may be like, job/ attributes they would have and to consider a character at that level		Status cards
	15 mins	Split into small groups and give each group a stimulus object, ask them to come up with a short improvised scene based on their status, mix as a group and influence on the object	Tutor observation	Random objects
	15 mins	Write up ideas into a script, but get individuals to write their own as their memories or interpretations will be different	Literacy	Pens and paper

Week	Length of activity	Activity	Assessment	Resources
6	5 mins	Intro – Using other stimulus material. Discussion on how we may choose to use influences from real life or respond to an image to create a play		
	10 mins	Give out a selection of photographs/ newspaper articles – students have 5 mins to brainstorm as many ideas as possible onto a sheet of paper in response to article given		Selection of photographs/ newspaper articles
	15 mins	Write ideas into a play script with a defined start, middle, and end	Peer observation	Pens and paper
	5 mins	Read script with partner		
	5 mins	Make any changes to the script that you feel could be improved on	Self-evaluation	
	10 mins	Sharing of scripts	Peer observation	
7	5 mins	Taking on board what we have learnt and taking a step into the surreal – introduction, get students to recap on what they learnt from the previous class and how imagination can be used to create ideas		Pens and paper
	15 mins	Repeat the exercise "What's in the box" but this time get the students to give the object a personality, e.g. the object might be a dusty grumpy book that has been left on the shelf for years never read or perhaps a noisy banjo who just won't shut up	Tutor observation	
	10 mins	Share characters created in group and pair together characters that may suitably work		
	5 mins	To look at each other's characters and to discuss how they might meet	Peer feedback	
	10 mins	Individually write own script with a start, middle, and end		
	5 mins	Share some play texts	Peer evaluation	
8	5 mins	Introduction —I have lots of scripts, are they any good? Group discussion, what makes a good play		
	25 mins	Tackling a two hander script – split group into threes, make one person a director, and give each group a play they have not previously worked on. Ask students to consider:		Photocopied scripts written by students
		Staging for effect – i.e. use of areas, levels, proxemics		
		The characters they are playing		
		The emotion they want the audience to feel having watched the play – this last one, get them to write down and give to you		
	15 mins	Share performances – peer observers to make notes on two things that worked well and one that could improve. Did the group achieve their goal?	Peer observation	
	5 mins	Feedback on plays – did the playwright agree with what they did, or did it help them to see their play differently?	Group evaluation	
		Does it keep to time?		

(Continued)

Week	Length of activity	Activity	Assessment	Resources
9	5 mins	Introduction – Polishing up a final script		
		Ask students to look back on the scripts they have written, state it is OK not to like ideas and that it is OK to discount and change a script if it does not work		
	5 mins	Ask the students:	Evaluation	
		To rate the scripts they have written in preference and to state why		
	15 mins	To take their favorite play and to ask:	Evaluation and development	Pens and paper
		Is the play actually 1 min long, or does it need editing?		
		Does the play have a clear start, middle, and end?		
		Do my characters have noticeably different personalities?		
		How should the audience respond to this play?		
		What changes, if any, do I need to make to this play?		
	10 mins	Rewrite	Evaluation and development	
	10 mins	Ask students to choose one play script they were less happy with, ask why and how they could change or develop the idea into a new script:		
		e.g. John and Jane went to the park to discuss their wedding but what would happen if they met a dragon?		
		Write up new idea		
		Ask students to have one script they are fully happy with for next class		
10		Get our plays on their feet		
	15 mins	Split group into smaller groups, share out scripts so that the writer does not work on their own scripts, and read through scripts		
	25 mins	Get each script onto its feet and roughly blocked following Week 8	Teamwork	
	10 mins	Share in a small class performance	Group evaluation and individual evaluation of own play	

Scheme of work kindly prepared by Jan Ansell (Head of Division, Media, Music and Performing Arts, York College, UK)

Appendix C

As we have mentioned, one minute plays require actors who can really focus as well as working as part of an ensemble. These next two exercises will help your actors improve their skills in both of these areas.

Sit On It

You will need: One chair for every participant

The aim of this exercise:

To help actors work collaboratively, share responsibility, and work intuitively under pressure

- Ask each participant to place a chair in the space you are working in using all the available area and sit on it.
- Pick a participant (one of the ones sitting at one end of your space) and ask them to vacate their seat and stand at the other end of the room.
- The participant, whom we shall call "The Walker," is now free to slowly walk back to their seat.
- The aim of the exercise is to attempt to prevent this.
- Other group members may leave their own seats and occupy the empty seat (they are allowed to walk quickly or run – where space permits).
- Once a group member leaves their own seat to fill the vacant seat, their own seat obviously becomes vacant.
- Once "The Walker" has noticed that a seat has been vacated, they may walk toward it.
- Once the Walker successfully finds a seat and sits, that round of the exercise is over.

This is an exercise about teamwork and focus. The Walker will eventually find a seat, because eventually panic and confusion will set in among the group. Often the Walker is tempted to run; do not allow this. Groups quickly learn to work together and to watch each other's moves and actions, reacting not just to the vacant seat but to the seat that might be vacated next. This is a great exercise for improving confidence and teamwork.

Appendix D

Bobby's Balls

You will need: Three to six balls or bean bags (juggling balls or bags are best, but tennis balls or similar will do)

The aim of the exercise:

Like *Sit on It*, *Bobby's Balls* is a game about concentration and focus. There are many variants of this game, but at its heart it's about delivering and receiving and being in the moment, the keys skills of the actor.

Part 1

- Arrange the group in a circle.
- Ask each group member to raise one hand.
- The group leader should now throw one ball across the circle.
- The person receiving the ball catches it, lowers their hands, and throws to somebody else across the circle with a raised hand.
- This process continues until everybody in the circle has received the ball.
- The last person throws the ball back to the group leader.
- Ask the group to remember who they threw the ball to and who they received the ball from and then repeat this rotation.

Part 2

- Once the group are happy with this rotation, add a second and then a third ball to it.
- The group are still only asked to throw and receive with the same two people, but the additional balls add extra stress, as the times between throwing and receiving are reduced.

Part 3

- If the group are comfortable with this, start a new rotation by repeating the first steps of the exercise with a different colored ball. Once this rotation has been established, introduce your original rotation (Part 1)

- The group now have to remember who to throw to and receive from with two separate balls.

Part 4

- You can now add more balls to each rotation (having two sets of balls with different colors really helps here). Alternatively, you can ask the group to count to 100 in increments of 1, starting with the group leader and progressing clockwise or counter-clockwise.

You can see that the permutations of this exercise are pretty much endless, and it's a fantastic way of showing actors that to work as part of a team, you actually have to concentrate on your part of the machine and not worry about the whole. What do you need to do, what do people need from you, are you focused on the right thing at the right time? This is an excellent warm-up exercise that actors will return to as they try to improve their teamwork. When working well, the catch and throw of the balls will start to form a natural rhythm, like one machine made up of many parts.

Notes about this exercise

- Throws must be under arm.

- Participants must not speak or apologize.

- No one should throw a ball unless they have eye contact with the catcher.

- No one should ever be holding more than one ball.

Appendix E

Hitchhiker

Create a "car" out of four chairs: two in the front and two in the back.

- One person begins as the driver; they need to maintain the physical action of driving the car (and looking at the road!) throughout their "term" as the driver.

- A second person hitches a ride (they get in and sit in the "shotgun" seat next to the driver). The hitchhiker should choose a clear, strong character trait; even (or especially!) something archetypical, e.g. a self-absorbed egotist, an ultra-conservative millionaire, a groovy hippie for whom everything is great; encourage actors to focus on traits instead of occupations.

- The driver gradually assumes those specific traits, while maintaining the thread of their conversation/relationship, and their driving responsibilities.

- A third hitchhiker flags a ride; they bring in a new, specific character with a clear set of traits. The others gradually assume the new traits, again without stopping to "wait" for the new traits, or losing the thread of what they've just been discussing. This third rider gets into the seat just behind the front passenger ("shotgun") seat.

- A fourth hitchhiker flags a ride, and is again a new, specific character with identifiable traits. Others in car assume these traits, etc. This person sits in seat directly behind driver.

- When a fifth person flags car for ride (bringing in new character/traits that others will assume), they enter and sit in the seat directly behind the driver; other car occupants rotate counter-clockwise, so that driver exits the car, the front seat passenger now becomes the driver, the person who had been seated behind "shotgun" now moves into that seat in the front, and so on.

- Each new hitchhiker follows this pattern, and passengers rotate counter-clockwise to accommodate each new person in the car.

- Participants can randomly flag a ride whenever they want, or guider can create a "line up" order of who goes when.

Tips

Encourage passengers in the car to be patient with "getting" the traits. If someone is driving, they may be tempted to stop looking at the road, turn around, and look at the person behind them in order to get the traits "faster." Having the driver-actor wait for the traits to reach the person in the passenger seat will allow them to experience the transitions more fully. Encourage passengers to continue the scene that they're doing until they are given a reason to change. Sometimes actors will come to a complete stop verbally and physically when someone new is entering the car. Again, experiencing the transition will be more beneficial to them.

Challenge participants to explore silent traits: something physical that isn't communicated as quickly, or a character who happens to be quiet. Fewer words can help them explore physical nuances.

Notes

Hitchhiker focuses on commitment, specificity, listening, trust, focus, observation, and awareness. For actors who are creating multiple roles in a single evening, it's a terrific exercise in committing, and working the muscles involved in letting go of a choice and committing fully to something new in fast succession while maintaining relationship and story. It's also fast and fun.

When it comes up (and it will come up), take the opportunity to discuss with actors the differences between archetypical behavior and stereotypical behavior. Not all blondes are "ditzy," not all teenagers are "slackers"; over time, encourage specificity within the bold character trait choices.

Appendix F

Three Character Interview

Two participants, A and B; one interviewer, one being interviewed for a specific job.

- A greets B, and A decides what the job is that B is interviewing for. B must commit to the circumstances of a) wanting to get the job, b) doing anything in their power to get the job.

- B begins with a specific and clear character. After a few moments, the Guider claps their hands, and B must switch immediately to new character traits. B *remains* the person who wants the job and is committed to interviewing for the job, but their traits are now entirely different; e.g. if they began the interview as humble and self-effacing, they may now be bold or arrogant. The given circumstances do not change; only the traits of the character.

- After a short while, Guider claps hands again, and B must switch immediately to yet a third set of traits. Participant A's character/traits remain constant, but of course they are responding in the moment to the changes in their partner.

- Guider can determine how many changes of character they want actors to experience, but we've found three at a time is a good stretch.

Tips

Encourage B to explore physical differences as well as internal ones. A shy person may indeed slide down in his/her chair; a confident and well-prepared person may well sit up straight, holding their head straight forward. Actors may find the change of physical choice will quickly lead them to the set of different traits.

Notes

Three Character Interview focuses on commitment, being present and listening, specificity, letting go of judgment, imagination, multi-tasking, focus, and stamina. Because the Guider determines when the clap happens, it also helps actors get away from pre-planning choices, allowing them to listen and be more fully present in the interview. Again, this is an excellent exercise for actors working on multiple characters, and helps strengthen their trust and confidence in their ability to make fully committed choices quickly and clearly. The fast succession of changes also helps them to experience how specific their choices are (or aren't), in comparison with the character they just embodied.

You may find that you need to remind participants of their objectives: "I want the job," "I want this person to reveal their true qualities (so I can determine if they're fit for the job)." Sometimes, in the rush of entertaining and hilarious character trait switches, actors can lose sight of the goal.

Appendix G

We've used one minute plays in many directing classes to explore the concepts of story as well as the seven fundamental categories of plot/story as per Christopher Booker's *Why We Tell Stories*:

- The Quest

  - A hero (usually along with some companions) is required or compelled to travel to seek and obtain a specific item of treasure. They encounter great challenges along the way and often must defeat a larger, darker force. *Deep into October* p. 117, *The First Step* p. 188, or *Lord of the Rings*.

- Rags to Riches

  - A sympathetic and usually poor protagonist takes a journey from humble means to great success. The "riches" can be personal and emotional, not simply monetary wealth. *Sunset in North Dakota* p. 167, *The Gold Doubloon* p. 317, or *Great Expectations* by Charles Dickens.

- Overcoming the Monster

  - Where the protagonist must defeat a monster that is a threat to them, to society, or to community in some way. This can be a literal monster, or a personal demon (alcoholism, etc.). *Fishing for Men* p. 275, *Diamonds Are Forever* p. 274, *Confrontation* p. 249, *Sleep Tight* p. 332, or *Harry Potter* (which could also absolutely be Quest or Voyage and Return).

- Voyage and Return

  - Protagonist travels to distant or unfamiliar places, and struggles to get back home. Usually encounters great challenges, and meets new friends who prove to be allies along the way. The experience gained on the journey is often what helps the protagonist get home again, and the focus of the story is more about obtaining experience rather than obtaining wealth. *Goldfish Quest for Domination* p. 256, *Listening off Beat* p. 132, *Welcome Home* p. 176, or *The Wizard of Oz*.

- Comedy

  - A lighter conflict that results in a happy conclusion. *Mirror, Mirror on the Wall* p. 139, *You're the Only One of You I've Got* p. 181, *Conversation* p. 272, or *A Midsummer Night's Dream*.

- Tragedy

  - A flawed character/hero who succumbs to ego, hubris, or temptation, breaks a law, and generally makes choices that lead to their own downfall, usually evoking pity. *Winter Coat* p. 180, *Pandora* p. 201, or *Hamlet*.

- Rebirth

  - Often an antagonist character who experiences an epiphany, leading to a change in their behaviors, resulting in redemption. *The Collective Memory of Humans, Being* p. 247, *In an Hour* p. 129, *King Kwik* p. 240, or *A Christmas Carol* by Charles Dickens.

Through analyzing these seven basic plotlines/stories in a series of one minute plays, the multiple examples help students hone analysis skills to identify the heart of a story/play with more efficiency. We recommend working with 20–30 samples. The economy of the storytelling in the one minute plays more readily reveals their structure and theme. In reviewing these multiple examples, students gain insights regarding the journey of a story and a play. When they return to full-length plays, they find that they are able to simplify and clarify their observations, guiding them to a stronger and more specific analysis of the story.

Appendix H

Liz Lehrman's Critical Response Process

CRP is a four-step process of facilitated dialogue created to support the development of an artist's work. Its goal is to nurture a dialogue between artist and responders that focuses on the work itself and the artist's goal for the work. There is the facilitator who guides the discussion, the artist who created the work-in-progress, and the responders (audience/invited audience). The dialogue is held immediately after the work has been presented.

Step 1: Statements of Meaning

Facilitator asks respondents what moments were meaningful, evocative, striking, exciting to them in the work that they've just seen. Facilitator guides responders away from language such as "I liked …" or "I disliked …" Lehrman writes, "all artists want to know that their work has meaning." Starting with Statements of Meaning instead of opinions helps to keep the focus on the work instead of the artist's feelings about the work.

Step 2: Artist as Questioner

The artist is asked to frame questions for the responders, trying to be specific to something the artist had been challenged by in the work. For example, instead of fishing for compliments such as "Did you like it when …," Ask "Was the transformation of the hero clear to you?"

Step 3: Neutral Questions

Responders are permitted to ask neutral questions without any embedded opinions. Liz Lehrman uses baking examples:

- "Why is the cake so dry?"
- Embedded opinion: "This cake is dry."
- Neutral Question: "What kind of texture were you going for with this cake?"

So to apply to the artistic work:

- "Why is the character Tara always yelling at Josh all the time?"
- Embedded opinion: "Tara yells at Josh too much and I don't know why."
- Neutral Question: "What is at the core of Tara and Josh's relationship?"

Step 4: Opinions

In this last step, which can be optional, responders use the following format: "I have an opinion about _____, would you like to hear it?" The artist has the option to say yes or no. Once the artist has said, "Yes, I would love to hear it," the responder is then free to offer their opinion about an aspect of the work. Guiders should take care that responders frame the opinion question without the embedded opinion! For example: "I have an opinion about the character Michael, would you like to hear it?" has no embedded opinion, while "I have an opinion about why Michael is so bossy, would you like to hear it?" *does* contain an embedded opinion.

The facilitated process and dialogue is a wonderful tool to support new writing and plays in development.

Appendix I

Using One Minute Plays to Explore Status
(Keith Johnstone's status, not sociological!)

This exercise can be adapted in many ways for acting, directing, and even improvisation classes. In acting and directing classes, the short plays provide a clear and economic exploration of status concepts in multiple stories. They also provide opportunities to use status to achieve objectives and make relationships clearer and more specific. In improvisation classes (after exploring concepts of status), students/actors inevitably ask, "Well, status is great; but how do I start to apply it to existing text?" We'll focus on one example here.

Use the play Nothing by Kevin Clyne, p. 143 in the Anthology section. This simple and clear conflict about two people in a relationship fight is universal and accessible to all. Mix and match gender throughout; the play works in infinite combinations. When we refer to "Him" and "Her" below, it's only for clarification of character names as the playwright has given them.

- Ask two people to read the play aloud going by first impulses/impressions; assign no status. Ask group, "What is this story about? What does he/she want? Do you think they achieved their objective by the end?"

- Use the same two people, and whisper status assignments in their ear; we suggest starting with "Her" as high and "Him" as low. Remind them that with an assigned status, one is looking for ways to raise status throughout if going for high, and ways to lower status throughout if going for low. Have them read the play again. Ask the observers the same questions and include "How did the focus on status affect the story?" "How would you describe this relationship?" Discussion will often include awareness of specificity of choices, how original perceptions of relationship have shifted, and greater awareness of beat changes (when a new tactic is being employed).

- Select two new people, whisper new status in their ear; try "low" for "Her," and "high" for "Him." Have them read play aloud. Discuss with observers: "How did status affect story this time? Who has the primary objective? Describe this relationship," etc. Be sure to mention that low status doesn't always mean one fails to get one's objective, and playing high status doesn't always mean one succeeds.

- Select two new people, whisper new status in their ears; try low/low and then high/high. Have them read play aloud again. Discuss: "What is this story about? How did status affect the story and does the story still work with the different statuses?"

Tips

Remind participants to still play their objectives and allow the status to support their actions in pursuit of objectives. Encourage them to observe closely and listen for opportunities to raise or lower their status even further and how that might help them get what they want.

Notes

Focusing on specific status in a conflict reveals the wide range of choices that are available to actors, and illuminates the concept of interpretation for directors. Participants find that shifting the status in characters changes the relationship, and therefore the story itself changes; and yet the story works every time (so long as participants are committed and specific with choices!). Through exploration, we've seen this story be about:

- A wounded "Her" whose longtime love, "Him," has disrespected her on her birthday and wants him to apologize and make it up to her;

- A "Him" who has been "played" by a manipulative "Her" and feels disrespected and wants her to admit fault and apologize;

- A clueless and passive "Him" desperately (and comically) trying to get "Her" to reveal what she wants so he can make it better;

- Two fiery people whose relationship is built on constant fighting, and the fight is integral to why they are together (i.e. this is not a rare event);

- Two shy people whose relationship is built on "you go first ... no you, no, you go ..." for whom fighting or disagreement is foreign and painful, and they are struggling to get what they want while avoiding conflict as much as possible; which is impossible while in a conflict!;

- A mischievous "Him" trying to get "Her" off the track so he can propose to her in the final moment;

- A "Her" who has been disappointed by "Him" many times in the past and is trying to find the courage to break off the relationship.

And that's just a few examples. No one changed a single word of text; they only changed the status of their characters and therefore shifted meaning in the text.

Adding status to relationship and objectives also seems to more clearly reveal changes of tactics and helps actors become more specific with actions. Status gives everyone something to do, and even in a moment when something may not be working, raising or lowering one's status further keeps the story fluid, active, and moving forward. "Transitions" or beat changes (changes in an action or tactic) can be challenging for actors and directors. Focusing on status helps ground those moments of change and makes them clearer. For example, in what specific moment did "Him" lose status? Did the actor playing "Her" take advantage of that loss to try a new action to raise her status further, and did that get her closer to her objective? Did "Him" recognize the loss of status, and did he try a new action in the next beat in an attempt to raise his status again? Did that get him closer to getting what he wanted?

The primal nature of status is in everyone; by exploring the countless possible "match ups" in a one minute play, it heightens awareness and empowers actors and directors to consider a wider range of possibilities when they next approach a scene/play. They will have experienced how many ways a story can work, and any concept of a story needing to be told "one way" will have lessened or vanished.

Bibliography

Atkins, G. (1993) *Improv! A Handbook for the Actor*, Portsmouth: Heinemann Press.

Ball, W. (2003) *A Sense of Direction: Some Observations on the Art of Directing*, Drama Publishers/Quite Specific Media.

Boal, A. (2002) *Games for Actors and Non Actors*, Oxford: Routledge.

Bonczek, R. (2015, June 11) Theater for the 60 Second Attention Span. [Interview]. Kristen Meinzer, Producer. The Takeaway with John Hockenberry, New York, NY: National Public Radio.

Bonczek, R. B. and Storck, D. (2012) *Ensemble Theatre Making: A Practical Guide*, Routledge.

Booker, C. (2003) *The Seven Basic Plots: Why We Tell Stories*, Continuum.

Gi60: The International One Minute Theatre Festival. Online video. Gi60Channel. www.youtube/user/gi60channel. Web. August, 2016.

Gottschall, J. (2013) *The Storytelling Animal: How Stories Make Us Human*, Mariner Books.

Hodge, F. and McLain, M. (2009) *Play Directing: Analysis, Communication and Style*, Focal Press.

Johnstone, K. (1987) *Impro: Improvisation and the Theatre*, Oxford: Routledge.

Lerman, L. and Borstel, J. (2003) *Critical Response Process: A Method for Getting Useful Feedback on Anything You Make from Dance to Dessert*, Tacoma Park: Liz Lerman Dance Exchange.

Miller, A. (1952) *The Crucible*, New York: Dramatists Play Service.

Pauly, Fred L. (1931) *One Minute Plays Requiring No Rehearsal*, March Brothers.

Robinson, M. B. (2012) *Directing Plays, Directing People: A Collaborative Art*, Smith & Kraus.

Spolin, V. (1963) *Improvisation for the Theater*, Evanston: Northwestern University Press.

Spolin, V. (1985, updated edn 2011) *Theater Games for Rehearsal: A Director's Handbook*, Evanston: Northwestern University Press.

Authors directory

Aakaash, Buffy   buffsters@me.com
Alberts, J.F   john.falberts@gmail.com
Allen, Matt   matt.liveartbistro@gmail.com
Allen, Oscar   oscar.allen@hotmail.com
Allen, Vic   mugwamp@btinternet.com
Ansell, Jan   ansell.jan@gmail.com
Ansell, Steve   screammedia@yahoo.com
Arieti, Olivia   o.arieti@alice.it
Ashmore, Liam & Price, Ellice   liama96@hotmail.
   co.uk, elliceprice@hotmail.co.uk
Avison, Rachel   rachelavison@hotmail.com

Barile, Paul   paulbarile@gmail.com
Bernstein, Alex   alexb0917@gmail.com
Bernstein, Amy L   alb457@gmail.com
Bezdickova, Lucie   lucienovakster@gmail.com
Boatride, Robert   erwygge@gmail.com
Borchard, Kieran   screammedia@yahoo.com
Bown, Jasmine   Jasminebown@yahoo.co.uk
Brewka-Clark, Nancy   nancybrewkaclark.com
Brown, Hedley   hedleybrown@hotmail.co.uk
Bryant, Joe   jb@dreamcountry.org
Burch, Ron   burchre@gmail.com
Burdick, Michael   lotofiris@gmail.com
Burn, Sean   burn.sean@googlemail.com
Bonczek, Rose Burnett   dinorosie@aol.com

Carbajal, Ruben   reachruben@gmail.com
Cardiff, Hugh   hcardiff@gmail.com
Carr, Alison   @AlisonCarr_
Carraway, Greg   g_carraway@yahoo.com
Carrozza, Tom   SayHiToTom@aol.com
Chisholm, Edgar   edgar.chisholm@gmail.com
Clyne, Kevin   kclyne50@yahoo.com
Clyne, Catherine   earthandsky@optonline.net
Collins, Terry   tr.collins@hotmail.co.uk
Costa, Allie   allie@alliecosta.com
Coyle, Julia   ralph.coyle@btinternet.com
Crose, Brandon M.   brandon.crose@gmail.com

Dean, Joel   joel.dean50@yahoo.co.uk
Dremann, Alex   info@alexdremann.com

Ehrlich, C.J.   www.CJ-Ehrlich.com
Elliott, Helen   helen.f.elliott1@virginmedia.com
Elliott-Hatton, Zachary   zachary.elliott-hatton1@
   virginmedia.com
Exilus, Mack   mack.exilus@gmail.com

Farrington, Sara   sara.j.farrington@gmail.com
Fazio Littlefield, Karin   karinfaziolittlefield@gmail.com
Feldman, Lauren   lauren.m.feldman@gmail.com
Flanagan, Mike   ms_flanagan@yahoo.com
Flourakis, Andreas   aflourakis@yahoo.gr
Floyd, Ramona   @ramonafloydnyc

Gabridge, Patrick   pat@gabridge.com
Geffen, Natasha   ngeff100@gmail.com
Gelo, Tom   thomasgelo@gmail.com
Gerhard, Tom   tgerhard60@gmail.com
Gijsbers van Wijk, Amy   www.amygvw.com
Gillard-Bentley, Paddy   paddy.gb@gmail.com
Girvan, Clare   claregirvan1@gmail.com
Grabowski, Bill   Wmgski96@hotmail.com
Gracia, Stephen   Stephen@dthreec.org
Grijak, Danica   danicadaystar@gmail.com

Harvey, James   jharvey@yorkcollege.ac.uk
Haun, Aren   arenhaun@gmail.com
Hawkhead, John   john.hawkhead@mypostoffice.co.uk
Hilton, Jessica   Jessica.hilton@ntlworld.com
Hosking, Sandra   sandrahosking@hotmail.com
Hsieh, Peter   phsieh1@yahoo.com
Huff, Helen   hhuff@nyc.rr.com

Ignatow, Amy   @amyignatow

Jolly, Arthur M.   info@arthurjolly.com
Jozwiak, Alan   jozwiakalanplays@gmail.com

Kaplan, Stephen   stephen@bystephenkaplan.com
Kaufman, Julian   brotherskaufman@hotmail.com
Kennedy, Janice   janice_kennedy@sbcglobal.net
Kimmel, Henry   hwkimmel@gmail.com
Konkel, Matthew   mydarkmaze@gmail.com
Krasauskas, Vincent   vincentk17@gmail.com
Krasauskas, Anton   ajkrasauskas@gmail.com

Lambert, Maude   ansell.jan@gmail.com
Lane, Stacey   Stacey@StaceyLaneInk.com
Lanfer, Stefan   sglanfer@gmail.com
Langsner, Meron   www.MeronLangsner.com
Lawrenson, Emily   emily_lawrenson@hotmail.co.uk
Lederer, Julia Represented by Stephanie
   Sinclair   stephanie@transatlanticagency.com
Lefer, Diane   dianelefer@gmail.com
Levine, John   www.johnlevineplaywright.com
Levine, Mark Harvey   markle96@hotmail.com
Ley, David   david-ley@outlook.com
Lockhart, Laurel A   lallockhart@gmail.com
Lunoe, Joan   joanyl2000@yahoo.com

MacCallum, Rhea   rheamac@yahoo.com
MacGregor, David   dmacgregor77@gmail.com
MacLarty, Andrew   @AndrewMaclarty
MacNerland, Jim   macshick2@aol.com
Maiella, Michael   mikemaiella@gmail.com
Manfredi, Rosanne   Manfrediro@yahoo.com
Markarian, Michele   michele.markarian@gmail.com
McLindon, James   jmclindon@gmail.com
Miley, Jessica   jmiley93@gmail.com
Misuraca, Thomas J   TomJMisuraca@gmail.com
Morra, Dan   morradan21@gmail.com
Muswell, Jo   jmuswell@gmail.com

Nickerson, Jay   nickersonjay@gmail.com

Pajka, Corey   corey.pajka@gmail.com
Palermo, Brian   pimo@verizon.net

Pattison, Rebekka   rebekka.pattison@gmx.de
Petryk, Walter   fotsrf@gmail.com
Ponzio, Anthony R   theparanoidpictures@gmail.com
Provenza, Jennifer   jenniferprovenza@gmail.com
Putt, Jr., Barry M.   barrymputtjr@gmail.com

Raby, Henry   henrythepoet@btinternet.com
Ramirez, Juan, Jr.   juanmanuelramirezjr@gmail.com
Ramsburg, Kat   katramsburg@gmail.com
Revell, Harry   harryrev@btinternet.com
Ryan, M. Rigney   rigney_ryan@yahoo.com
Rivera, Jose A   Jarivera21@gmail.com
Russo, Jennifer   jen.russo.jr@gmail.com

Sedgman, Kirsty   info@kirstysedgman.com
Shearer, Bruce   bruce.shearer@lexisnexis.com.au
Shotter, Anna   anna.shotter@hotmail.co.uk
Silva, Altenir   altenirjs@hotmail.com
Solfanelli, Eugene   solfanelli@gmail.com
Stewart de Peña, Aurora   aurorahello@gmail.com
Storck, David   d.storck@yahoo.com

Thorne, Russ   russellsthorne@gmail.com

Vale, Ivy   mygenerationproductions@gmail.com

Wadley, Gary   akmenaiv@bellsouth.net
Weagly, John   jmweagly@hotmail.com
Webb, Loy   loyawebb@gmail.com
Wenskus, Ted   ewenskus@rochester.rr.com
White, Christopher   urbanastronomy@gmail.com
Widney, Chris   chriswidney@gmail.com
Winter, Theeda Phe Kali,   stephenandkali@hotmail.com

Yancey, Dwayne   dwayneyancey@yahoo.com

Ziegler, Irene   iziegler2@gmail.com

Index